DATE DUE

Demco, Inc. 38-293

MAR 3 1 2010

Straight Talk to Teachers

Twenty Insane Ideas
for a Better Classroom

Bruce J. Gevirtzman

ROWMAN & LITTLEFIELD EDUCATION
A division of
ROWMAN & LITTLEFIELD PUBLISHERS, INC.
Lanham • New York • Toronto • Plymouth, UK

Published by Rowman & Littlefield Education
A division of Rowman & Littlefield Publishers, Inc.
A wholly owned subsidiary of The Rowman & Littlefield Publishing Group, Inc.
4501 Forbes Boulevard, Suite 200, Lanham, Maryland 20706
http://www.rowmaneducation.com

Estover Road, Plymouth PL6 7PY, United Kingdom

British Library Cataloguing in Publication Information Available

Library of Congress Cataloging-in-Publication Data

Gevirtzman, Bruce J.
  Straight talk to teachers : twenty insane ideas for a better classroom /
Bruce J. Gevirtzman.
     p. cm.
  Includes bibliographical references.
  ISBN 978-1-60709-037-3 (cloth : alk. paper) — ISBN 978-1-60709-038-0
(pbk. : alk. paper) — ISBN 978-1-60709-039-7 (ebook)
  1. Effective teaching. 2. Classroom environment. I. Title.
  LB1025.3.G438 2009
  371.102—dc22   2009027624

∞™ The paper used in this publication meets the minimum requirements of
American National Standard for Information Sciences—Permanence of Paper
for Printed Library Materials, ANSI/NISO Z39.48-1992.

Printed in the United States of America

Contents

Acknowledgments

Tom Koerner, my editor at Rowman & Littlefield Education, saw this insanity for its constructive potential and took a chance on it; my whopping thanks goes to him for his courage—and for making sure I wasn't needlessly offensive.

Kudos to my best friend and teacher ultra-deluxe, Eric Jordan, for helping me to begin my book-writing career two projects ago, when just about everybody else thought I was too old or, well, too insane to accomplish anything.

Steve Cisneros, thank you for being a terrific publicist, and for not nagging me into the ground, even though it's quite tempting.

And to the absolute love of my existence, my wife Janis, who is quite *sane* in her ideas, but still the best teacher I know: Thank you, my love, for allowing me to write books.

Bruce J. Gevirtzman
May 7, 2009

Note: Most names have been changed to protect the privacy of those mentioned. Although many are about a compilation of individuals, all stories are true.

Introduction

The Truth May Drive You Insane

After reading this book, you are going to think I am a very wise man. *Or* you are going to think I am a crazy old codger.

Ultimately, you will be the one to decide whether I have anything to offer the teaching world in the way of sound philosophical wisdom and concrete advice—or if I have flipped my lid.

What did former vice president Dan Quayle say? Something like, "The mind is a terrible, wasteful thing to waste, as it's better for the mind to be used than for the mind to be wasted!"?

Perhaps, someone else had once said this better, or the slogan ran fluently when first articulated, but we should not lose sight of the essence of Mr. Quayle's convoluted utterance: *The mind is important.* If you fix the mind, you may have a remarkable effect on healing the body; they go together. And sometimes, when the mind is functioning on all six billion cylinders and the body is working with a renewed strength and vigor, great things happen.

That's what this book is about—great things happening. It focuses on the mind: the overall *attitude*, the *mental* stamina, and the *emotional* stability of America's teachers. When these elements operate well—in unison—a teacher's classroom functions like a well-oiled machine and is a place students *want* to go.

My experience in the classroom (thirty-six years teaching English) and extra-curricular commitments (debate advisor, head baseball coach, theater director), have provided me with unique perspectives on education as per role of the teacher. The intention here is to improve the professional lives of teachers and, thereby, the successes of their students.

Both practical and philosophical, some of these ideas may ruffle a few feathers, but *this book* should wake up those educators who are already asleep at the blackboard.

Politically correct, this book definitely is *not*!

Weeding out the bad ideas from the good ideas is needed today more than ever in public education; anyone who takes even a cursory glance at what is emerging from the schools knows something is not quite right. But rather than placing all the blame on any one particular entity (such as parents or socioeconomic factors, etc.), it's time we talk candidly about what teachers can do to make things better. Certain powers only teachers possess (although I also maintain that teachers can work around some of those constraints and impediments they believe are not within their control).

The time for someone to tell the *truth* is long overdue.

This book tells the truth.

What is sorely lacking in the realm of public education these days is *honesty*. Finding truth in the education world is akin to finding nutrition in chocolate donuts. Honesty in education is like getting a World Series ring with the Chicago Cubs. It just ain't gonna' happen, man!

Sometimes honesty *can* be brutal ("Mr. Gevirtzman, like, as a teacher, you, like, really suck, dude")! For many teachers, however, honesty may be a refreshing change from all of the watered down, pasted over gobbly-gook in educational jargon—full of buzz words, pseudonyms, acronyms, and plain ol' poppycock. How invigorating to be advised in a straight-forward, direct, no-nonsense manner, cleaning up the mess of political correctness that has sullied the education community! (There is no trendy teacher trick for when a student has to go to the bathroom. When a kid has to go, *he has to go*; don't let him go to the restroom and experience a *new* kind of mess—this one in your classroom.)

What it boils down to more often than not is *attitude*. The attitude teachers have embraced as they walk into their classrooms everyday and their frame of mind as they have anticipated their challenges predict the overall level of success they will attain as a teachers. I can't emphasize this enough. I am washed out by workshops and conferences where so-called dynamic teachers demonstrate their pet lessons in their self-proclaimed unique styles. I can barely tune my brain into what's happening at these places! It would be nice, indeed, if we *all* had the perfect captive audience of eager learners who had volunteered to be in attendance that day—all of them comfortable, healthy, well-fed, and generally free from any hor-rendous burdens at home.

The *reality*, of course, is that most of our students do not fit the learning profile of the average professional conference attendee. As a result, we have to adjust our own attitudes to anticipate what we actually have to deal with each day, and under what (less-than-ideal) conditions we have to deal with it.

And that *is* the truth.

The most common questions about this book revolve around its title: "Why use the term *insane* ideas for a better classroom?" people ask me.

"What does *insanity* have to do with education?"

"Are *you* insane?"

In order to qualify as an *insane* idea for this text, the proposed concept must meet at least one—though they usually met more than one—of the following criteria:

1. The idea has rarely been considered.
2. The idea has been considered, but very few—if any—have dared to try it.
3. The idea reeks of being impractical and unworkable.
4. The idea appears too bold and audacious—even a bit scary.
5. The idea seems unrelated to education, schools, teachers, or students.
6. The idea has attracted the support of crazy people.
7. The idea had been implemented in some fashion before and (supposedly) failed.
8. The idea (when implemented) would cost an inordinate amount of money.
9. The idea would not garner any public support.
10. The idea would get enthusiastic support from teachers' unions or the Democratic Party (making it the craziest idea of all).

On that last point, I'm just joshing you a little.

Throughout all the years of disciplining myself to stand before a room of media-saturated, hormonally charged teenagers, I have achieved some success by implementing many of the insane ideas found in the twenty-one chapters of this book. Read about these ideas. Contemplate them. During this process, have some fun. You may take even bits and pieces, adapting them to your *own* style. Since many of my suggestions for developing a better teacher also pertain to making a happier, well-rounded human being (critical for being a first-rate teacher), you should see a marked improvement in the manner you deal with life in general. It has to do mostly with self-confidence and self-respect; they tend to go hand-in-hand. When you are finally more comfortable as a teacher, you will experience a knowledge that you are also much more competent—even terrific—at what you have chosen as your life's profession.

And you were not as wacky for making this career choice as you thought you were!

1

✚

Pinch out a Little Gratitude: You're a Teacher, Man!

The familiar sounds of those pesky roosters have awakened you. Hugging your pillow, you savor the warmth of your bed for a few precious seconds, only vaguely aware of your own name and too groggy to register the time on the clock. You are precariously close to a state of comatose.

And then it hits you!

You bound out of bed with a spring that would impress even the staunchest fans of Spiderman. That once solemn—albeit near-dead—expression on your face has transformed miraculously into a look of sheer ecstasy. Your eyes sparkle with a newly realized excitement. You have had your epiphany; the day is yours to conquer.

It takes you twenty minutes to shower, put on some of your best clothes, and gobble down a bowl of Cheerios. Not too long ago, these pleasing pursuits of your wake-up routine would have taken you much longer because of your desire to relish each of them for their contributions to your personal satisfaction. Lately, however, you have bypassed any interest in enjoying these morning luxuries, for your life has taken on a much greater profundity.

You are one of the few.

The fortunate.

The privileged.

You are a teacher!

Uh, is that corny enough, or what?

Maybe "corny" is the wrong word. Mixed in with a bit of hyperbole (perhaps, far too much hyperbole), the truth about this teacher's career

1

satisfaction appears to be out of sync with someone else's perception of her satisfaction. There are those in any profession who enjoy their work—and, of course, those who don't. Is it possible for a teacher to have such love, such passion for her job that she actually does look forward to flying out of bed with glee at the first sign of sunrise?

The truth: On any given morning, some teachers would prefer battling terrorists in Afghanistan to facing students in their classrooms. Sure, this observation could apply to people of any profession, but teachers work with *children*. When teachers fail to mask their unhappiness or dissatisfactions, *children* suffer the consequences.

When it comes to irate, miserable teachers, an interesting dichotomy is at work: On the one hand, teachers have been blessed—they have so much to be grateful for; on the other hand, their grumpiness often results from unfulfilled, wide-eyed expectations over their career choices. Teaching is tough, grueling work, and when that tough, grueling work comes unaccompanied by public gratitude, parent support, political acknowledgement, and student appreciation—especially as teachers get older—what often follows are personal resentments and second thoughts about how teachers have chosen to dedicate the better part of their lives.

Disgruntled veteran teachers begin to express their dismay years before they finally retire. Their realization that they have not perceptibly changed the world gnaws away at them; after all, by this time they had hoped to part seas and move mountains. They now sense, however, the reality of their miniscule effect of being a tiny ripple in a very large pond.

In the beginning of my career, the word "grateful" did not adequately describe the pure elation I felt about being a teacher. What more could I ask for than my own classroom, my own students, and my own agendas? Unfortunately, I soon had my own conceptions about my new colleagues. I listened to them constantly crab about their jobs. Usually—but not always—this incessant griping came from veteran teachers ("Old Farts," as I then affectionately alluded to them and call myself now). Here is a sampling of that tired grumbling—the moaning and groaning—I overheard in the lunchroom, around the lounge, or at faculty meetings, along with some thoughts I harbored at the time:

- "I could earn more money managing the McDonald's over near the cow pasture on Rosecrans Avenue!" (The nearby cow pasture, in all its smelly glory, would be an improvement over the atmosphere in this teacher's classroom.)
- "I could have made more money, if I had gone into the restaurant business with my brother!" (Willy Loman bemoaned that he had failed to follow his brother Ben into the diamond mines of Alaska. And just how did *Death of a Salesman* end, hm?)
- "There isn't one administrator at this school who knows his ass from his elbow!" (This teacher is adept at recognizing an ass when he sees one,

including when he looks in the mirror. Actually, recognizing his elbow is not required.)

- "Anybody with brains wouldn't go into education administration; that proves none of those people over at the district office have any brains!" (As if this teacher's cerebral contribution to the world of education has had a momentous impact.)
- "If you cut out half the administrators, we'd have enough money to buy some textbooks for these kids!" (If she cut out half the worksheets she copies for these poor kids to do their boring class busy work, we'd have enough money to buy new books every year.)
- "Jeepers (or some other archaic word), there isn't one kid in my classes this year who cares about learning!" (And, jeepers—amazingly—there isn't anybody in this teacher's classroom who cares about *teaching*.)
- "You should see all the losers in my fifth period classroom!" (Yes, well, this statement speaks for itself.)
- "Can't the teachers get any support around here? Who's running the show: the adults or the kids?" (Sometimes it's hard to tell the difference between the teachers and the kids. In the classrooms of *good* teachers, the teacher is always in charge, no matter how weak the site administrators.)
- "It's the parents' fault!" (Often this is true, but it's the teacher's job to soften the blow of a dopey parent. Sometimes the parents' contributions are nonexistent or even counterproductive. That's when the teacher fans the fires of his passion even more ferociously.)
- "They don't trust my judgment. Humph! In any other profession, I'd be treated like a professional!" (This teacher wouldn't *be* in any other profession. Could you honestly see this guy changing a flat tire or fixing a leaky pipe?)

These were comments I heard then—and they are, oddly enough, the comments I hear now. The difference is now I am one of the "Old Farts," and I find *myself* saying these things! Most of the time, I don't really mean these criticisms; they are uttered out of sheer exasperation or exhaustion. Overall, I'm glad I'm a teacher; in fact, I'm *thrilled* about being a teacher. When I was ten years old, an old chalkboard hung from the wall in my bedroom; I used it to play school with imaginary students. I prepared a completely made-up subject matter and even kept student record books, filled with the names, test scores, and progress grades for fictitious students.

A large wooden paddle hung from a nail on my bedroom wall. I sometimes removed the paddle from the nail and proceeded to beat my stuffed animals senseless, pretending I was their classroom teacher. (Forgive me; I'm kidding about the stuffed animals, OK?) Occasionally, my younger sister and some of our neighborhood friends would play my students, which turned out to be a lot more challenging than dreaming up people who didn't exist; however, real children or not, I persisted in being the teacher, and knew this is what I would be doing with my life a thousand years in the future.

So those hostile comments: Ignore them. Most veteran teachers, even in all their well-honed grumpiness, don't really mean what they say; and those who do probably would have been miserable, complaining, cantankerous old buzzards, even if they had decided to do something else with their lives. If we have unhappy personal relationships, if we have debilitating problems, or if we have lousy dispositions, we will hate what we're doing—no matter what.

I don't know what would happen to my family and me, if I ever have to get a *real* job. I can't imagine myself changing the flat tire or fixing the leaky pipe either. I count my lucky stars for my aptitude for classroom management and burning desire to teach young people. I don't *want* to be doing anything else.

Last summer, I helped my father-in-law stock some of his vending machines (a business he is extremely proud of). One afternoon, during the heat of August, we visited an aluminum factory that housed one of his soda and snack machines in its tiny lunchroom. What struck me was that during the middle of the summer, these men and women were *working*—had actual jobs that required doing tedious labor and physical effort. Teaching, of course, is work, too, but the psychological ramifications of watching people in a factory go about their strenuous, mundane chores presented me with increased gratitude for my own job status.

During my days of being a young, hip, swingin' single, I spoke with inquiring women who wanted to know what I did for a living. I found their responses to be mixed:

- "A teacher? Too bad you guys don't make any money!"
- "Why would you want to be a teacher?"
- "I'm sorry."
- "A teacher? Oh."
- "Wow, I'd like to do that someday, too!"
- "I really admire teachers."
- "I was going to be a teacher, but then I got a job herding sheep."
- "A teacher! Take me! Take me in your arms!"

OK, perhaps, that last one is a bit of an exaggeration, but teachers do stand out in society, and almost everybody takes notice of us. They may not think we have it marvelous financially (which is partly true, depending on our monetary goals in life), but most people have positive reactions to good teachers, those who help to establish our special place in the universe. The key is to channel this inwardly, to use this acknowledgment of our worthiness as a catalyst for the inspiration and energy needed to improve our teaching.

We need to like what we do and be proud of it, taking enough advantage of these validations to propel ourselves forward. It becomes a motivation/inspiration bank account we can draw from later.

If you love your job, your students will see it on your face almost everyday. This doesn't mean that you prance around the room, emoting ludicrous commentaries about the incredible beauty of life; it does mean that you show a genuine willingness to do what you're presently doing, displaying a visible satisfaction with the life choices you have made. This is why those conventional teacher jokes will make you laugh. You know they are not true about *you*; regrettably, you have discerned their accuracy in relation to some of the *other* teachers you work with every day—but not *you*.

Remarkably you have ignored all those predictable comments made by the miserable wretches in your school. You have courageously overlooked the barrage of criticism levied against teachers by talk radio jocks and daily newspapers and magazines. You have earnestly attempted to turn your friends' incessant wisecracks about your selected profession into positive, refreshing reinforcement for your having chosen to suffer six years in college earning your teaching credential.

But you're still kicking yourself in the gluteus .

So what can you do now?

Heed the following five reasons that you should be grateful—ever so grateful—you are a teacher:

1. THE SALARY AND BENEFITS ARE RESPECTABLE

The *average* public school teacher's salary in the state of California in 2006–2007 was $58,000; the base pay for a novice, his emerging year into our profession, came in as high as $46,500, while the top tier on the teacher pay scale ran up to $95,000.[1] This does not include extra pay stipends, such as those for coaching sports or helping to polish the principal's shoes (known as merit pay). It also does not reflect salary for the summer session, which can boost a teacher's wages as much as $6,000 or $7,000 dollars. Another financial fact: These base figures are usually for a ten-month period—not twelve months. Most average people in America hold twelve-month jobs, minus the two weeks they pack their wailing children into the minivan and drive almost nonstop to visit Indian reservations in the middle of the desert.

And you want to talk about medical benefits? The vast majority of the districts in the United States provide full medical benefits for credentialed teachers in the public schools, with most districts offering dental care programs and even vision plan insurance. Of course, teachers usually have to pay a portion of their salary for these programs, but usually the cost is minimal, averaging about one hundred dollars a month to cover a family of four or more.[2]

Term life insurance is usually included, and teachers' pensions are among the best for all public servants (except for the police and firefighters who risk their lives in other ways), and very often the school districts kick in perks, such as mentor pay, extra sick days, vacation allowances, and even reduced fee private disability insurance policies.[3]

Almost every state in the country, if adjusted for inflation and to the standard of living for that state, offers comparable benefits to its teachers. Private schools, particularly religious schools, pay much less across the board than the public school sector; however, teachers may work without official certification in private schools.

The bottom line: Although certainly not as lucrative as becoming a crooked stockbroker or defending O.J. Simpson in yet another trial, teachers do surprisingly well financially. Teachers themselves usually instigate jokes, complaining about how little money teachers make, because teachers can be very funny, self-deprecating people, hilarious jokesters who want others to feel sorry for their economic status, thus, giving them tacit permission to extract even more money from the public trough.

But you already knew that, didn't you?

2. TEACHERS GET LOTS OF DAYS OFF.

Of course, you already knew this, too; that's probably the main reason why you wanted to become a teacher in the first place: *I have the summers to travel, or write the great American novel, or read by the pool, or be with my kids more. With the whole summer at my disposal, I can . . .* Just finish the sentence. Assuming the teacher wishes *not* to spend his vacation time with Satan's children in summer school—or does not find himself in such an economic bind that he can afford the luxury of skipping summer school altogether—two months or more free from the stresses of work can induce even the most obstinate among us that a teacher's schedule contains luxuries that other professions may lack.

3. TEACHERS ATTAIN IMMORTALITY.

We all remember our teachers; for better or worse, we all have teachers we will never forget. Even dozens of years later, these memorable teachers trigger strong reactions and stir powerful emotions in us that sometimes cannot be explained.

This is, after all, a *good* thing. Even Clair May Tracy, my freshman algebra teacher who looked—and probably was—about three hundred years old, is molded into my memory bank. She embodied both fear and awe at the same time, generating a mind-boggling respect from teenagers that hardly anyone can imagine today.[4]

And Mr. Necterline: He was my history teacher who slid tearfully into our third-period class that Friday morning in November and informed us that President Kennedy had just been assassinated in Dallas. Before that moment, I had never seen an adult man cry.

How can I ever forget Mr. Necterline?

Many of us have etched our teachers into the scrapbooks of our lives, although at the time we may not have known it. Perhaps, we *resented* them for myriad reasons; perhaps, we even hoped that one of them might delight us by dropping dead right on the spot. But we remember them.

Good teachers never die.

Sometimes they *wished* they were dead, but we'll cover that condition in a later chapter.

4. TEACHERS WIELD AWESOME POWER.

The abuse of power for the purpose of perpetrating evil (or simply because someone is temporarily ticked off) repeatedly warns us that power can be an awful thing when it gets into the wrong hands; however, because you're reading this book and, presumably, strongly desire to become a better teacher, I will make the assumption that power in *your* hands portends nothing but good for the rest of your teaching days.

You have the power to change lives.

I used to hate those old teacher shows on television like *Lucas Tanner*[5] and *White Shadow*,[6] because those teachers always went to the kids' houses and worked miracles in the fifty minutes (minus commercials) it took for the program to air. On the one hand— when I was much younger—these TV shows provided an impetus for making me kinder, more understanding, and, yes, a little more snoopy about the lives of my students, hoping that I might hop into my 1983 Honda Civic and take all those troubled kids out for cheeseburgers and a superb motivational talk; on the other hand, I knew clearly that TV and movie teachers smacked of a commercialism that was only a vague reflection of reality. This defied my capacity to take any of them seriously.

However, consider the pragmatic range of your power:

A. You have the *power* to motivate kids to want to learn.

I use the word *power* here; I don't *guarantee* successes because I can't predict that any individual teacher will use his power wisely or skillfully. Conversely, teachers also possess the power to make kids *not* want to learn anything—and, understandably, those kids usually grow up to be teachers, themselves.

I can't believe that I just said that.

B. You have the *power* to impart knowledge.

Assuming you deem your knowledge to be worthwhile in the first place—of great value to kids—this can be awesome.

C. You have the *power* to encourage good values—and discourage bad values—in children.

No matter what your subject matter, good teachers shape values in our youth; Role-modeling good behavior is the very least a teacher can do for his students; some teachers even stress a values-based curriculum within their specific subject matter. An aging math teacher in my school has found this to be a vital component in his instruction. His justification: Numbers often lead us to ethical quagmires. This math teacher figured out something new and wound up doing something bold: Along with teaching the computation of numbers, he threw in a strong brew of ethics.

D. You have the *power* to thwart destructive decisions.

Kids make bad, destructive decisions all the time, mostly because of their impulsivity. You can intercede and, perhaps, even save a life or two. I mean, it is terrific that teachers, of course, always display remarkable self-control and patience while making important decisions in their *own* lives. Right?

E. You have the *power* to move kids forward—or to hold them back.

Nothing during my teaching career has taxed my stress levels more than knowing that the grade I had given—or was about to give—a student would remove him from the high school graduation ceremony that he and about 22 million members from his extended family from every corner of this world and Jupiter were planning to attend . Although it may not seem like it at the time, even an elementary school teacher's decision about social and/or academic advancement can—and does—have critical ramifications for younger children.

F. You have the *power* to inspire kids to become teachers themselves.

Oh, well, so not all that power is good after all.

G. You have the *power* to make kids like school.

At least, you have the power to make them like *your* class. And if they like your class, they like school at least a little bit. They may find your class difficult, frustrating, challenging, fascinating, scary—you name it. You have the power—and the *obligation*—to inspire your students to want to go to your class . . . for something. Examples of how to do this are provided throughout this book. A kid may attend school every day, simply because of you.

H. You have the *power* to shape curriculum.

Some schools and school districts give more latitude in this arena to teachers, and others give far less; however, all educators, from top to bottom, desire input from teachers, even if they wind up ignoring it later. No matter what they tell you in faculty meetings and district-level in-services, most teachers have the ability to close their doors and teach what they deem viable. Today's teaching-to-the-standardized test is easily masked, while more profound, student-friendly topics can be effectively taught for the overall good of the kids.

I. You have the *power* to determine the quality of the future.

We hear it all the time: "Mr. Doofus turned my life around. I wanted to sell crack cocaine for a living, until he showed me the way and the light. Now I sell hotdogs on a street corner instead; I'm a hotdog vendor. Thank you, Mr. Doofus—wherever you are!"

J. You have the *power* to represent—wth dignity—an important segment of America.

The Woody Allen character in the film *Crimes and Misdemeanors* tells his preadolescent niece, "You don't always want to focus on the horrible and miserable in life, but if you *really* want to feel pity for the horrible and miserable, just take a good look at your school teachers."[7] Teacher jokes aside (for a brief moment), this profession begs us to be a positive, splendid model of the best of the best. The "worst" capture the limelight all the time: surgeons who botch operations; lawyers who defend child killers; actresses who drive drunk into telephone poles; teachers who involve themselves romantically with their thirteen-year-old students (lots of that lately, too; some thirteen-year-old boys have become quite the studs they didn't know they were).

As a teacher, you have the power to aid your fellow sufferers by establishing reputations for fairness and hard work, displaying a visible passion for life and job, role modeling through being a stalwart member of the community, and having the capability of delivering a demonstrative tongue-lashing that would frighten even Dr. Laura.

5. TEACHERS COMMAND JOB SECURITY

Let's have a show of hands: How many of you actually wouldn't mind writhing on the floor in a fetal position, agonizing over the loss of a job or the destruction of a career, worried sick over how you're going to feed your family?

Hmmm?

Next to the fear of prostate cancer and going bald, the third greatest trepidation harbored by American men is their fear of losing their jobs. Most Americans would rather make less money and have more job security than vice versa. Teachers hardly ever lament such fears, because teachers hardly ever lose their jobs—at least, compared to those who must entertain insecurities and irregularities in other areas of the employment market.

An honest argument can be made that teachers actually have far too much job protection; short of a natural disaster or a nuclear holocaust, it's exceedingly difficult to get rid of the lemons out there. That said, the life of a teacher is normally free from the stress of pending job loss, as long as he doesn't hop on a table and dance nude. The term teacher *tenure* is, in reality, not tenure. Not really. It actually means *due process* rights teachers retain before they can be dismissed from their employment.[8]

In most states teachers can be fired for almost anything during their first two years of employment in a school district; however, the first day on the job of their third year gives them what is universally known as "tenure."

Whether or not you are philosophically in accord with the tenure laws and teacher job protection statutes really is not the issue here. No matter what arguments you give for or against tenure in a philosophical/academic debate, you benefit from those due process laws. Sure, you may like to point out that if you're a good teacher who always follows the rules, you don't have to worry about losing your job; the facts, however, unmistakably report to us that before "tenure" laws, even great teachers had been fired for all sorts of quirky reasons, sometimes merely on the whim of some colossally stupid administrator. Due process laws were designed precisely for such an eventuality.

So even if you are the most terrific teacher since Aristotle (or whoever), the peace of mind you have as a teacher after the first two years on the job is a bonus practically no other employees in any other segment of the job market ever receive (unless, of course, they work for a state social services department—in which case they maintain their employment status even fifty years after they have been dead).

Being grateful you're a teacher requires some introspection, reflection, and self-deprecation. Making the effort is worth it, though. You will be able to handle the kids more easily, do your job more efficiently, and digest your meals more thoroughly, while consistently deflecting those evil teacher jokes that come your way, responding with some rather crass, heavy-handed lawyer jokes in return. (What's the difference between a lawyer and a sea urchin? *One is a bottom-dwelling, scum-sucking parasite . . . and the other is a fish.*)

In *Annie Hall*, the Woody Allen character Alvy Singer remarks, "Those who can't do, teach; those who can't teach, teach gym."[9]

You will learn to find such comments amusing; for from the deepest crevices of your soul, to the outer reaches of your most reprimanding, authoritative voice, you are *glad* you are a teacher.

NOTES

1. National Education Association, *NEA Newsletter*, November 14, 2006, at nea .org.newsrelease/2006/NR06114.html.

2. Figures are based on the 2008–2009 contract for the Norwalk-La Mirada Unified School District, a district of average size and spending capability in Southern California.

3. *Ed Data for 2008*, "Teachers in California," December 2007, at ed-data.k12 .ca.us/articles/article.asp?title=teacher-%20in%20california.

4. Rumor has it that Mrs. Tracy is still alive and even appeared in the last scene of the 1997 film *Titanic*.

5. *Lucas Tanner*, NBC, ran one season (1974–1975), starred David Hartman.

6. *White Shadow*, CBS, (1978–1981), starred Ken Howard.

7. Woody Allen, *Crimes and Misdemeanors* (MGM, 1989).

8. A. Hermitt, "Is Teacher Tenure Fair to Students?" (*A–Z Education*, December 17, 2007), 1.

9. Woody Allen, *Annie Hall* (United Artists, 1977).

2

Prefer Professionalism

We hear stories about teachers' parking lots around public schools all over America; we listen to how they're crowded with luxury cars: Mercedes Benzes, Corvettes, and Honda Accords—I love *that* car—just to name a few. But around my school the newest looking so-called "luxury car" is an ancient Lincoln Continental with a big dent in the driver's side door.

Most of our teaching staff and office workers aren't mourning about the mostly dumpy-looking vehicles in our faculty parking lot, so, frankly, I don't know where all these stories about opulence come from. My guess is that these rumors are concocted by a few teachers who only *wished* that our teaching salaries allowed us the flexibility for buying those allegedly pricey automobiles we drive to work daily; or maybe these fibs are spread by disgruntled citizens who never went to college and figure *everybody* should wallow in economic mediocrity, college graduates notwithstanding.

The truth of the matter is most teachers don't have enough money to buy one-hundred-thousand-dollar cars. They would like to earn that kind of money, but they knew when they launched their teaching careers—and probably long before—huge piles of money that could be allocated for high-priced automotive toys would be out of their realm. Still, it's tempting to lament how awful we feel because we can't even afford today's gas prices, let alone a car that costs more than some people's homes.

The financial lot of a teacher, of course, is really not that bad; in fact, it's quite good compared to many other professions and jobs. But every once in awhile, all of us get dreamy-eyed with neon dollar signs flashing in the

13

not-so-far reaches of our psyches. And if we're trying to support a family on only one salary, a teacher's earning power—though creditable—dictates a budget of monetary decisions requiring the self-discipline of a monk.

OK, if you had gone into law, you would be making at least twice the salary you are making now. If you had decided on medicine, you would have been in school until you're thirty—if you hadn't committed suicide—now earning a salary that pales your teacher's wages. But you didn't choose these other professions, so logic would now dictate you are not going to reap the monetary benefits of those other professions (no duh)!

You are a teacher, pure and simple (if there really *is* such a thing as a pure and simple teacher); so when you hear the soon-to-be omnipresent griping begin—many of you have already heard it—brace yourself and maintain your own professional composure:

"Humph! If they expect me to act like a professional, they ought to be treating me like a professional; they should be paying me a professional's salary! Humph! Do you know how much money Dudley Davis is making now? A first-year lawyer! I could have been a lawyer! I don't know why I didn't become a lawyer! I would have been a *good* lawyer!"

What was the name of that episode on the series starring Jerry Seinfeld: "Yada, Yada, Yada . . "?

Lawyers—once again, lawyer jokes aside—go to court, carry brief-cases, speak with educated vocabularies, and foster professional dignity (most of the time). But that doesn't happen naturally. If anything, three to four years of law school may suck any semblance of dignity right out of a person; yet, attorneys manage to receive preferential professional status (along with the accompanying professional-size salary) to that of a teacher, no matter how loudly we teachers scream about wanting others to respect our special talents and skills.

For starters, when a lawyer goes to work, he wears a uniform; so does a doctor. A lawyer's jacket and tie or a doctor's coat, adorned by the stereotypical dangling stethoscope has become the trademark of the profession—the label identifying who she is or claims to be. What do we teachers wear in the classroom, illustrating the trademark of *our* profession? Hmmm? We wear what we darn-well please: sports shirts, slacks, shorts, T-shirts, loafers, tennis shoes . . . whatever delights our fancy for any particular day on the job. Some male teachers have been reprimanded for putting on tank tops or wearing shorts that show off their underwear; some female teachers have had to face the dress code police for their expression of, well, what they, unfortunately, wished to express with a particular type of attire. Sometimes this requires us to purge ahead into unmentionable topics for debate—in public—and that alone is not good for the teaching profession.

To be sure, some teachers wear coats and ties, classy dresses (I have heard of male teachers in my district who have worn classy dresses on special days like Halloween, but, perhaps, that's a topic for a different book.), or nice pants with a dress shirt and loose-collar tie; however, this is not the norm. For the most part, public school teachers, though they desire professional status, refuse to don professional attire.

I firmly believe—and I truly mean this with the utmost seriousness— the way teachers dress impacts the learning climate they should be cultivating in their classrooms. It *has* to. Teachers develop a rapport with their students—or they don't. I'm not saying that good teachers wear suits to school, and bad teachers wear blue jeans with holes in them (as a matter of fact, one of my own favorite high school teachers dressed like a slob, patchy blue jeans and all); but we teachers establish a certain disposition, a tone, an atmosphere in our classrooms and in the relationships we hold with our students, not to mention the image we project to the general public. Dressing well—a professional look—is one of the most important distinctions of that professionalism. Can we really keep a straight face, as we argue for respect and public support, pointing to doctors and lawyers and CEOs as examples of those who have the status we would like to attain, as we stand there, looking as though we'd just thrown on some old clothes before driving over to the supermarket?

The kids watch us very carefully. High level school district administrator Roger Federwisch talked about tough student dress codes: "Our expectations for students are so high, we can't be hypocritical and expect less of teachers." Federwisch, often hears complaints from parents about a double standard.[1] In *USA Today*, Olivia Barker wrote, "Kids are looking to teachers for direction and guidance, not to be their buddies."[2] Occasionally, dressing down is good. Students need to know we are human, too; that we don't sit around the house all day in a tie, like Ward Cleaver did in *Leave It to Beaver*.[3] However, professional attire is a significant element in projecting our professional status and attaining respect for that status; it can make the difference between being viewed as a professional—or a simple slug.

One teacher I spoke to shuddered at the suggestion of having to wear a tie with a (gasp!) sports coat to his class: "But it's hot! And we don't have any air conditioning! If the folks at the district in their cool and cozy and nice air-conditioned offices, would just . . . "

Then how about *this*? When it's unusually hot, dress down; otherwise, you should dress like a professional. Even when it's hot and muggy, cotton dress shirts offer casual comfort; and a soft, light tie hardly carries enough heavy weight to hurl male teachers into an abyss of climactic despair. Besides, as students notice their teachers adhering to a professional dress code even in hot weather, they are less likely to offer those lame excuses for wearing spaghetti straps, no straps, or straps that cover very little of what should never have been lightly strapped in the first place. When a female teacher finds professional solace on a hot day in a pretty, cheerful sundress, patterning the current season of the year—but not announcing to the world she is dressing to attend a rave party in somebody's sultry garage warehouse—she has killed several summer birds with one rock (or whatever): A woman can be cool, casual, and professional, while looking good at the same time; teachers can still role-model professional dignity. And now students must follow suit without rationalizations for dressing in sluttish clothing.

Professionalism in the teaching ranks goes beyond the way one dresses. Incorporating the dress code directive, I have come up with ten rough guidelines for professionalism:

DRESS WELL: MEN, WEAR A TIE; WOMEN WEAR DRESSES (OR VICE VERSA).

It would be easy to dismiss the significance of dressing as a professional— as many people, mostly teachers, have already aptly demonstrated in the past; however, our students complain all the time about those dress codes imposed upon them, because they claim that their ability to express themselves has been impugned.

Consistent with this logic, teachers who wear other than what connects appropriately to their jobs seem to be going out of their way to "express themselves" in a contemptible fashion; for example, how much respect for his church does a man convey when he attends a place of worship in Bermuda shorts and a white t-shirt? And a teacher who shows up in her classroom with a tight-fitting blouse and her navel piercing in full view—or a raggedy, torn pair of pants: What is she projecting about reverence for the school in which she works or respect for the students she teaches?[4]

EVEN THOUGH YOU HAVE A FIRST NAME, IT IS TABOO FOR YOUR STUDENTS TO CALL YOU BY THAT NAME.

Ernie Gorin, an eighth grade woodshop teacher, made his permanent mark for one thing—and one thing only: He physically assaulted his students. Mr. Gorin didn't attack them with an actual weapon; he used an open hand to slap them about their face. Paradoxically, Ernie Gorin was a small, somewhat sheepish looking man with horn-rimmed glasses; but when set off by a student, his predictable response had been to slap his students—male students—until they ran from him in fear or pain.

What would set Ernie off?

Just that: *Ernie.* Woe to the kid who found out Mr. Gorin's first name and—even in jest—called him *Ernie* instead of Mr. Gorin! Of course, this happened over forty years ago—things were quite different then—but even if one of Ernie's students had verbally referred to him as "Mr. Creep," Mr. Gorin would have responded rather passively.

In those days many male teachers kept wooden paddles hooked on the wall just above their chalkboard, and most of these teachers did not hesitate to use those paddles when, uh, necessary.

For Mr. Gorin, calling him by his first name conjured the word *neces-sary*—not for the wooden paddle—but for angry, rapidly delivered slaps to both sides of an offending student's face.

When Mr. Gorin was asked—as he had been several times—why he re-acted so aggressively when a student referred to him by his first name, he replied with his patented, amicable shake of his head, "It just isn't right; it just ain't professional."

Lesson learned: Teachers who allow their students to call them by their first name or a cool nickname forfeit a huge part of the teacher-student dynamic. I don't remember ever referring to one of my medical doctors by his first name: "Hey, Jack, good to see ya', dude! Need you to check out my aching back."

Most doctors wouldn't have slapped me in the face for this; however, they would have wrapped their stethoscope around my neck and pulled it into a knot with a forceful energy unbeknownst to most of their other patients.

At least, I think so.

USE OTHER THAN THE TELEPHONE TO COMMUNICATE WITH YOUR STUDENTS.

With the advent of email, the technology now exists for keeping (forever) detailed records of written communications. Telephone conversations, on the other hand, rarely provide us with accessible means for recording and preserving our most common correspondences. When teachers com-municate with their students in their students' world (telephones, text messaging, etc.), they succumb—in a sense—to the level of their students; they have relinquished a bit of their professional edge.

DON'T MINGLE SOCIALLY WITH YOUR STUDENTS.

As a rule of thumb (although I have no idea what thumbs would have to do with this concept) teachers and students should not socially mingle *at all.* Especially younger, hipper (not in anatomical measurements, but in coolness), and friendlier teachers possess the notion that social interaction with their, uh, teenage students somehow makes them younger, hipper, and friendlier. Besides the obvious age disparity—even among the just-out-of-college set and seniors in high school—there is a professional line of distinction that broadcasts, "Me *teacher,* you *student.*" When that line becomes blurred, and the natural order of things dissipates, there is a tendency for students to lose respect for their teachers, and other teachers to lose respect for this so-called socially hip group of teachers.

KEEP MOST OF YOUR PRIVATE LIFE, UH, *PRIVATE.*

Although the particulars of their private lives are rarely their students' business, the sharing of an event or pattern of experiences in teachers' personal portfolios can illustrate valuable life lessons.

Mr. Rojas once stood on the front lines of the protest marches against the war in Vietnam; he later stood with a rifle on the front lines *in* Vietnam! His life experiences, his notions of valor, his concepts of patriotism, his intermingling of differing personal values became invaluable lessons for his students.

I could never figure Mr. Rojas out either. On the one hand, he appeared to be one of those flaming liberal, left-wing, aging hippies who often drove me to bopping my head against padded walls; on the other hand, he sometimes came off as a died-in-the-wool, "Stars and Stripes Forever" patriot who would no sooner crunch a war protester over the head with his own picket sign than be willing to flash peace signs with him (and those folks made me crazy, too). Mr. Rojas's abrasive personality and mystifying mixture of attitudes and beliefs always kept his students guessing—all the while his interesting paradoxes helping him to be an excellent history teacher.

Mr. Rojas had fascinating stories to tell, but for the most part, teachers do not need to share information about their love lives; the same holds true for their financial woes, extracurricular weekend romps, weird relatives, and family conflicts. Sometimes when teachers disclose interesting stories about their own families, they help to foster a valuable lesson, substantiating that teachers are kind of human, after all—making it more possible for their students to like them. And when teachers share personal downfalls or mishaps (such as when I left my wallet on the trunk of the car and drove away, only to have my intact wallet personally delivered to my doorstep a few hours later by a Good Samaritan), they sometimes may steer impressionable young lives in a positive direction.

USE ELEVATING LANGUAGE AROUND STUDENTS; DON'T CUSS LIKE A DRUNKEN SAILOR (OR A DRUNKEN TEACHER)

This, my friends, is a toughie. Not that teachers swear more than do people in other professions (although teachers believe they have better reason to), but their stress usually rises equivalent to their desperation to self-contain, so their tendency to, well, emote, becomes more pronounced.

One teacher I know is actually *known* for his use of foul language. And I do mean *foul* language. I'm not going to list the specific words here (as much as it would feel really good to do so), but let's just say that he sometimes hurls a string of obscenities in his classroom that would have made the late George Carlin proud.

To be clear: This guy is one of the most admired and well-respected teachers in his school. He's funny, well liked, and revered by students and other teachers. Delighted by some of his positive and *honest* contributions at faculty meetings, other teachers talk about him in glowing terms. He has been a wonderfully successful varsity sports coach for years, and his players adore him (despite his colorful rants after a loss, or sporadic spews at officials during a game). His penchant for using those four letter words in and out of his classroom has attracted some negative attention from concerned parents and bossy administrators. But when push comes to shove, no parents want to sacrifice their child's place in his classroom, since he is such a popular—and effective—instructor. And no administrators wish to confront him for his antics, lest they become an unwitting subject of one of his tirades.

Overall, however, teachers should maintain verbal professionalism. Every time I have slipped (yeah, right) and uttered a cuss word or two around students, I later regretted it. Sticking my bloated, eleven-and-a half, triple-E foot in my mouth is a pastime I'm not proud of; furthermore, after hurling an unnecessary obscenity around the vicinity of my students, I have always felt a little less professional. This is not to say that teachers who swear at school are bad teachers or bad people; it is to argue, however, that verbal obscenities in the classroom do not hail as evidence of watershed professionalism.

Next time, as you are about to let those ugly utterances fly from your mouth, first ask one of your students to wash your mouth out with soap.

DON'T PUBLICLY BERATE OTHER TEACHERS OR STAFF

So you assume what goes on at private, religious institutions should be filed under the label "Perfection"? And you carry visions of professional excellence at those schools sporting names like Mother Teresa's School for Girls?

Think again.

After receiving a rather dismal written evaluation from one of the leading teacher assessors at a most distinguished Catholic girls' school, a young male instructor—we'll call him Mr. Grim—burst into the dining hall at the height of a busy lunch hour and strode with strident purpose in the direction of his recent evaluator, Sister Mary Masters.

The clanking of plates and the buzzing of busy conversations screeched to a complete halt, as very loud, angry words fumed from Mr. Grim's fiery nostrils right in the direction of nun *and* head honcho teacher supervisor, Sister Mary Masters.

"Sister!" he yelled in deafening decibels. "Don't you *ever* walk into my classroom again without first giving me some notice! Do you understand what I'm saying? *Do you?*"

To be fair, Sister Masters was probably 180 years old; if someone wished to be heard by Sister Masters, he was forced to aim his words—with extraordinary volume— right in her direction. And Mr. Grim, not even thinking of—or caring about—Sister Master's age impediment, attacked her in his loudest, most raucous, threatening voice. It took the nun a moment (or a couple of hours) for her to register his intense anger and the circumstances to which he had been referring.

Evidently, Sister Masters had decided to observe Mr. Grim for the purpose of his semiannual evaluation on the Friday morning of the biggest football game of the year: the homecoming game with the school's crosstown rival. Understandably, Mr. Grim's students were not in the mood for geometry, and the math teacher had been sensitive to the nonacademic ambiance in his classroom; he proposed some laid-back, nonthreatening math games, a few requiring enthusiastic participation and *loud* input from his already geared up students.

Sister Masters, however, had viewed this flamboyant activity as a detriment to the teacher's ability to discipline and control his students—and a major weakness in Mr. Grim's teaching ability.

Mr. Grim continued to spit fire. "You had no right to say what you said about me. I'm hereby quitting this job to work at a sewer dump—a step *up* in the quality of my work environment! And, Miss Mary Masters, you and the rest of this pathetic school can expect to hear from my lawyers in a matter of days, because I'm gonna sue you for every penny you have!"

No lawsuit ensued.

Mr. Grim quietly slipped away to teach at a public high school (making twice the amount of money he had made at the Catholic school), and Sister Mary died about six months later, presumably not hastened by Mr. Grim's verbal assault.[5]

STIFLE THE WORKPLACE GOSSIP

It's obnoxious. The more you tell stories about others you work with—true or untrue—the more likely they will tell stories about you; and they will increase in their ugliness as days go by. This is, of course, an old standby nugget of wisdom about life in general; but when gossip hits the fan *at school*, young people, impressionable ears, the sons and daughters of your peers, want to hear—maybe even participate in—the scandals, too. Senseless claptrap will flow from your mouth, and your remorse is sure to follow. Foot-in-mouth disease follows teachers everywhere they go. And most of the time when the kids tell others about your dumb comments in class, they are not lying. But here's the caveat: Those occasions when your comments or actions have been distorted, destroyed, or disguised compare weakly to those countless other times you managed to escape unscathed from a situation for which you *should* have been chastised. A perfectly innocuous, "Had the South won the Civil War the slavery problem would have lasted, perhaps, for decades longer than it really did," turns into, "Did you hear what Mr. Smith said today in class? Well . . . he said, 'It's too bad the South didn't win the Civil War. It would have been really great if we could have kept slaves for a few more decades!'"

All teachers have been victimized by the confused student, the non-listening student, the overly zealous student, or the lying, vindictive student. The truth: Unless they spice up their teachers' words or questionable behaviors with smidgens of sensationalism, or they twist what their teachers say or do way out of proportion, many kids find the *real* deal boring.

Teachers and other participants in the school workplace would do well to utilize the following gossip antidotes:

A. Refrain from discussing students with other teachers, unless there is a shared educational need. Sometimes teachers need to discuss students they have in common just to check on their potential for achievement or aptitude for success in other subjects. But it never bodes well when a teacher says something like, "That Steve Frampton! Man, if I had a kid like that at home, I'd chain him to the bed (although, keep in mind, in reality, this may be an excellent idea)! Another taboo remark: "Did you hear about Emma Slunk? A few of her classmates told me that she got drunk at Friday night's party and slept with every guy on the basketball team." It's tantalizing to take this route; but in the end, it's counterproductive.
B. Refrain from discussing non-school-related incidents with other staff members (and, of course, with students) unless your words have purpose. Obviously, if a teacher becomes seriously ill, people

will talk. But to spread word that Mrs. Martin's husband beat her up
yet another time may have no merit, a malicious intent, and destructive consequences. Refrain from discussing among your colleagues
all those negatives. Admittedly, this is an incredible amount of fun.
As teachers finally reach the golden plateau of old fart status, they
have earned the right to moan, groan, complain, and even gossip.
The problem is, while gossip at school may extend to you a sense of
relief—even pleasure—it achieves nothing substantive and makes
your work environment hostile.

AVOID SEXUAL INNUENDO OR JOKES ABOUT POOP, PEE, AND OTHER BATHROOM STUFF IN FRONT OF STUDENTS.

The surest way to avoid having to deal with teenagers when it comes to
issues of sex, intimacy, homosexuality, or body gases is to not discuss
these subjects at all. However, since this is not feasible, nor is it recom-
mended from an education standpoint, you should consider the following quick advice: *Be careful.* When you sense that something bad is about
to escape from your voice box and have even the slightest little doubt you
should say it, *don't.*

Practically nothing else makes a teacher look more unprofessional than
a mixing of gratuitous sex into his classroom curriculum. Discussions
about—or mentions of—sex for the sake of learning self-control, self-
containment, and self-respect are valid and even desirable. But alluding
to sex with a wink and a nod, or a reference to an *American Pie*[6] film, does
not exactly project a teacher's image with visions of Mr. Tibbs or—that
classy, dignified fictional guy from another profession—Atticus Finch.[7]

Some high schools and middle schools are still teaching our children
how to correctly slip a condom on a banana; your making wisecracks
about the size of the banana may be a hoot, but the professionalism police
will throw you in the poky.

FIRMLY SET THE TONE: YOU ARE THE TEACHER; THEY ARE THE STUDENTS. YOU ARE THE ADULT IN THE ROOM; THEY ARE THE CHILDREN IN THE ROOM. (REPEAT: *YOU* TEACHER; *THEY* STUDENTS.)

Consider the following scenario on the first day of school: The students
are seated, nervously awaiting the first words from their new instructor.
The kids have already played and replayed so much drama regarding the
new school year, when it comes to levels of angst, one episode of "Getting

to Know the Teacher" pales by comparison. But the teacher can wreak lots of havoc in a kid's life, so what she talks about today—and her personality type—may be a precursor of either good times or bad times ahead.

This teacher has grabbed her students' attention; she then speaks in a moderate, but authoritative, voice.

Teacher: Okay, here's the deal. I'm not one of those teachers who comes here every day thinking of ways to put you guys down. I'm not sitting around dreaming up ideas to make your lives miserable. In fact, it's cool; we're all people here. We're all human. So the first thing we're going to do is decide on ten rules; we'll make the rules *together*. And if you don't like the rules, then we can throw them out and start over.

A student: Why are we gonna do that?

Teacher: (smiles) Because I want to show you I have respect for you, too; that we all have to abide by what we come up with. I want you to feel comfortable in here. I am not the boss; I am the facilitator.

Another student: You mean, if we don't like a rule, we can ignore it?

Teacher: No. I mean if you don't like a rule, we can throw it out or not even write that rule down in the first place.

First student: But you're the teacher, man!

Teacher: Hey, it's cool. I'm cool. And we're going to have a cool year.

Silently—in unison—the kids are drooling over their potential opportunities. They know this teacher is dead meat. Any teacher who—especially on the first day of school— doesn't take complete charge of her classroom, laying down law and defining order, will *die*. Children look for weak teachers like this one; they don't respect them, but what school child wouldn't like a teacher who looked him in the eye and told him she was "cool," they were going to have a "cool" year—and, in fact, the whole universe was, well, *cool?* In fact, it won't be long before this teacher's students won't *like* her either. Kids—especially high school students—see teachers who behave this way as weak or condescending (even though they may not even know what that word means). They may not know what to call it; they even may not have thought of it before, but their strongest feelings of safety lie in situations where the adult is in control. They want to know there's a difference between the adult in control and the children who are running around the room shooting spit wads at each other or having farting contests. A sure sign of professionalism on the part of a teacher comes in her clear, stern stipulation of authority, commanding presence, and unwillingness to compromise on issues she knows better—what's better for the students, the school, and even her.

One of the most oft-uttered criticisms of public school teachers comes from those who don't see us as behaving in a professional manner—and most of these (I believe) valid criticisms reflect the ten points delineated in this chapter.

Teachers will become an endangered species when either (A) computers can crack funny puns and, at the same time, walk around the room with a ruler; and (B) no one else in the universe sees teachers as professionals; they view us as adults who couldn't make a living elsewhere, so we had to denigrate ourselves by working with (gasp!) children.

Sometimes even *I* see us this way!

And that should scare you.

NOTES

1. Roger Federwisch, "Schools Enforce Dress Code for Teachers" (*USA Today*, August 25, 2003, Life section) 1.

2. Lorraine Lotowycz, "School Enforces Dress Code for Teachers" (*USA Today*, August 25, 2003, Life section), 1.

3. *Leave It to Beaver*, CBS from 1957–1962, ABC in 1962–1963; Ward Cleaver was played by Hugh Beaumont; the show was listed in *Time* magazine's 2007 unranked list of one hundred best TV shows of all time.

4. "Dress for Success," July 31, 2007, at English-test.net/forever/ftopic19182 .html.

5. Mr. Grim, as of this writing, has been teaching high school for thirty-two years. One of the most respected teachers in his entire (large) school district, Mr. Grim doesn't seem to be any worse off today for his encounter with Sister Mary Masters.

6. *American Pie* (Universal, 1999); After taking my wife to this movie, she came the closest she has ever come to divorcing me.

7. Two famous film characters known for their dignity: Mr. Tibbs, a teacher, played by Sidney Poitier, in *Call Me Mr. Tibbs* (United Artists, 1967), and Atticus Finch, a lawyer, played by Gregory Peck, in *To Kill a Mockingbird* (Universal, 1960).

3

Emote Passion for
What You Teach

It's not an accident that I'm an English teacher. It's also not an accident that I'm a teacher, as we discussed in chapter 1 (as an unrelated matter, it's not an accident that I'm about twenty pounds too fat). We are a product of our choices, often driven by our passions and desires. My entire life I have loved words: their sound, their look, their power—all of the creative and interesting things we can *do* with words, such as make people laugh with our puns and cry with our poems.

I seemed compelled to somehow incorporate this fascination into a career. Writing, of course, is the paramount avenue for this endeavor. It is a glorious method of self-expression, but not a guaranteed vocation. We all, however, need a way to pay the mortgage; we don't want to wind up on a street corner with one eye shut tight, drool rolling off our chin, and holding out a tin can. Teaching is a satisfying career, and contrary to the grumbling we often hear, we do make a decent living. I decided that teaching was how I would earn food and rent money; writing could be done on the side.

Teaching English has become my passion. I could not have been a math teacher, because I hate numbers; they bore me. History was a possibility, but its scope was too limited, especially compared to what I teach now. Teaching English affords me the opportunity to boldly pontificate my values and theories about life (through literature and writing) while I help kids learn new words and show them how to use those words. What could be better than that? During those occasional moments I am down, personal compensation comes in the knowledge that I may impart something solid—of substance—to my students that day, information and ideas I find interesting and important; in fact, many times I have told my classes, "We're doing [this] today, because I love it, and if you happen to enjoy it or learn from it—good." Of course, my tone is jocular, and they truly believe I'm joking. But in a sense, I'm not joking at all; I *mean* it.

Students know when their teachers are robotically going through the motions. They see us for what we are at the moment: public servants merely trying to get through the day (or hour), so we may collect our paychecks on the first of the month. Many of our students wonder why they are compelled to master the subjects we teach them; and if we don't provide them with a good answer (for it is a *very* good question), we will have lost these kids from the very onset.

Obvious, ridiculous fabrications may be worse. Take the following tenth grade English class scenario:

Teacher: Open your books to Act I, Scene 3.

Johnny: (from the center of the classroom) Mr. P., why do we gotta read *Julius Caesar* anyway?

Teacher: (showing some exasperation) Because it's good for you.

Johnny: How?

Teacher: Just do what I tell you!

Johnny: But—

Teacher: Come on; let's get going. We have a lot to cover today!

So what is the big lie here? The comment from the teacher about *Julius Caesar* being good for Johnny? Nah. Johnny already knows it's a lie, unless the material is imparted in such a way that Johnny himself recognizes he is learning something worthwhile. "We have a lot to cover today"? Nope; that's usually the truth. In English classes there is hardly a shortage of material to get through in a single class session. In this instance the lie had emerged earlier in the school year, when the teacher, via handouts and maybe a few spirited sermons, told his classes how vital and interesting the course was going to be for them. The truth is simple: If the teacher hates the play *Julius Caesar*, or if he dislikes theater (or literature, in general), the kids are going to sense this and probably hate *Julius Caesar*, too.

Recently, one of my students in the eleventh grade American literature class raised her hand during our discussion of a Wallace Stevens poem and commented, "You don't like this poem, do you?"

A bit rattled by her words, I lied. "Yeah, I like it. Why?"

She continued, "Well you don't like it nearly as much as some of the other stuff."

"How can you tell?"

She smiled. "Because with most of the other things we read in here, you're more excited, shouting—even jumping up and down. Today you look kinda bored."

I *was* bored.

I didn't like the Wallace Stevens poem, but I thought it was important enough to remain in the course because its theme usually triggered some good peripheral discussions about perceptions and reality. Obviously, however, I had not generated enough enthusiasm in my conveyance of these ideas to my students, and they easily detected it. Sometimes my students surprise me with their perceptive observations; they're not stupid.

Not usually.

Loving your subject matter will make it easier for you to plan your lessons, teach your students, and (gasp!) grade papers. When you assign writing topics that have piqued your own interest, you enjoy reading them, sometimes aloud to the students. They know you love their writing on these subjects; they can see it in your eyes and body language. When you are reading or studying stories, plays, or poetry you do not enjoy, your students respond accordingly.

I know this is true for English classes. I suspect it would also be the case for any other subject. There are math teachers at my school who actually walk around with a gleam in their eyes. *They like math!* The same goes for some of the government teachers, P.E. coaches, and foreign language teachers. Our most popular Spanish teacher takes extended vacations in Mexico at his own expense, so he can learn more Spanish. He didn't start out as a Spanish teacher either (he has a master's degree in American history!), but he has come to love so dearly what he does, he dreads the thought that one day he might be reassigned to the history department.

The advice here does not pose challenges of great cerebral proportions: You soon-to-be teachers must address this issue by carefully selecting your college majors and subjects for your credentials (teacher certification). You (college students) should lead with your passions and not necessarily the areas of your greatest aptitude or familiarity: Perhaps, you are gifted when it comes to computers and advanced levels of technology, although that is not where your heart is. The Civil War and other landmark moments in time really *do* float your whatever. You should become a history teacher. Not by mere coincidence will your technological knowledge infuse your history classes with extra excitement that would not have been possible without your expertise about the Internet, PowerPoint, audio-visual media, and maybe even some experiences with virtual history episodes. (By the way, just exactly how such virtual history episodes can be accomplished is way beyond the scope of *my* understanding. This is why guys who know computers command respect and adoration in the world of education. Hardly anybody understands what they do. I barely know how to *describe* what they do!)

But for experienced teachers who are bored with what they teach, here are two direct, but politely worded, suggestions:

BECOME AN EXPERT IN YOUR SUBJECT

Recently, my cousin analyzed our professions (she's a teacher, too) for a mother of one of her daughter's school classmates. She said, "Well, it's this way: When you teach children, it's different from teaching adults or college; you need to know about teaching itself—the how-to-teach thing. With college students, you need to know your subject matter well."

I asked her (initially, rather indignantly) whether this meant primary and secondary school teachers, even if they happened to be total morons in the subjects they were teaching, could simply wing it with their personalities and teaching charm. She surprised me by saying (thankfully, not in front of the other mother) she thought this was normally the case; that, for example, high school and middle school teachers need to stay only a page or two in the textbook ahead of the kids. If they were quality teachers, their results—although not necessarily commendable—would at least be acceptable.

Elementary school teachers certainly have to know how to humor tiny kids, wipe runny noses, and patch up boo-boos; the truth is, they don't have to be Rhodes Scholars in Play-Doh, multiplication tables, or abstract literary elements found in *Dick and Jane* books.

My premature mortification over my cousin's somewhat flippant disregard for my smarts (after all, I *do* know my subject matter!) was later somewhat mollified as I recalled my very first teaching experience: I had taught high school biology to a bunch of juvenile delinquents in a reform school near a big lake resort. The only thing I knew about biology was some malarkey about muscles in the human body. (Isn't that biology?) So, I made the little criminals in my classes learn about the various muscle groups, which they later trivialized by mischievously referring to certain unmentionable appendages on the male body as muscles.

Later—because I had lots of ant farms when I was a teenager and figured that I knew ants like the back of my hand—we spent an inordinate amount of class time on red ant colonization. This idea swiftly came to a crashing conclusion, when one of my student felons hurled a jar of ants at another one of the class's other demons, drawing a few trickles of blood from his forehead. The topics of muscles and ants, rather tenuously related to the subject of biology, dissipated into a total debacle; even these kids could see right through my lack of knowledge (and enthusiasm) for the subject I had been assigned to teach them. Of course, these cretins may also have mutilated just about anything anybody attempted to teach them, since more than half the class already had been convicted of at least one violent crime by the age of sixteen (just a guess; although I hate going out on a limb, this may also have had a little something to do with my abject failure in my feeble attempt as a biology teacher).

Truly knowing your subject makes you an expert in the eyes of your students and boosts your self-respect way off the charts. No one is going to fool *you* anymore—certainly not a bunch of hormonal, baggy-pants-wearing sixteen-year-olds—because *you* know more about your subject than anybody else you're aware of in (at the very least) the immediate vicinity of your classroom.

You will radiate passion.

And that's what the kids like to see: passion in their teachers. They like to see it a lot, and every so often it's contagious.

No wonder so many teachers rue the idea of getting up in the morning and going to work. If they honestly surged with excitement about the ideas they had planned imparting to their students that day, rousing from the sack would be much easier. Not having a handy grasp on their subject matter—only peripheral knowledge—taints even the slightest notion of radiating true passion for their work. Sure, they might be passionate about teaching, but most kids don't give a rat's behind about that little tidbit. The kids want to know that their teachers are really, really into *what* they're teaching them; if not, how can they be expected to like learning in general, let alone the drab, lifeless material that graying, balding, four-eyed geek in the front of the room is spewing in their direction?

Teachers must become, if they are not already, experts in their fields, *so* . . .

- Go back to school and get another degree in what you're teaching.[1] If you already have the highest degree and you still aren't the expert, pursue some additional courses in your subject or related fields. It won't kill you, and there are tremendous benefits for you and your students from your having delved back into the college environment.[2]
- Team up with another teacher in your department who has aced her stuff. Admit to her that you still have a lot to learn and can benefit from her experience and wisdom. She will gladly help you. This sort of adulation can't be ignored, especially by a female physical education teacher who looks like the lesbian stereotype portrayed in the movie *Porky's*.[3]
- Read books in your subject area. When I first began teaching, I bought this very geeky book called *365 Days to a Better Vocabulary*. I

actually forced myself to learn one word a day. I even did the nerdy word exercises in the back. I stuck with it for a full year and now offer those same words to my own students today. I now reveal to my students that I learned a word a day on my own, and, naturally, they scoff at my intellectual compulsiveness.[4] He who scoffs last scoffs best, so, naturally, I get the last scoff, since I still demand the same from them: one word a day; they must *own* the daily word in their written and oral discourse.

- Live what you teach; like it a lot. Do you teach science? Conduct some experiments at home (perhaps, with your own children) with some of those chemistry sets that you buy in the toy stores. I hated science when I was a kid, but the gift I most wanted for my tenth birthday was this totally cool-looking chemistry set with test tubes, ominous-looking powders and liquids, and the instruction booklet's warning that if I wasn't careful, it would blow off half my face. That was all I needed to see. I *loved* messing with that chemistry set!
- Do you teach a foreign language? Go to a foreign country and learn more about their language.

My Spanish teacher friend tells me that nothing made him a better Spanish teacher than spending all that time conversing with Mexicans in Mexico; in fact, when they weren't making fun of his Anglo accent, they actually tried to help him with his Spanish.

VARY YOUR INSTRUCTION.

Loving what you teach does not necessarily mean you must love the subject matter itself. Of course, it may help tremendously to love the actual subject, but let's face it: you're already here, and you're stuck. If you loathe your assignment or you find yourself lapsing into a coma because of boredom, you'd better have a plan. You are—like it or not—compelled to adapt. This could mean making the best out of another day teaching middle-schoolers how to "appreciate" seventeenth century art (actually, as I wrote those last few words, my own head drooped forward, and my eyes disappeared into their sockets).

So, as you begrudgingly begin another day of sticking those worn slabs of sticky stencils on the much-too-loud-and-annoying overhead projector, try this idea on for size: *Don't use the overhead projector!* That's right. Have the kids file by the pictures and gawk at them while they're standing or walking around. Sure, they'll probably be poking each other in the ribs and other places. (Freshmen boys like to play a game I affectionately refer to as "Grabsies." As they prod and jab each other's bodies, I tell them to stop playing "Grabsies," which, not surprisingly, brings their energetic, little activity to a screeching halt.)

The point: Do the things that *you* love to do with your students. Constantly change it around. Even within an hour of class time, have a variety of activities and methods; kids get bored after about ten minutes of the same thing, and you will, too, especially if you already don't care that much for your subject or the required curriculum. Pretty soon you'll find activities that are fun for *you*, and—viola!—your affection for what you teach will have increased immeasurably because you now love how you teach it.

The actual implementation of these ideas demands preparation and sacrifice on your part. Loving what you teach requires hard work, if it does not come to you naturally. But then again, you always have choices:

A. Teach something different.
B. Quit teaching altogether.
C. Suffer day in and day out (as your students suffer, too, because you're inevitably going to stink as a teacher).
D. Incorporate the ideas presented to you in this chapter for developing a love, passion, and thirst for your job, because you have procured a love, passion, and a thirst for what you teach.
E. Check to make sure the exhaust pipe on your car is working.

Really: Those *are* your choices.

And just remember this: The kids are watching every move that you make.

NOTES

1. The many other benefits of going back to school—and the best ways to achieve this goal—are discussed in detail in chapter 15.

2. Kevin Zhou, "When Teachers Go Back to School" (*Harvard Crimson*, November 28, 2006), at thecrimson.com/article.aspex?ref=516018.

3. *Porky's*, Astral Productions, 1982, directed by Bob Clark. The highlight character of this irreverent parody of American high schools in the early 1980s is the female physical education teacher.

4. I have searched extensively for this book, online and elsewhere; after forty-some years, apparently, it has ceased to exist.

4

✝

Stay off Your Tush

When you really think about it, many of us refer to other people's posteriors, rear ends, or buttocks, as one of the main—if not, *the* main—body apparatuses for catalyzing energy and force.

You often hear comments like these:

- "Hey, Joe, get off your butt, will ya'!"
- "Steve was hit by a car because he didn't move his butt fast when he was crossing the street."
- "Bill, hurry! Come on! Shake your ass!"

You never hear anyone yell, "Bill, hurry! Come on! Shake your *buttocks!*"

Politely, someone *may* command, "Please move your *tush.*"

But that would only apply to writing books like this one; here the word *ass* flies as completely inappropriate. Still, there's a lot to be gained by veteran teachers, new teachers, and would-be teachers when it comes to the simple concept of moving one's, uh, okay—*butt*—in the classroom. My bank account would be full if I had the proverbial dollar for every time I wanted to say to another teacher, "Your students would actually learn something from you—well, at least they'd have a better chance—if you would get up off your tush!"

Lazy teachers hurt our kids. There are billions of ways to define "lazy teacher," and even a few zillion examples to fit each of those definitions. Frankly, if you are sluggish enough to cause parents to shake their heads in consternation, principals to write you memos, students to crack jokes about you—and worst of all—other teachers to deflate in an embarrassment for the entire profession because of you, you should ditch your job immediately; in fact, stop reading this book now. If it's still new enough, maybe you can con the store into giving you a refund. You're wrecking the system. Yes, thank you for reading so far: for knowing what a terrific profession you had chosen; for learning about ways to love the subjects you teach; for understanding the importance of appearing to be a professional. Yes, thank you for all that.

Too bad, however, it may have all gone to waste.

Nothing you can do—*nothing*—will compensate in the long run for being a lazy teacher. Your wisdom, your creativity, your ingenuity, your knowledge—all of those pale in comparison to your slothfulness. But here's the really cool part: You can change it; you can become a teacher *known* for her energy and enthusiasm. You can garnish a reputation for being a bubbling ball of balm. As with practically anything else in life, ultimately, behavior alters emotion.

So let's examine the part of you that stipulates—broadcasts to the world—whether you are a faculty workhorse or not: your tush.

Standing, walking, jumping, skipping, pacing, running, twirling . . . all constitute examples of being *off* one's tush. The converse of this, of course, is when the entire body is supported by the buttocks, while the buttocks rests comfortably in a chair. This is an example of being *on* one's tush. For primary grade teachers, this tip may seem absurd; after all, the very nature of working with small kids—especially toddlers—requires grade school teachers to move to and fro and all about constantly. Some second grade teachers, for example, claim they have undergone what is tantamount to a tough aerobics workout before they are able to sneak away for a few moments to have lunch in solace with real, live adults. Sadly, however, some elementary school teachers move around the room about ten feet a day—total! Movement is less common among middle school and high school teachers, who mostly like to stand, emulating the lecture approach while instructing their classes. (Forget college teachers; they never move—period. I once ran into my college astronomy teacher in a movie museum and couldn't tell the difference between him and a wax figure of that bald guy on *Star Trek*.)

Shifting around the room—at least, standing—constitutes a multitude of advantages:

1. YOU EMBODY THE LOOK OF *THE* PERSON IN CONTROL.

While watching a televised baseball game, just how often have you observed the manager of one of the teams sitting—especially during a particularly crucial part of the game—on the bench in the dugout? The manager is in control, and he must look the part, too. Resting on his tush contradicts that image.

2. YOU CAN SCAN ALL SECTIONS OF THE CLASSROOM.

Consider what several of my students have told me—what goes on in other teachers' classrooms (which, of course, never, ever goes on in mine): Students have described teachers who were clueless about students' text messaging—persistent, even during exams—actual game playing on the cell phone or other such hallmarks of modern technology, students poking each other (in various places and for sundry reasons), cheating on assignments or tests, doing homework from other classes, writing nonsense notes to other kids, drawing/doodling, playing with video game devices, listening to iPods, eating, drinking coffee, kissing (sometimes passionately), making paper airplanes, using substances that have been banned by the school district.

Several years ago in a nearby school district, a student in woodshop class was videotaped by another student while the unsuspecting student rolled a marijuana joint (which today would have been relegated to YouTube). A huge brouhaha erupted, and instead of admonishing that specific woodshop teacher for not knowing what was going on right under his nose, the school district instituted a new policy about unsolicited, undercover videotaping, making it virtually impossible for those who work on school yearbooks—even teachers—to take candid photographs of students on school grounds.[1]

A teacher whose posterior had not been glued to a wooden chair for sixty-five consecutive hours would have, undoubtedly, noticed a student who prepared pot to serve up as his morning delicacy.

3. YOU CAN SEE EVERYBODY.

Some students pique our desire to look at them more than we look at other students. For aesthetic reasons alone, it's easy to fall into a trap . . . or two . . . or three, when it comes to looking at our students. As a teacher, one of your responsibilities is not to be easily beguiled by the attractiveness of your students. However, human nature—or whatever—being what it is, teachers must be especially careful to look around at all the children. While teachers lecture, check busy student groups at work, or flow about the room during students' seatwork, professionalism requires teachers to use their eyes all over the place, and not to hide one student behind the other—though tempting it may be.

While you walk around the room, all students may see you—and you may see all students!

See how well that works out!

4. YOU LOOK MORE IMPOSING.

Teachers constantly complain about their discipline problems, linking their failures to their own body size or physical stature. Especially female teachers make this complaint: "If I weren't so small . . . ," they whine.

My wife teaches high school; she currently is working nights at what is charitably referred to as "the adult school," and her students are not exactly, shall we say, of Harvard Graduate School caliber. For most of her students, this is, after numerous chances, their last stop; they will either graduate high school, or they will fail her class and wipe out completely. So these students definitely have a huge stake in their experience in my wife's nighttime English course.

Most hardcore discipline cases do not develop in my wife's class. Despite the fact that Mrs. G. is barely five-feet, two-inches tall and weighs about 112 pounds, she ordinarily has her students eating from the palm of her hand. But when she finally plods through the door to our home around ten o'clock at night, she is utterly exhausted. She's outputted a maximum amount of energy and a seriously high level of exertion in the few hours each evening that she spends with her students. Along with her remarkable class preparation (discussed at length later), she has propped herself up as a very visible sight in her classroom.

She moves!

One of these days I am going to ask her to wear one of those pedometers while she's teaching. The space she's covered and the number of calories she's burned could reach astounding record heights.

The bottom line: When it comes to looking imposing, someone six feet tall who lounges in a chair the entire hour cannot hold a candle to a midget who stands and hovers over her students, energetically, vigorously, striding from one place in the classroom to another place in the classroom for almost the entire length of the class period.

So what are you saying, Bruce? Are you telling us that sitting down at your desk for most of the class period every day is a sign of a teacher's ineptness?

Yes.

5. YOU POINTEDLY IMPLY WHO'S THE BOSS— NOT BRUCE SPRINGSTEEN; HE'S "THE BOSS"

There can be only one boss—one person in charge. And indisputably contrary to some of the pabulum emerging from Blowhard Talking Heads Education Central, it's the *teacher* who captains the ship—or *should*.

The classroom is not primarily a collaborative effort. Sure, everyone has to work together to achieve maximum success, to reach goals, to raise local property values by getting higher scores on standardized achievement tests; but when push comes to shove, whenever we get a bunch of people together—especially when the "bunch" consists of oily-skin adolescents—the adult in charge must be, well, *in charge*. He may take suggestions, ask questions, and offer propositions, but, ultimately, he is the final arbiter, decision maker, judge, rule-setter, god-in-charge, and third base coach, deciding whether to send the runner home from second base on a ground ball up the middle.

The key: He must look the part.

Again ask yourself: Who fills the role of "boss" better? The teacher sitting meekly behind her desk, every so often craning her neck to check her students' behavior, *or* the teacher standing firmly before the class and then toddling about, briskly going from student to student—whether it's to look a student in the eye, pat him on the back, ask him a question, or grab him by the hair, and then twist him around and throw him to the floor? Just who plays the part of boss better? (By the way, in case you have any doubt, that part about grabbing by the hair and throwing to the floor is a joke. Besides, it won't work; some kids don't have enough hair.)

6. YOU OFFER PERSONALIZED HELP FOR EACH STUDENT

Yes, this may be accomplished with the teacher sitting on her posterior while sucking on a frozen candy bar for the entire class period; theoretically, she can help students individually as they come up *to her*.

But they won't.

And she won't.

Moving about creates an impetus for actually doing something, once you have used the power of inertia to get your body in motion. Imagining a teacher in motion, but doing nothing once he has arrived at a specific location in his classroom, may conjure up an image of Billy Crystal in *When Harry Met Sally*: He's clueless, dancing around the room with an animated, forced smile—something he called, "White Man's overbite."[2]

Teachers who *move*, help their students' needs. They actually lessen the distance between them, treating their students as though they were human beings.[3] I highly recommend a good deodorant and mouthwash, however; you wouldn't want your students to back away from you in a retreat reminiscent of Santa Ana's soldiers at the Alamo.

7. YOU REVEAL TO YOUR STUDENTS THAT YOU ARE WILLING TO WORK HARD FOR THEM

Jeanna Bryner of Fox News said in *Live Science* that American teachers have captured a reputation for being lazy. She wrote, "In a high school class, one out of every three students is sitting there and not interacting with a teacher [who is also sitting there] on a daily basis."[4] It's not news to us that many parents think we sit on our butts all day reading the newspaper and listening to our own iPods. And parents have this notion because they get it from their children:

Parent: So, Marnie, what kind of a teacher is Mr. Borders?

Marnie: He's really smart. But he's such a lazy ass!

And why is Mr. Borders known as a "lazy ass"? He sits around all day; or, at least, that's how his students perceive him. He may actually be on his feet half the day, but if he's sitting the other half, the kids have the overall impression that he sits around "all day" twiddling his thumbs.

And it's not just the iPod that labels him as being lazy—or reading the newspaper: Hank, an extraordinarily bright student, spoke to me about his geography teacher, Mr. Sling, (not his real name), an unpopular teacher at his school. He evaluated Mr. Sling as lazy because he sat around a lot.

"And what is he doing while he sits at his desk?" I asked Hank.

Hank simply shrugged and answered, "I don't know; I think he's grading essays or something."

Which means . . . he is working.

But that doesn't matter. To Hank—and countless other students of Mr. Sling—a teacher sitting at his desk for sizable chunks of time fosters an extremely unfavorable impression.

Carla said, "I like hard-working teachers. It makes me want to work harder, too. I mean, if my teacher is just moping around all period, it sucks the energy right out of the classroom.

8. YOU CATCH BEHAVIOR PROBLEMS
BEFORE THEY MATERIALIZE OR ESCALATE.

"Paul's a chicken."

"Why do you say that?"

"He just is."

"Not good enough. You call somebody a *chicken*, you gotta' back it up."

"OK, OK. The thing is, he's always hitting people, saying bad stuff to the girls, and he even threatened Oscar [the school geek] a few times when you weren't listening."

"I wasn't listening?"

"Nope. You're never listening, Mr. Slug. You're always sittin' at your desk, hardly paying any attention to what's going on in the room."

But Mr. Slug *was* paying attention to what was going on in his classroom. He could see—from a slight distance—that things were fine. His students busily worked on the Xeroxed handouts he provided them, and discussions in different sectors of the room allowed him to believe learning had been taking place.

The problem: Some kids are excellent at hiding their no-goods. "No-goods" are those tricky little maneuvers that set apart some of the bad kids from some of the good kids. The good kids would never do a no-good behavior: physically assaulting other students; stealing money; encrypting the desks with slogans and pictures no one in a normal state of mind could ever decipher; sticking chewing gum under the desktops; mischievously commenting under their breath to students around them; instigating a fight with words; profanity—you get the idea. From afar, most teachers don't stand a chance of discovering no-goods. But rocketing off their tushes, teachers have a dandy chance of deterring no-goods. Most kids will not attempt to steal a quick look in their backpacks at their text messages, if they suspect you would trot directly toward them in a surprising instant. If you're too fast for them—a rarity, especially for old geezer teachers—they will simply take their shenanigans to the classroom of the dolt who is teaching next door.

9. YOU INTIMATE A MOTHER (OR FATHER)
FIGURE TO YOUR STUDENTS

One may fairly argue the validity of that last statement. Many kids find their parents sitting on their derrieres, too. The days when mother worked all day in the kitchen cooking meals and then took precious time to darn socks, do laundry, and decorate the house (after thoroughly cleaning it) may be over. This is not to say that mothers are not working hard at their jobs or careers; their children just don't get to see the domestic part of them very often.

The same is true for fathers: Dads who mow lawns, fix leaky pipes, and change engine oil may have gone the way of the single-screen movie house.

But here's why teachers suggest parental ideals when they move around the room, never sitting at their desks: They are perceived by their students as caring. Hard work, physical exertion, individualized instruction, careful assessment, casual conversation, comments of praise, warnings of danger, offers of extra help—all of these behavioral images, tempered with the knowledge that the teacher who instigates them does so lovingly—come from the teacher who is in charge. He rules the roost; he makes the rules—and wants what's best for his students. He protects these kids, and they trust him.

Those teachers who perch their bottoms on those creaky wooden chairs by the elevated, smelly old desks: How can anyone trust those guys?

10. YOU SHED CALORIES, DEVELOP STRONGER LEG MUSCLES, AND BUILD UP ENDURANCE

This, by the way, is not as much of a joke as you may think. I always look forward to the beginning of the school year, for I know I'm going to shed some unwanted pounds right from the get-go. All that constant—and I mean *constant*—walking, standing, and arm waving can't help but turn me into the slim, trim hunk that I'd been before sliding into the ice cream, sodas, cheeseburgers, tacos, inactive physicality of summer vacation. In a few short weeks, I'm once again ready to adorn magazine covers, showing off my trim, svelte body.

That aside, please go back and read item number seven again; it may be the most important justification for getting you off your tush.

I'll just sit here on this soft, plush chair and wait for you.

Honestly, if the students see you working hard, some of them may actually contract a rare childhood abnormality, the guilt pang, for being so lazy, nonresponsive, and apathetic to your instruction. One or two kids may think to themselves, "If Mr. G. has all of this energy and is working so hard to teach me, then I ought to do something, such as, like, reach over and pick up a pencil. I mean, like, that's the least I can do!"

One former student I've become very close to also became an English teacher. One of her other English teachers (not I) was actually a model for her own, personal classroom style; however, he was a negative model. While this guy lectured or conducted class discussions about literature, he sat in front of the room at his desk, sipping from a can of soda and munching on a Snickers candy bar (a dark chocolate Milky Way, I could fully appreciate).

Besides the fact that she and the rest of the kids wallowed in digestive distress because they had become hungry and thirsty, my former student told me she would sit there and think, "How lazy can he be! How does he expect us to work hard, if he sits there stuffing his face and never gets off his rear end!" (This former student would never have even thought in terms of the word "ass.")

My friend is a mover and a shaker in her own classroom; and although there is always the physical temptation to want to plop into a chair and rest for a moment, she never submits to the urge. She can't; just the notion of being anything like her lazy English teacher has become abhorrent to her.

To acquire motivation for forming better teaching habits, even teachers need role models. It's not always easy, but physically active teaching ranks as one of the most significant factors in healthy American classrooms. Getting motivated to be dynamic, throwing off the reigns of boredom, is a challenge. Columnist John Stossel concluded, "Working hard for public school students has to be [a teacher's] own reward. Because a lazy teacher is paid as much as a good one—more if he has seniority."[5] And working hard sometimes requires a physical effort.

There are a few ways that you can move around freely, naturally, without the students beginning to think you are wired by something you illegally digested that morning:

Move While You Are Lecturing

Good speakers do this anyway. They rarely stand in a stationary position. It works off lots of nervous energy, seduces boredom, and burns calories. You may be thinking to yourself as you move to the right, to the left, up the middle, and so on, "Hmmm. . . . I might not really have to do the treadmill at the gym tonight! Maybe I won't even have to go to the gym tonight at all!"

Seriously.

In addition to these advantages to you and your students from your constant movement, you also place yourself in the strategic position of being able to, when necessary, bop an inattentive or disruptive student on the back of the head.

Move About During Group Work

You probably are not soliciting my personal view of "group work" or "cooperative learning," as "they" refer to it, so I will not provide it here.

Let it suffice that most of you are doing—or planning to do—at least some group activities with your students. What any expert in this field will readily tell you is that for your students to be optimally successful in their communal endeavors, you, the teacher, must constantly move from group to group. You do not sit at your desk. You do not walk out the door for a moment and check the weather (I do that often, sorry to say; I, too, love the smell of napalm in the morning)! You do not talk on the telephone. You move from group to group. Even if the little rascals are doing well, you should periodically ask them if they have any questions. Even if you stand there and peruse their busy activity for a few seconds, they will get the idea you are monitoring them. They may not even look upon you as a snoop, an unwanted interloper; they may get the notion that you care enough about what they are doing to actually observe it (which is a lot more than most of their other teachers have been doing)!

Move About During Individual Seatwork

This may be one of the very few opportunities you have to get to know your little darlings personally. You don't need a hushed, overtly serious atmosphere in your classroom for this either. I sometimes go from seat to seat while the kids are working and talk about things that are completely irrelevant to what they are doing: "So, did you hear the game last night? The Angels blew it again!" or "How did your job interview go yesterday?" or (to a boy) "I like your bangs." or "Did you hear anything about the ASB prom selection site?" or "Gained a little weight there, haven't you?" Whatever. Merely relate your questions and comments suitable to their personalities; you don't want to irritate a kid with a silly, offensive quip that makes him want to punch you in the nose. The bottom line: Keep moving from desk to desk!

After each class is over, you will stagger over to your desk and sink into a chair with a loud sigh—of exhaustion. This happens whether it is at the end of the day or near the start. If it doesn't occur, if you are not completely pooped out, temporarily depleted of your energy—evaluate your previous hour of teaching.

You probably weren't doing your job!

NOTES

1. If you ever run into me and ask about this, I'll plead the Fifth in order to stop you from any further probing: I won't name the district here, but anyone reading this who knows me personally will know exactly which nearby school district had been involved in this scandal.

2. *When Harry Met Sally* (Castle Rock Entertainment, 1989); Harry, played by Billy Crystal, mentions this phenomenon of very uncool suspended dance motions and facial expressions.

3. Jeanna Bryner, "Live Science," *Fox News*, February 28, 2007, at foxnews .com.

4. Ibid.

5. John Stossel, "Teachers' Unions Are Killing the Public Schools," February 15, 2006, at realclearpolitics.com/commentary/com-15-06-JS.html.

5

Spotlight Reality: If It Doesn't Matter, Don't Teach It

Remember the science teacher on an old TV show called *The Wonder Years*: the guy who droned on and on and on . . . and on in front of his middle school classes about—nothing? Remember how boring he was? Remember the apparently *meaningless* information he imparted to his eighth graders?[1]

If you ask yourself, "What matters the most in my job? Why am I a teacher? Why has my career been devoted to children?—the answer is hardly startling. That teacher in *The Wonder Years* is a caricature of teachers throughout the United States; most of us have had teachers just like that. They are the ones we shudder about, while making fun of them years later (if we remember them at all). Then we seemed to know they were just, well, there—doing some rote, routine exercise in order to bide their time—blatantly clueless about what their students really needed to learn to make their lives better.

I had an epiphany about twenty years ago when I almost decided to quit teaching and actually work for a living. I was tired, frustrated, and confused; most of all, however, I had come to a head with a daily feeling of spinning my wheels. I perceived what I taught the kids had some importance, but I wasn't sure how much substance or why, and—worse—I didn't have a clue how to persuade my students to grasp the significance of what they had learned in my class. Yes, there were those daily lesson plans, course curriculum guides, state standards, and department meetings in which fervent—sometimes hostile—discussions about what we were to teach took place.

But there was something wrong.

And that's when it hit me: I had a new personal credo, a new insight, a new goal: *I would always teach kids what they most needed to know*. Hours had wasted away, as I rambled on endlessly about ostensibly worthless material for which my students would never have any pragmatic use: conjugating verbs, predicate nominatives, introductory adverbial clauses, assonance, meter, clustering.

This wasn't a game; we weren't here to memorize data or absorb concepts and then discard them later. There was no purpose to that kind of classroom. The kids knew it; I knew it. Nobody was fooling anybody else, and *everybody* knew, with a wink and a nod, that the jig was up.

As you courageously attempt to integrate this philosophy about the curriculum into your teaching, you may want to sit down, let out a deep sigh—I like to grab a Diet Pepsi and some sunflower seeds for this—and consider the alternatives. There are basically two ways of approaching this philosophy and coming up with a tangible plan of action: (1) *You* decide what matters in these kids' lives and assemble materials that will complement your transmission of those ideas; or (2) You reverse that route by examining the materials you *already* possess and use these resources to develop issues pertinent to the lives of your students. In other words, find out what you need and then get it—or find out what you already have and figure out how to use it.

The result should be the same: Your goal is to speak to the passions and necessities existing in the everyday world of your students. This is a far cry from saying (if you are a geometry teacher), something like this: "We need to study angles and measure their sizes because one day many of you may be, uh, architects."

Yeah, right. Like Guito Zanguini in my first period class is going to become an architect! Guito can't even keep track of his escalating pants size, let alone figure out how to calculate an isosceles triangle.

Remember, your ultimate accomplishment will have been for your students to learn the subject in practical, reasonable terms that actually make some realistic sense to them; your secondary goal will be for them to actually *know* you've done this. And by way of residual reward, some of your students will not only realize they are learning that which is worthwhile to them, they will *talk* about you and the course matter with family and friends, asking them for their input, soliciting their opinions about what you have imparted to them.

Again: You need to decide what truly matters to your students and then go with it—one-way or the other. Before I give a few across the curriculum examples of topics that matter to teenagers, consider this five-step process for making your decisions about your class's—or your entire department's—curriculum.

1. PUTTING THE ACTUAL COURSE YOU ARE TEACHING COMPLETELY ASIDE (FOR A MOMENT), JOT DOWN A SHORT LIST OF WHAT ALL CHILDREN THE AGES OF YOUR STUDENTS SHOULD LEARN IN PREPARATION FOR LIFE

Forget for an instant that you are a high school or middle school teacher (which, depending on your circumstances, may temporarily bring about feelings of total bliss). Try hard to squirm away from this potentially euphoric moment and be totally honest with yourself: What do all children—the ages you are teaching or would be teaching *if* you had been a teacher—need to know in order to prepare them better for life? Two or three topics will immediately zip into your mind: how to be a better friend; how to get along with my parents; how to plan for my future. You probably can think of dozens of topics that matter in real life to these children.

2. EXAMINE CAREFULLY THE MATERIALS YOU ALREADY HAVE AVAILABLE TO YOU

Presumably, your courses have been supported by a textbook or two. You have probably collected magazine articles, newspaper clippings, multimedia slides and videos, portfolios, DVDs, computer graphics, pamphlets, books, notes—and who knows what else—in order to wow your students. How many ideas that you wrote down for number one actually have matches in number two? In other words, of those areas you deemed important—maybe even vital—for your students to learn (because they matter in real life), how well were they supported by materials you already had assembled for your course?

In all honesty, a meticulous inspection of your stuff should reveal a surprising number of matches and volumes of materials you can use to teach children about what matters in real life. That old essay in *Runner's World* magazine from essayist George A. Sheehan, dying of prostrate cancer at the time he wrote the piece, certainly brings home ideas about mortality and gratitude, and introspection.[2] Aren't these the inspirations that make life more meaningful? And just think about how many stones you knocked off with one bird—or whatever: You've taught the kids to read, think critically, and maybe even expanded their vocabulary (all these dealing with *standards*, of course), while you have inspired them to take their own lives more seriously.

3. CONSIDER WHAT ELSE YOU MUST PROCURE TO TEACH THESE CONCEPTS

There's a wealth of information out there; help dangles from every crevice of American society. I'm not talking about those mathematics flash cards you buy from those boring education supply stores; I'm referring to, for instance, a major film about blackjack that advanced some sharp, high level mathematical concepts that had spurred gamblers on to win millions of dollars. OK, don't advocate gambling; but perhaps having a mock blackjack tournament, using both modern card counting techniques and the principles in blackjack that dictate when you should hit your hand or sit on your hand, would be amazingly helpful to your math students. It would be fun, too.

I'm about to make a rather embarrassing confession here. But please believe me when I promise you I will make absolutely sure nothing bad comes of it. As insurance to that claim, I have my wife, who—if I don't guarantee this turns out benign—will kill me. At any rate, I have been teaching my six year-old son the ins and outs of blackjack—what gamblers call "basic strategy": when to hit; when to stand; when to split; when to double down; and when to take insurance against a dealer's ace card. I've also advised him—not about card counting per se, but card value approximations—to carefully watch tens and small cards as they flow from the deck. He has learned how to count to twenty-one faster than any adult I know, and he can predict with a degree of accuracy the size of the next card the dealer wields from his hands.

Assuming my little first grader doesn't grow up to be a crazed, addicted gambler, knowing how to add quickly and having some idea about number values helps him in a practical endeavor he can readily understand; for his limited world experience, he has absorbed the importance of rudimentary mathematics. I do like using flash number cards for teaching addition and multiplication tables; card counting, however, beats those traditional methods of learning numbers and simple math hands down.

So whatever you need—games, books, newspapers, taped audio interviews or readings, guest speakers—get them. On your federal income tax return and in most states you can write your school expenses off on your taxes. Considering the parsimonious position people render toward education these days, extra money is hard to come by. In the long run, you may wind up funding your supplementary enterprises yourself; however, eventually, you have the kids eating from the palm of your hand. And you'll be saving lots of money on blood pressure pills and other medical expenses. Just knowing that you're teaching skills and ideas that truly make a difference in children's lives is better medicine than any doctor could ever prescribe for you at a pharmacy.

4. DURING YOUR PLANNING, STREAMLINE YOUR NEW IDEAS TO THE STANDARDS FOR THE COURSE YOU TEACH

A glut of ideas about planning will be discussed in depth later; however, here we should be thinking about what you *want* to teach the kids and how to adjust those ideas to the course standards on which you, the teacher, are going to be evaluated. When your supervising administrator comes into your classroom to do her biannual observation of your teaching, and you happen to be playing moderator in a trivia game with sports content material not even apparently close to your subject matter, you had better have a handy justification for your unconventional lesson. Finding standards that cover oral presentations is quite easy, and they would apply here nicely. Upon first glance, however, the visiting administrator may be in the back of the room scowling like Alex Rodriguez of the Yankees after he had gone one for sixteen in the 2005 American League Divisional Playoff Series.

5. REVIEW WITH YOUR STUDENTS WHAT YOU HAVE DONE, AND HOW YOU DID IT

This is quite easy. If you are way off the charts nuts in the approach you've taken to your subject matter, you may want to occasionally—and I do mean *occasionally*—justify to your students (and by virtue of that approach, probably their to parents) what you're doing. You could say something like this:

> Today we had a mock presidential election, practiced exit polling techniques, did an analysis of the results, and compared those numbers to the actual outcome of the mock election. In a history class, it's important to understand how leaders wound up in positions of power, whether they had been duly elected by the people—which does not happen in despotic regimes—or came about as the back side of a coup. In America, democracy thrives, mainly because of the way we conduct our elections.

Or, "Today we made greeting cards for parents and family. You had the opportunity to practice your creative side, writing techniques, and computer design. But most important, you made something nice for some of the people who matter to you in your lives."

You have refreshed everyone's mind as to the academic validity of your approach, and actually taught your students what matters in real life. There's no need to allude to a specific standard or read it aloud. Only the most anal-retentive teachers would go that route—and the most eccentric administrators force you to comply.

OK, enough theory on this subject; here are some rough lessons that encompass real-life topics and skills students will find useful:

1. Students give various types of oral presentations, covering topics that matter: product demonstration, job interview, persuasive speech, life's statement (a speech about their core selves). Lengths of presentation and expectations about writing mechanics differ, depending upon the assignment, but all are related to their real world. Teenagers, for example, not only love talking about themselves (though they'll deny it), they adore presenting their thoughts and feelings about social issues on the micro level: dating, relationships, marriage, divorce, parenthood, fooling around with each other, etc. Give them a formal structure for presentation, and with experience, they learn about formal speaking, thinking under pressure, and so much more.

2. Students are constantly writing. Topics are prompted from major newsmagazines, social journals, newspapers, and DVDs—topics pertaining to modern interests and problems: abortion, rights/responsibilities, war, crime, racism, sex and dating, etc. Again, topics can come from them or you or both. Don't complicate things by forcing a heavy-handed, overly "scholarly" approach down their fifteen-year-old throats.

3. Values are expounded from the literature: These are not perfunctory discussions; all discourse on the literary works matters. Instead of reading Walt Whitman's "Song of Myself" and answering the questions at the end of the piece, we probe the ideas and essential values that can be garnished from this poem: themes about death and immortality are dissected and written about. Most students have interesting personal stories to tell about these topics. Even if they don't, when you put ideas in the realm of *their* real world, they will take an interest.

4. Group problem solving gives all students a stake in the class: My students normally are not involved in a great deal of group work; however, a wonderful research and oral presentation exercise can be developed through the use of asking the students to find solutions to specific problems. As an example: A group of five is asked to read

an article by Mortimer Zuckerman from *U.S. News & World Report* about the impact of absentee fathers in American homes.[3] They are told to outline the problems Leo cites and then develop solutions to solve those delineated problems, through the use of a specific format I had previously taught them on problem solving.[4] More writing assignments can be fueled by this activity.

5. A well-known person in the school (student, teacher, secretary) has died; now we will read about death and coping with loss. A tremendous body of literature (Thornton Wilder's *Our Town* and Robert Frost's "Out, Out—" are just a couple of examples) flourishes on this topic. Students can talk (or write about) their own experiences on this issue.[5]

6. During a unit on the Holocaust, disseminate supplementary materials to your students—not about the Holocaust, per se—but about racism and discrimination right here in the United States. Studying history in a history class, as your learned history teachers already know, does not have to be all about dates and places. Circumstances breed other—even worse—circumstances, and which of these circumstances in America today make us ripe for social destruction or another holocaust-type scenario? Even apparently benign situations like high school clique stereotypes can be examined with these probing questions: *Should we judge a book by its cover? If it walks like a duck and quacks like a duck, is it a duck?* Obviously, there is no patented answer to either of these questions.

7. In a science course, teachers usually get around to discussing the great inventors. How often do they get around to talking about their inventions and various subsidiary issues that spring from those inventions? What if Albert Einstein had not fled to America? How would have Adolf Hitler's possession of the atomic bomb have impacted the outcome of the history of the world?

   Understanding science as a social phenomenon—and the ways it affects their lives—rallies kids to the side of the teacher and garnishes trust in what they are being taught. Belching and flatulence have social strata, too. And they are a part of science—no? What is funnier to teenage boys than the act of laying a fart in public?

   I rest my case.

8. The tedium of studying and understanding mathematics shoves lots of young people into other courses of study. Even children talented in math—kids who know numbers and know them well—surrender to ennui. Math teachers must find relevant problems to allow students to discover the worth of finding their own pragmatic solutions. For example, some kids find the science of weight gain and weight loss fascinating.

Please—if you're a math teacher—is it not possible to teach children how to add, subtract, multiply, and divide by going into serious studies of weight control, such as exercise, food intake, and other forms of dieting? When we get into fat, carbohydrates, protein, and all the other components of digestion, food use, and weight control, math suddenly becomes important to kids.

And we shouldn't stop there. Frankly you shouldn't give a rat's behind what the course curriculum mandates that you use as examples; you can provide interesting, pertinent illustrations of math-knowing necessities in subjects these kids really care about. And you know what else? They'll *want* to come to your class because of that; they'll learn all those nifty math skills in spite of themselves (or the out-of-the-loop dopes who wrote your curriculum).

The bottom line: Make the assignments meaningful to your students; if you do, they will respond. Too often, students have related to me their unfortunate experiences with teachers who bore them to tears. These students almost always say this is because they see no reason to spend so much time and effort learning material that will not matter to them—ever.

They may see a poem about a tree or a sunset as a mere exercise in "having to study a poem." And it is. Truthfully, who *cares* for a poem about a tree? If you're some sort of weird duck who rhapsodizes about trees so intensely that you have to write it down in poetic form, well, good for you.

I guess.

If it matters, give them some reasons. Show them how it affects *their* lives. Motivation is key; however, motivation is not difficult to provide, if there is relevance. When you plan your lessons, you can simplify this entire process by asking yourself three basic questions:

1. What do I want them to learn today?
2. How will it matter in their lives?
3. What is the best way for me to teach it?[6]

If you ask and answer these questions, you will have won most of the battle. Students will look forward to your class. They will tell you that your class is the only one they've shown up for today. They will laud you to others, and will come in after school to bestow more praise upon you. They will bring you hot food and bake you cookies. They will shower you with gifts, some of which will make you independently wealthy, so you can quit teaching and actually get a life.

You didn't know it could be *that* good, did you?

NOTES

1. *The Wonder Years,* ABC-TV, "Dance with Me," Season 1, Episode 6.

2. George A. Sheehan, "And Miles to Go Before I Sleep" (*Runner's World,* March, 1995), 18.

3. Mortimer B. Zuckerman, "Attention Must Be Paid" (*U.S. News & World Report,* August 18, 1997), 92.

4. The reference is *8 Steps to Effective Group Problem-Solving,* by Bruce J. Gevirtzman; This master's thesis can be found in the Whittier College Library.

5. *Our Town,* a play by Thornton Wilder, and "Out, Out—" a poem by Robert Frost, deal with similar themes: the fragility of life; the certainty of death; and slowing down time by having gratitude.

6. For detailed lesson planning—the whys, hows, whens, and wheres of lesson planning for relevance—see suggestions in chapter 16.

6

Entertain an
Acting Requirement

While you were in college, did you take an acting class as a perquisite to participation in the education program? Did you take any acting classes *while you were in* the education program? If not, you should have. Acting classes should be mandatory for obtaining teacher credentials.

William Shakespeare must have been talking about schoolteachers when he wrote, "All the stage is a classroom and the men and women there are mere *teachers* (or something like that)."

Good teachers do good acting.

In the introduction to this text, I described one of the most difficult days of my life (my mother's death), a day that also coincided with the very last session of a summer school term. Inside I was a palpable mess; outside I unsuccessfully bantered and cajoled with my students the same (I thought) as I'd always done before. The kids possessed keener intuition than I had figured, but acting is a skill every teacher should develop and then store in his arsenal.

What is acting? You portray a different person; you transcend the real and project moods and emotions you are not actually feeling at all. *You fake it.* You are what you're *not.* You conjure emotions appropriate to the moment, even though, in reality, you may not be, to even the slightest extent, experiencing those feelings.

The best actor is a bit of a liar.

The best teacher is also a bit of a liar.

A faker.

If you have not had the following charming moment yet (and I can't believe that you haven't), you will soon, so be patient: The kid in the back of the class is not paying attention to anything you're saying. Worse, he is snickering and making faces, because he is engaged in a sidebar conversation with the guy in the seat next to him. Worse still, both of these goofballs are dispensing expressive reactions to each other's comments, which further infuriate you, because their mere inattentiveness has now transmogrified into teacher abuse. A couple of the other children laugh at one of their remarks, and, as usual, you are unable to hear the inflammatory wisecrack. The real you wants to stop lecturing, run back there, grab the offenders by their shirt collars, and heave them into the nearest wall, as you run off a stream of obscenities that would make any Al Pacino movie character proud.

Of course, you may have noticed that you are *not* Al Pacino, although you do have a different sort of actor in you. The actor in you does not do the Al Pacino thing; in fact, it is the actor in you who manages self-discipline that even Jesus would admire:

You: (quietly and with a wry smile—and notice—not even raising his voice) Jimmy and Fernando, that must be a pretty cool conversation you're having back there. . .

They halt their exchange, but neither one verbally responds.

You: (with pleasant sincerity) Can I get in on some of it?

Again, no response from the offenders.

You: (sweet, almost hurt) Is there something I should know about, guys?

Jimmy: (finally) Nooo.

You: (another smile) Because I hate to stop one of my lectures for nothing. *(Through your teeth, but with great sincerity.)* See, I lose my train of thought when something out there distracts me. Funny, somebody in here sneezed a little while ago . . . and did you see how I lost my concentration?

No answer: It didn't happen; no one had sneezed.

You: Fernando?

Fernando: No.

You: (looking forlorn to the rest of the class) Well, it just goes to show how everybody loses out when someone creates even a *tiny* distraction while I'm talking. *My* problem, I guess, but—until I can do better—will you try to be careful so I don't lose my very fragile concentration? Jimmy . . . ?

Jimmy: Yeah.

You: Fernando . . . ?

Fernando: Yes.

You: (still hanging on to his saccharine tone) Great. Let's see . . . where were we . . . ?

Every year this scene repeats itself until my students eventually understand that bugging me bugs *everybody*—and bugging everybody won't be tolerated.

It always works the same way. Secretly, I want to take both of these teenagers over my lap and thrash their behinds with a large mallet; outwardly, I come across to them as candid, controlled, and—amazingly—*right*. Some students detect obvious sarcasm in the way I handle these situations.

Keep rehearsing your part, however, until the sincerity outshines any possible range of sarcasm. Sarcasm may have its place, but not here. If you yell and scream at your students at every infraction of your rules for classroom decorum, you will begin to sound like a raging lunatic. And they will turn you off, as they are mentally framing a picture of Jessica Alba on the TV screens of their minds, forgetting that *you* even exist at this particular moment.

Just as you begin one of your frequent verbal attacks, they silently will be saying to themselves, "There he goes *again*. [sigh] Oh, well. Now what *should* I be thinking about right now that would be a heck of a lot more pleasant than this professional nag with the short stubby legs? Hmmm. . . . Jessica Alba in a bikini comes to mind. . . . I wish this guy would just *shut up!*"

Acting is a biggie. Here are some common situations in which acting helps you to communicate better with your students and eventually gets them to respect you more; these ideas may be the difference between your showing up for work the next morning with a pleasant smile on your face, or finally accepting that offer to work for your brother's fertilizer company:

1. YOU ARE PHYSICALLY ILL

If you at all can help it, you must not *sound* sick. Actually letting your students know you aren't feeling well may be a huge mistake. A few middle school kids are like that chick in *The Exorcist;*[1] they are evil. They thrive on stomping on other people, especially teachers, when they are sick or hurting. By letting on that their health is in the dumps, some teachers expect their students to suddenly conjure up pangs of empathy. While a kid or two might, indeed, be in tune with your pain, don't bet on it; even if among your students there are patches of well-wishers, the chances that these kids will have a perceptible positive influence on the others are slim. Always remember this: These are *teenagers* we're talking about! *Teenagers!*

2. YOU ARE EXTREMELY TIRED

You must gear yourself up to be almost obnoxiously perky. Stifle that impending yawn, never put your head on the desk, and smile a lot; of course, you may collapse and die right after class, but you will cross that bridge whenever.

3. YOU HATE TODAY'S COURSE MATERIAL

Ironically, this is the day you show your students that this topic is the most interesting part of the curriculum, because you are *acting* as though it is the most interesting part of the curriculum. Of course, this may reinforce your students' notion that you're nuts, but most of them already thought that anyway.

4. YOU ARE HAVING A BAD DAY

Not only are you *not* going to tell your students you are having a bad day, but you are behaving and sounding in class as though it is the *best* day of your life. You may slightly convince even yourself that life should go on . . . sort of. If you allow your students to know you are suffering from recent events, trust me: There will be at least one kid in class who will salivate at the possibility of making your *bad* day a *horrible* day—or even your *last* day, if he has any say in the matter.

Remember, some kids have a twisted, warped, demented sense that if they play your mood, they have a greater chance of getting noticed by you. Here "getting noticed" often has a most peculiar way of rearing its ugly head. Ultimately, some of your students will make your bad day much *worse*. Sounds cruel, huh? Again, we're talking about *kids*! And if these kids happen to be of the teenager variety, sadism may very likely creep into the equation.

5. YOU DON'T KNOW THE ANSWER TO A QUESTION

Naturally, it is sometimes okay to admit to your students that you don't have an answer to their probe, but this is only for an unusually tough question or an idea you would like for them to explore, possibly with you. A query in a basic science class, such as, "Mr. G., how many planets are there in our solar system?" is a question, that if you cannot answer immediately, you should consider being the next teacher to ride on one of those Challenger shuttle rockets.[2] On the other hand, a student's inquiry about the different gaseous components in the ring around Saturn may provide a legitimate justification for your promise to look up the answer tonight and provide it for him in the morning.

Remember, if you often admit you don't *know* the answer, they begin thinking you are not as smart as they thought you were. You had them fooled until now; don't blow it. In fact, eventually, they may consider you stupid.

The scene *should* be played like this:

Student: Mr. G., do you use a semicolon inside or outside the quotation marks?

Teacher: (*sounding confident*) You put them in a consistent pattern in the manner you have used semicolons before—or other punctuation marks in similar situations.

Of course, this did not directly answer her question, but you sounded smart, even though you really didn't know the answer!

Student: Huh?

Teacher: (*forcing a deep, contemplative sigh*) Put them after quotation marks in certain situations and before quotation marks in other situations. We'll analyze this in specific examples as they arise.

Then you furtively take out your teachers' text, look up the rule, and supply the right answer at a more convenient (so you don't look so lame) time. If you have already blown the answer, give the correct directions later, as you politely adjust your original comments. You'll still sound brilliant— and even a bit human (or as close to human as a teacher can sound):

Teacher: Hey, Bill, you know that answer I gave you before about the semicolon?

Student: Yeah.

Teacher: Boy! Did I blow it! Was I a friggin' idiot, or what! I mean, if I were any dumber, you could use me on a bowling lane!

A lack of any logical coherence to the last comment aside—and recognizing the overkill in self-deprecation on the part of that teacher—you get the basic idea here: Once you've already clearly blown it, admit your mistake and fix it.

6. IT'S THE CLASS YOU LIKE THE LEAST

Sometimes a student will publicly ask me—for no particular reason, "Are we your favorite class, Mr. G.?" Of course, it is always my *least* favorite class (and my least favorite student who asks) when that question arises, so how do I respond?

I usually quip sarcastically, "Yeah, right!" Which for many students, because they do not understand verbal irony, instills some doubt as to the truth of what I really believe. In this case the deliberate ambiguity works, because nobody gets hurt. Sure, some of the kids may not know the whole truth, but so what? Would it be better to retort meanly, "Are you kidding! I despise this class! This is the worst group of kids since *Village of the Damned!*"[3]

Sometimes a teacher's good common sense is his best ally. You may have to try harder to be a good actor during the class from hell, but this is true for every popular movie star who has been forced to accept roles she and her career could have done without.

7. YOU HELP YOUR STUDENTS THROUGH TRAGEDY

One of the toughest aspects of being a teacher is that really bad things are going to happen to some of your students, even those kids you have grown to love. Unfortunately, kids are killed, often in automobile accidents and sometimes from drugs or acts of senseless violence.

One morning you will receive a note in your mailbox or a phone call from the counselor that Jackie, a sweet, bright student with a promising future as a political advocate or, perhaps, a prosecuting attorney, was struck and killed the previous night by a drunk driver. You will be devastated. As the kids file into class, they will be hit with something they rarely focus upon: their *own* mortality.

The loss of their precious friend and classmate, along with the sight of her empty desk in the center row, will generate more visible grief than you may have expected from these children.

But it is incumbent upon you to persevere. Though you feel like crying, perhaps raging against drunk drivers—even God—the kids and their parents are counting on you not to fall apart. Maybe you can use this horror as a learning experience, instructing the students about the fragility of our existence and a need to appreciate our lives as they hang by that proverbial thread.

I have often used our literature to explain senseless death and suffering, and most of my students have probably never forgotten that part of the course. Most significant: Maybe—just maybe—it helped them to make a little personal sense out of life and death.

8. YOU ARE DEALING WITH AN UNCONSCIONABLE PARENT

This will tend to wear your teeth down during the middle of the night; it may also encourage you to claim aloud, "I should have been a lawyer!" on more than one occasion. You often will utter to others, while you are in tremendous pain, "*Now* I know why Sally turned out the way she did!"

Which is the truth! Parents: We need 'em more involved in the schools, but, gee, wish they would just do their job right at home and stay the heck away! You will muster your acting talents for two types of parents you may come into frequent contact: (A) the portentous parent, who thinks she knows more about teaching and your curriculum than you do, and (B) the inept parent, who is not involved in her own kids' lives, or—worse— is completely counterproductive in her role modeling. Dealing with these so-called adults can sometimes be the most taxing part of your job.

I remember a parent who tried vociferously to persuade me to change her son's grade from F to an A (yeah, you read that right). She had convinced herself she had a persuasive case; ultimately, however, I told her politely that she was wrong, and I could not justify her reasons for a grade change to *myself*—let alone to others. She then responded—and these are her exact words; I remember them well—"You *could* go in that office right now and change the grade in the computer while no one is looking."

I wanted to tell her, "Well, lady, now I know why your son is headed toward abject failure for the rest of his miserable life!" But, of course, I conjured some good acting reserve and made the best out of a pitiable encounter.[4]

9. YOU ARE READING ALOUD TO YOUR STUDENTS

Acting, in its most literal application, usually requires enthusiasm, animation, and passion—none of which you may be feeling at the time you are sitting in a classroom full of lingering body odor, stagnant perfume, and thirty-five pairs of glazed adolescent eyes. Blandly reading (or telling) a story to children of any age not only will bore them; it is an invitation to disaster. Disciplining children becomes more difficult if they are experiencing tedium.

Simply put, make anything that you read—whether it's a fairy tale, a newspaper article, or a paragraph from a literature book—exciting. Use inflection, variation, and if the situation demands it, different voices and accents. Always ham it up. Inject jokes, over-interpretation, nonsense—occasionally "read" something that's not even there!—as you give it all you have! Acting! The actual material you are covering really stinks up the joint, but so what? You have made it fun!

10. YOU ENCOUNTER ANOTHER TEACHER, ADMINISTRATOR, OR STAFF MEMBER—IN FRONT OF STUDENTS

The only time this will require your acting graces is when you actually despise the person, or if he is somehow harassing you. But young, malleable eyes are looking upon you, and it is your professional duty to, at least, be *civil* to each other—distasteful to you or not. Many teachers and site administrators, especially those who seem unfriendly, unnerving, or unqualified to head the staff of a school, challenge us to don our most creative, introspective acting faces. When we fail to do so, we usually wind up behind the eight ball, despite our status (or personal sense) of intellectual superiority over the students—and the administrators who run the show.

The instability, insatiability, and immaturity of children tend to raise the stress levels of most beginning, and some veteran, teachers. Leading a classroom in worthwhile instruction is difficult enough, without having to go on a battlefield unequipped for duty. Perhaps, the theory I have advanced to you about honing your acting talents is also rather intimidating, since many of you believe you do not have the slightest talent—and even less experience—in the acting realm. Relax. The good news: Acting—this brand, at least—is a learned behavior developed by experience, not necessarily an innate talent you can market to Broadway. The more time you spend with the little tykes in your classroom, the more proficient you become at what you do.

Masking your true thoughts and feelings while you are teaching has become an imperative. The actual methodologies for achieving the level of actor you think you must become are varied. Some people already possess inborn qualities that make acting chillingly easy for them; others can't act their way out of a wet paper stage curtain. But across the board, a vital, inherent ingredient that forms a *base* for requisite acting success for teachers to achieve is . . . self-control! Just because we feel a certain way doesn't mean we should behave that way.

Even a modest flicker of hope of being someone else (happy, bubbling, passionate about long division, seemingly incapable of killing the first little brat who sneezes in her face), is often snuffed out before it has the slightest chance of gaining momentum, because many teachers have resigned themselves to an overload of responsibilities and the depravity of a system that seems to work against them.

But we owe it to our students to do better than that.

I will forever maintain: Anything wrong with the youngest generation of Americans is merely the consequence of the abject failure of the generations that have preceded them. Teachers must zero in on this truth, storing this critical knowledge in the back of their minds; then they are more motivated to sharpen their acting talents—even if they severely lacked them in the first place—and work harder to infuse some electricity into their classrooms. Even if they think their lackadaisical, lackluster, loser students don't deserve an enormous effort from their teachers, they will have so much more fun during their everyday classroom performances.

It is vital to our students that we develop a consistent pattern of success in this endeavor. If it is true that more enthusiastic teachers turn out higher-achieving students, teachers must master a skill that will make them better at their jobs day in and day out: acting. Our obligation on the job is not to "be ourselves"; it is to provide effective, worthwhile instruction to our clients, even if—in order to do so—we have to *act* like someone or something else.

Even higher education—normally clueless about the true needs of America's teachers—recognizes the worth of acting. Some colleges and universities offer Acting for Teachers courses, which are nothing more than how to curtail destructive behaviors and appearances, and replace them with behaviors and appearances that will spawn better rapport—and, ultimately, more successes—with young people.[5]

The kids who walk into my classroom never quite know what to expect on a given day. The one constant, however, is they are certain of being met by an instructor who seems to have relentless—perhaps, inordinate—enthusiasm for the day's activities. And, yes, many of my students believe I'm loony. They watch my crazy, energetic, silly, non sequitur behaviors in class, and they think I'm a bit touched.

Perhaps, I *am* insane.

I like to keep them guessing.

NOTES

1. *The Exorcist* (Warner Brothers, 1973); Think of that guy in your neighborhood who plays loud, booming rap everyone can hear, whether they want to or not: Linda Blair's character in this film was a lot meaner than he is.

2. If you understood this tasteless quip, I'm sorry. If you didn't get the comment, I'm also sorry for dragging your attention to an endnote that would urge you to further think about it.

3. *Village of the Damned* (MGM, 1960; Universal, 1995); I've seen both versions but was more terrified by the John Carpenter remake, because I think some of my students appeared in that one.

4. Bruce J. Gevirtzman, *An Intimate Understanding of America's Teenagers: Shaking Hands with Aliens*, (Westport, CT: Greenwood, 2008) 208.

5. Karen Agne, "Acting for Teachers," Plattsburgh State College Course Catalogue 2008, at http://faculty.plattsburgh.edu/karen.agne/sy575.htm.

7

+

Internalize Affection for the Kids: Love 'em Up!

Jack had become a high school principal for one primary reason: He wanted to make substantial contributions in improving the quality of instruction students received in public education. In plain English this means, Jack wanted to help teachers become better at their craft. He knew, as principal, he would be evaluating teachers and then making recommendations for enhancing the quality of instruction in their classrooms. He found the prospect exciting, but daunting. When Jack had his own classroom, he had affected only one teacher's students—his own; but as a high school principal, the potential to impact the lives of so many other teachers' students drove him back to college in order to earn an additional credential, this time in education administration.

But Jack soon ascertained that his proportional role in making teachers better was far below his optimistic expectations. School principals, he discovered, did not make a significant difference in the quality of teaching that happened at their schools.

He shook his head dolefully, his hands folded, leaning forward over his office desk, "It's the reason I got into education administration, and now it's the reason I'm getting out. The perks of this job are not that great—unless I hold on to my idealistic notion that I can make a huge difference in the classroom; that in a kind, benevolent way, I can make teachers better. They should know I'm on their side because I'm on the side of kids—their students."

He lowered his head slowly; a heavy sigh followed. "But I learned quickly there are some things I can't change, no matter what," he said. "I won't go into the dynamics of the kids' family lives or the teachers' private strife. . . . But when a teacher comes to me and is angry and bitter and says, 'I hate the kids. I work very hard at my job, but I just can't *stand* my students,' what in the hell am I supposed to do about *that*?"

Pragmatically, a principal can't do a heck of a lot to force teachers into liking children, if those teachers wished their students would somehow disappear from the face of the planet. It's an inherent dysfunction. Disliking the kids is not something a teacher practices, nurtures, or covets; it simply happens. It just *is*.

Theoretically, if you had risen to success in your teaching career, children would have been the souls who lit up your life—at least, occasionally; unfortunately, young people are often catalysts for taking a torch to your life, smoldering your patience, wearing and tearing at your goodness. No matter what you do, no matter what mindset you carve out in your brain, the little, gum-chewing, obscenity-spewing creeps cause your insides to churn and bile to form in your throat.

And the kids know it; they can smell you from a mile away.

You may never reach the pinnacle of teaching you already dreamed about when you were that small tyke in your parents' home, or that stoic young adult, impatiently treading through under-graduate school, putting up with your weirdo professors, praying to anyone who would listen to you that you would never resemble them, unless. . . .

You like the kids!

Correction: *You really, really like the kids!*

Oddly, it is not money that motivates an excellent teacher. It may be the impetus for getting a job in the first place, but higher teacher salaries have not been linked to better teacher quality.[1] No study has produced results that conclusively prove this.[2] Every anecdotal example I can think of has pointed out a success ratio between teachers who demonstrate they care about their students, and how much better these students do in their classes (just as with parents who intensely love their children and sacrifice for them, and how much better off their children do in life). Both are subjective judgments, but they are apparent, obvious in their conclusiveness.

"Gee, Bruce . . . if ya' don't really like the kids, can't ya' act like ya' care about kids? Can't ya' just sorta' like 'em? You're all into this teacher acting stuff."

Whatever.

But, no, if you don't like them, you won't care about them. Since when do we show how much we care for people we loathe? "Yeah, dude; I really can't stand Danny, . . . but I care a lot about him and what he does with his life!"

Sure.

It's not enough that you sigh mournfully and resign yourself to wiping the snot from the noses of your kindergarten brats, struggling to see the light at the end of a long day's tunnel. It's not sufficient for you to take a deep breath and meander through your biology labs, acting as though you are busily helping those nonresponsive, ungrateful, creepy teenagers.

None of this is good enough.

I recently heard one teacher put it in a (unintentionally) humorous vein: "I know I could be an incredibly good teacher, if I just liked my students. But I don't; I can't stand the little mutants!"

Upon meeting people, whenever I tell them I'm a high school teacher, they gaze at me as though I've just escaped from a mental institution. I know what they're envisioning: three dozen sexually obsessed, bubble-gum-chewing, possibly homicidal maniacs, sitting in front of me in a small room, daring me to teach them something. And they're right! I *am* crazy! Frankly, I do become energized in positive ways by that particular vision of what I do, but I know most people do not. Most of the general public only comes into contact with teenagers when they visit a fast-food diner, forced for twenty minutes to endure kids, dressed as though they had recently stepped off the set of a bad science fiction movie: loud, cussing, sloppy, cackling adolescents, who have reputations for mugging people in the parking lot.

Some movies, beginning with such gems as *Blackboard Jungle* and *To Sir, with Love*, which are tame by today's teenager high school movie standards (have you seen *The Substitute* or *187*?), have kicked good people, who were borderline in the first place about entering the teaching profession, into boring telemarketing or computer technology.[3] Even those precious little tykes have the potential for sending us home from work in body bags. If you've ever been in a restaurant, you already know what it's like to sit around a couple of six-year-olds who don't know how to behave, even when their parents are supposedly in control; the thought of trying to teach thirty-five of them in one classroom invokes in me an inviting image of deliberately dropping headfirst into the Grand Canyon.

So where do you learn to love (OK, "like" and "care about") the kids?

The answer to this question is divided into two separate categories. And if you don't fit into either one of them, you shouldn't become a teacher.

Unless you are a shoe-in for an Oscar at the next Academy Awards ceremony, you had better now qualify for at least *one* of the following:

YOU ALREADY LIKE THE KIDS, BECAUSE, WELL, YOU JUST LIKE THE KIDS.

Either it's in your nature, or it's not.

Some adults love children; some don't. Some adults tolerate children, but would rather—if they could legally arrange it—send them all off to Siberia. The latter group is not a category for housing promising teachers.

Here are comments from several teachers on the secondary level; I asked them their impressions of their students, their views of their job, and their opinions of teenagers in general. As you can readily perceive for yourself, their observations are mixed. So are my annotations to their observations.

- "My students are all individuals; some of them I like a lot—some of them I don't like at all. You either like them, or you don't; you either respect them, or you don't. In general, I do like kids, though". (female, high school teacher)

  This teacher has zeroed in on a truth. Adolescents are people, too—and they are certainly, as she said, *individuals*. Overall, kids are likeable—and even human—to her, which is a notch above the way some others teachers look at children.
- "I wouldn't be in this line of work if I didn't like kids. It's not even work to me; my career has been an honor, and working with educators has been a blessing." (male, high school administrator)

  This assistant principal has been in the hot seat for less than five years; like marriage, the seven-year itch for administrators usually begins, oddly, in about seven years. Also, this V.P. has never had to work from the discipline office, which normally speeds up the seven-year itch to about a one-year itch.
- "Are you quoting me on this, Bruce? Because if you are, don't use my name. I'll just say this: I've been teaching for [a long time]; every year the students get worse. They don't listen to directions, and in my class that, because of the hazards, could end in a real disaster. They're crude, rude, and obnoxious. Their parents are crappy—and as you know, the apples don't fall very far from their trees. I started out teaching liking the kids; I really did. But lately, it's hard to like them—and getting harder every day that I hang on." (male teacher, high school)

  Focusing on the term "hang on," may be pertinent here, since a teacher this old is doing just that, "hanging on." He understood his subject (he taught various science courses), but his mounting antipathy for his clientele has fairly certainly signed on to his death warrant—metaphorically speaking, of course.

  I think.
- "I have three children of my own and seven grandchildren. They are all—all of them—precious in their own way. When I greet my students each morning, I see them through those eyes. What if these were my children or my grandchildren?" (female, high school teacher)

  This teacher sees her students as actual people—with loves, hates, desires, dreams, goals, needs, pains, sorrows, frailties, and strengths. At the precise moment one of these sixteen-year-old human beings sprouts horns, she thinks of her own family and is reminded of the kid's humanness. He could have been *her* child. But this teacher's special sensitivity is innate. And when describing a quality as "innate," it means that most people don't have it.

- "No teacher likes all the kids all the time. There are those days I don't like anybody, including other adults. And as an eighth grade teacher, everybody always calls me crazy, reminding me how difficult teaching eighth grade is, as though I didn't already know that. But it's not as bad as people think. Just yesterday a boy told me that his father is coming home from Iraq this month, and he can't sleep at night because he's so excited. I mean, when I saw that gleam in his eye, I was reminded of all the times he looked so dead in here. And now I know why. This kid—he was so nervous and excited in his telling about his father, he stuttered all through it. I just wanted to pull him close and hug him. I do love my job, precisely because of moments like those." (female teacher—middle school)

God bless any eighth grade teacher with an attitude like hers. Most teachers of eighth graders immediately figure out that those creatures sitting in the desks of their classroom are mutants. They're no longer little children, and they are not quite young adults. Some eighth grade girls have the full bodies of beautiful, voluptuous young women; others have not reached puberty. The boys are still babies, but their voices are beginning to change. Many eighth grade boys still run around the classroom grabbing for each other's rear ends and like pinching girls instead of kissing them.

The teacher here understands the developmental process of children; these kids still have to live a while before they evolve into actual people. And who knows? Maybe eighth graders *are* the Missing Link.

Miracles happen, and that most great teachers really care about their students substantiates such miracles. We don't know with total certainty that Moses parted the Red Sea, but we see every day millions of teachers who have given their hearts to those eighth graders they have been employed to impart knowledge, values, and wisdom. You think it's a big deal standing under great duress with a staff at the shore of a great body of water, while praying to God for a miracle? If you do, try teaching algebra to a classroom full of thirteen- and fourteen-year-olds.

I dare you.

You can dislike children, particularly teenagers, in regular public contacts, and still maintain your composure and go about your job in the classroom; however, how effective will you be at teaching them anything? Teenagers are people, too (a moot point, I know), as are younger children; and you were once a teenager yourself. How lovable did you feel? Chances are, you were short on self-esteem, hated to see your blemished, sleepy face and scrawny body in the mirror every morning, and you felt no one in the world loved you as much as everybody else in the entire universe was being loved right at that moment.

During those times, what would one very special, attentive, caring teacher have meant to you?

YOU CAN *LEARN* TO LIKE THE KIDS.

Hand ringers infest all corners of the planet with their boundless despair and expressions of contagious pessimism. In the teaching profession, these people congregate in the faculty lunchrooms and staff lounges all over America; their downcast faces publicize their unhappiness, and their sloppy attire punctuates their waning professionalism. Misanthropic values permeate their humanity and dominate how they personally view life. To observe that these malcontent teachers don't like teenagers would be almost as much of an understatement as saying European Jews felt a disdain for Hitler. They want to *be* teachers but don't like children. Their only chance, therefore, is to *learn* to like the kids; if they choose not to try, they would do us all a favor by fleeing from our profession.

The odd thing is, when we leave college and first begin teaching, we're barely free from our teen years; yet, here we are, the ladies and dudes who suddenly must play the part of adults—usually the only adult—in the room. In a matter of a few months, we will have become an illustrious leader—the person in charge. And we even get paid for it. So if we don't like the people we're teaching, and for some reason we still want to be a teacher—that adult in charge—it's time for us to sit or get off the top. (I just thought of that; don't bother to look it up in Benjamin Franklin's *Poor Richard's Almanak.*)

Anyway, it may be time for *learning* to love the kids: The following is tried and true and maybe a bit crusty. It's my A B C's for liking kids. Actually, instead, we'll call them *The P P Ps.*

Positive—Potential—Pretend:

A. Savor the POSITIVE traits children have to offer:

Here are some examples: their sense of humor, their innocence, their trusting nature. These qualities can be enduring in and of themselves. Small kids, especially, come up with gems that have to make us laugh, no matter how badly our day is going. My six year-old son recently asked me, "Daddy, how come all the other kids have such young daddies, and my daddy is such an old daddy? Are you going to be an old daddy forever—or just for a little while? And when you die, will you *still* be an old daddy?"[4]

That was a deep sigh and throat clearing sound you just imagined—but very funny stuff I must respond to him about . . . eventually. In a similar vein: Recently one of my high school students said, "Mr. Gevirtzman, you're, like, the oldest teacher I've ever had, but you don't look nearly as old as you appear to be." Part of the fun of teaching is trying to figure out comments like this one—and attempting to answer kids' questions in a manner that can actually teach them something about, well, *something*, and at the same time, preserve some of my own dignity. It's their innocence, their naivety; they can be *very* endearing.

So don't kill them on the spot.

Don't fight them either.

Just relish them.

Teens want to like you, since they have to spend so much time *with* you; and they also want you to like them, especially since you're giving them a letter grade for your course that may send them to college—*or* off to work in every fast-food franchise in the Western Hemisphere.

Just for once—maybe while they're taking a test or working busily on an in-class project—stand in front of the class and watch them. Look indirectly at them. Don't comment, ask questions, or make any noises. Blow a soft sigh of your own, lean back on your feet, and watch them. Instead of thinking of them as your daily challenge, your barrier to happiness, your ticket to the funny farm, objectively observe them: their chatter, their movements, their facial expressions, their *humanity*.

Looking at these kids and seeing what they truly are—lonely, afraid, confused, dubious, untrusting, hurt, chidden, defeated, exhausted, pensive—will help you to connect with them, if only for a few minutes. It will provide you a brand new perspective on these precious souls who are—by the luck of the draw, a simple twist of fate—with *you* day in and day out. They trust you. They *need* you.

And they desperately want you to like them.

B. Savor the POTENTIAL in Children

Squirrelly kids can learn to settle down; quiet children can learn to speak up; bad children can learn to be good. And some of your students will become doctors, lawyers, social workers, mothers, fathers, and even teachers. (You may wish to deny or ignore that last comment.) One of them may go to Mars (and, if you're lucky, he will be the adult version of the kid you'd like to send to Mars right now). Another may become a war hero, saving others' lives on the grotesque plains of a battlefield.

A few years ago, a new kid joined my class late, and I thought to myself: "Why, me, God!" Seriously. The child had a couple of hooks up his nostrils, something metal hanging off his lower lip, and two earrings I could have used as dumbbells during my weight training sessions; his swagger to the front of the room had to have been practiced repeatedly, because no kid would have been able to walk like that without "Special Forces Scary Intimidation Walk Training" for at least six months.

To make a long story somewhat shorter: Julio and I wound up getting along splendidly. I eventually teased him by mocking his walk in front of the class, and he came up and made fun of my teaching by replicating (with gross exaggeration, I hope) some of my rather flamboyant gestures, facial expressions, and voice patterns. Julio wound up being a part of one of my readers theater productions in a technical capacity (he ran the lights.); what may have been a complete waste of his classroom time (and talents), and a fate worse than death for me, his English teacher, turned out shockingly well for both of us. I figured he had some potential, and that gave both of us a chance to develop it.

Technically, all young people have potential. But the potential must turn for the greater good of all and not just the immediate, if-it-feels-good, temporary, selfish pleasure of one darling little child. So here are five key signs for recognizing in your students true potential for—if not great-ness—a boundless step forward, a leap over the line that divides people you'd want to cozy up next to and cuddle, from those you would rather send to an isolated thousand acres in the hills of Pakistan.

A Kid Who Doesn't Give Up Easily (Yes, an Obvious One)

Not to downplay his failure in just about everything he tries to do, this child keeps going, doesn't stop, never surrenders. And sometimes the other students make fun of him for it. But he endures; and when he finally singles with the bases loaded, clasps his high school diploma, or lands his first job, those who knew him smile with approval. They secretly knew he could do it, and some of them even encouraged him—when no one else would—at the time. In cases like these, everyone turns out a winner.

Specific Barriers Holding Her Back

And those "specific things" can be conquered, opening the door to life's successes. Usually a child's bad homelife makes her school life an ex-tra—even horrific—responsibility, and she isn't free to fully focus her efforts in the directions they need to sail in order to help generate enough positives in her life.

Very often when a kid grows up and flees the nest, her whole life opens up for her, with geography alone freeing her from burdens that previ-ously held her back. As a teacher you don't need to judge her potential; just know it's already there. Once you have discovered inherent impedi-ments in her life, work on them with her. If not soon, eventually she will flood the universe with her abilities—at least, she has the potential to do so. And that's all you're diagnosing: her potential. As drab and dreary as her life seems in the present, remember that in her future she may be a different person—one that you would really, really like!

His Life's Course

Check out his recent behaviors. Find out where he's been already. Some children gravitate to those who are especially needy because—for whatever the reasons—they are interested in *helping*. They choose courses of study that will lead them to the so-called helping professions: doctors, lawyers, teachers, nurses, garage mechanics, and therapists. We hear familiar comments about these kids:

"Mike is such a sweetie; he's so kind."

"Mary is always thinking of others; she always puts other people first."

"Blake is a really nice boy; he seems to feel other kids' pain, too."

Whether or not these children are doing well in your classes—and some of them may be doing extraordinarily well—the fact that you may not like them (because they can't or won't calculate equations) is more of a commentary on *your* character and personality than it is on the potential of these kids. If you care about making the world better—though maybe you don't—you should understand that *these* children will grow into adults who may actually do just that: add something positive to humanity.

Or not.

The Kids Who Flock to You

For most American children—particularly teenagers—the idea of chumming around with a teacher is right up there with the notion of an American adult taking an international terrorist out to lunch; in fact, the possible horrors that may come from their having been *seen* behaving in a civilized manner around a classroom teacher is the thing of which adolescent nightmares are made. Occasionally, however, students will stay after class to ask you questions about course material or to chat about a provocative comment you had made; sometimes a student will ask you questions about your personal life. Most often gregarious kids are inclined to approach you with information about themselves—stories or situations they need to share with someone else—and they trust you to listen with an open ear and an open mind.

Consider a conversation I had with Sart: Sart stood about five feet tall—if that tall. Pimples covered his already acne-scarred face; his hair hung loosely over his forehead. I knew the encounter held some dramatic potential when he politely commanded me to speak with him for a few minutes, until his ride would pick him up outside the school.

"All right, Sart," I sighed, more business-like than before. "Let's have it. What's going on?"

"Well, Mr. G.," Sart practically whispered, "it's all about me. That poem. I don't have a father like the guy in the poem. You know what my dad says, Mr. G.? He says that I'm ugly—that I'm a—no offense—a 'total loser.' Sometimes he calls me a 'faggot.' Like the other day. I couldn't move a heavy box that *his* new drill machine came in, and he started calling me names; his favorite one was 'faggot.' That's why I can't seem to get anywhere, Mr. G."

Thinking that I wanted to pummel this boy's father into pancake batter, I managed to say, "Your father is a jerk, Sart; chalk it up to that."

And then it struck me: "Besides, Sart. You can do whatever you want with your life. Maybe lifting heavy boxes isn't your thing. Ask your dad to come in here and figure out a poem by William Carlos Williams; see how well he does! As you get older, your youthful challenges [like his zits] and your temporary, indiscreet immaturity [like visibly picking his nose] will disappear. You have to be confident that, whatever happens to you, you will have had control over your own destiny."

Once you've gone through a traumatic discourse with a kid like this, you will begin to develop a relationship with him. Having begun to understand his frailties, you will grow akin with him. After you've invested in this emotional stock, it's difficult not to see a child's potential for escaping the excrement in which he currently lives; besides, the sense of accomplishment you'll inherit from the work you've done may build up a fondness for more than just this teenager. After all, how could this boy *not* have some potential? He decided to come to *you*.

Upon a Connection, Your Instinct

When I coached debate, I called it the "X-factor." There was simply a nontangible quality in some of my students—and other students I observed and got to know around the country—that compelled me to buy into their existence as a *promise*. I—and just about everyone else around them—knew they possessed attributes destining them for a fruitful life, a productive future, a set of flourishing contributions that would distinguish them from most other people on our planet. I'm not big on instinct when it comes to human behavior; animals run on instinct, not people. But likable, charming—almost beguiling—traits held by a few chosen (chosen by *whom* I have no idea) children mark them for brilliance.

A few of those children have—if you allow yourself to see it—the potential to be more than a bunch of odd, rude, annoyances in your busy life, as you barely scrape by a living in the confines of a classroom full of body odor, human gases, and perfumes that would kill even a large horse.

C. PRETEND You are a Kid Again.

If you remember what it was like to be desperately needy, hopelessly naive, frantically confused, and regularly frightened, you are probably magnanimously empathetic toward children. At the beginning of a relationship between you and a teenager, a small amount of empathy goes a long way.

Being a student yourself while you're teaching, is helpful in this regard. It enlarges the empathy factor, if you tune in to what it feels like on the other side of the classroom.[5] Sometimes when the kids are giving oral presentations, I sit in the back of the class in the hard wooden chairs at the desks my students use for six hours every day, and I think about what it would be like to be a student in my own classroom. I imagine this old, grumpy man standing at the whiteboard, his face twitching with passion; he's gesticulating, wildly and furiously, his voice, loud and booming; I try to envision what it would feel like for me to be an easily intimidated, self-effacing teenager, rather than a loud, pompous, confident-looking teacher.

Most kids want you to be consistent, fair, reassuring, and predictable. If they sense you like them, want them to succeed, and are not out to, oh, sentence them to ten years of hard labor, they will feel safe, sound, and secure while you are teaching them. So as I sit there and think about being taught by *me* (my initial reaction, of course, is to want to run very quickly to the bathroom), I gauge the amount of synergy (or whatever they call it) that flows in the classroom because of my presence, and ponder what I can do to make me (as a student now) more comfortable.

You either have a natural liking for children, or you will need to create one. Either way, this is a prerequisite for making you a good teacher.

On a personal note, I cannot imagine what it would be like to go to work each day and be around a bunch of people I can't stand. In reality, I don't like a few of my colleagues, who are vastly more irritating and obnoxious than most kids, but, fortunately, I'm not around these adult boors nearly as much as I am around my students. I mean, if I had to socialize with most of the folks I've worked with, I probably would have been locked away deep under the earth in solitary confinement long before now. And I would have asked *them* to throw away the key.

I'm not being sanctimonious here; I'm sure some of my colleagues have felt the same way about me.

Besides, you can get by if you don't like most of the staff.

You will be miserable, however—and probably fail—if you don't like most of the children.

NOTES

1. David E. Bosley, "Better Management Policies Produce Satisfied Teachers," *USA Today*, February 13, 2008, Opinion section, 1.

2. Studies may indicate that more money attracts teachers to a school or school district; however, no legitimate studies draw a link between more money and making bad teachers better.

3. All four of these films feature teenagers from hell. The difference: In the latter movies mentioned, the teachers *die.*

4. The exact words of Viktor S. Gevirtzman, age six.

5. Kevin Zhou, "When Teachers Go Back to School," (*Harvard Crimson*, November 28, 2006), at thecrimson.com/article.aspex?ref=516018.

8

Strive to Be (Gulp!) Fair

Students at my high school recently responded to an interesting survey, asking them what they viewed as the five most important qualities in a teacher. The study contained subjective, open-ended questions, but the results brought very few surprises. While the kids mentioned that they loved teachers with a great sense of humor, teachers with nonexistent homework assignments, teachers with bodies like Brad Pitt—none of these broke into the top three (sense of humor, however, placed fourth). The top three qualities teenagers admired in their teachers: high expectations of their students; passion for the subject they teach; and . . . at the top of the list—*fairness*.

To be fair, I'm not sure what our students meant by *fairness*; in fact, I'm not sure what *I* mean by *fairness*. If the ball is not foul, it's fair. If her skin is not dark, it's fair. But if a teacher favors (whatever that means) one particular student over another student, is she fair? If a teacher employs rules that seem plausible, but not too rigid, is she fair? If she bends a rule or doesn't enforce a rule because of an extenuating circumstance or in order to exact a specific result, is she fair?

What, exactly, is a fair teacher, and why do teenagers like them more than, say, hot oatmeal with cinnamon in the morning? (Notice, I didn't make an analogy to pizza; nothing beats pizza when it comes to teenagers' preferential tastes.)

And are you fair? Will you be fair when you become a teacher? Were you once a fair teacher; but now that you are retired, is the only "fair" you care about the one that comes once a year, has all those high-velocity rides, greasy foods, and baby piglets?

The concept of fairness in education is so overwrought, overworked, over-employed, over-discussed, and over-analyzed, just a mention of the word *fair* brings on a yawn that easily resists stifling. What's so novel about attempting to treat your students fairly, with a form of due process? Seems obvious, right? I would think so, except for the irksome reality; once again, the reality awakens us: Many teachers don't consider a passion for fairness to be an important quality—not in their own teaching. And most teachers stray from—or forget about—*any* fairness concept at one time or another, sometimes for protracted periods of time.

Devastating for your classroom environment, without fairness, your rapport with kids may shrivel faster than a male member in a swimming pool. I would cut the melodrama here, but for those emphatic condemnations I've heard from students about a lack of fairness in some of their teachers—and some lip-service reverence paid to fairness throughout the education process.

My focus on *fair* here is not the same as the concept of *fair* as it, for example, relates to the criminal justice system, although it does have a smidgen of those elements, as well. (Numerous teachers have fantasized the use of the death penalty as a suitable consequence for obnoxious classroom behavior.) When I speak of fairness, I conceive of four distinct characteristics of fairness:

> *First:* You promote clear, understandable policies for punishment and reward in your classroom.
> *Second:* You possess flexibility for extenuating circumstances.
> *Third:* Your patience and understanding pave the way for a secure, safe classroom environment, void of great fear and trepidation.
> *Fourth:* Your model of pragmatism and evenhandedness in dealing with the curriculum breeds an expectation of fairness and trust from your students.

Let's elaborate it, baby! This is good stuff!

1: You promote clear, understandable policies for punishment and reward in your classroom.

You may disagree with this (as you may with any other suggestion in this book), but I don't post a list of nitpicky rules and regulations on the wall and then proceed to harangue my students on the first day of school about tearing their limbs slowly from their bodies—just before they are crucified—for breaking *Rule 4-B, Little 2*. Nor do I send a Xeroxed sheet of paper home to their parents, pompously bragging about what a great teacher I am: that I demand respect; that their children may cry out in pain in reaction to the thorny whip that thrashes across their backs—for their failing to raise their hands prior to leaving their desks. I try to simplify things.

I've found that many educators honestly believe the more complicated something sounds, the more worthwhile it probably is to know. But of course nothing could be farther from the truth.

The first day of school I pass out a piece of paper, indicating there are only two rules that count majorly (Is that a word?) in my class; then I look the kids squarely in the eyes, put on my meanest teacher face, and read the two rules from the paper:

> *Rule Number One:* Be polite. If someone else is speaking, you are to wait until the proper time to interject your comment.
> *Rule Number Two:* Keep your head up. Put your head down on the desk, and you will wind up outside. Feel like sleeping? Do it at home.[1]

And I enforce these two rules. I don't inundate the kids with lots of minutia; if they know what's expected of them, what's most important, they will adhere to my regulations. Naturally, however, a time comes when the interpretation of rules has to be flexible enough to cover other eventualities:

> *Me:* Jimmy, please don't get up and stand by the door before the bell rings.
>
> *Jimmy:* I'm not standing by the door.
>
> *Me:* Standing by the door, after I've asked you not to, is inconsiderate, Jimmy.
>
> *Jimmy:* But—
>
> *Me: Sit down.*[2]

Jimmy then strolls back to his desk and slowly slides into his chair: no fuss, no muss; no argument, no pleading. You don't make a fool of yourself in front of everyone within earshot of your begging and pleading. Right should prevail here. But in front of the entire class, a challenge should be tackled with logic, with grit, with honor—and with a semblance of authority. If not—if you forget about logic, grit, honor, and authority—the kids will side with the perpetrator; and you, the teacher, the lone, miserable authority figure in the classroom, begin to look like a character from one of those low-budget teenager movies. You know the genre: Every adult, especially parents and teachers, looks like the biggest buffoons on earth.

The differences among our children are massive. But these differences have little or nothing to do with culture; they have everything to do with *behavior.* Let's face it: You will gravitate toward some children more than you do others; this is inherent in the human psyche. If someone treats you better than she treats someone else—is nicer, kinder, friendlier, more polite, more generous, more empathetic—you, in turn, will feel a greater affinity for this person. Unfortunately—or fortunately, depending upon your own point of view on the subject—this leads to "favorites," "teacher's pets," accusations of brownnosing, and the ultimate teacher slander, "You're not fair!" And I *do* mean this is not a good thing to be accused of. As I have already harangued ad nauseam, children think highly of fairness.

And so should teachers.

The harm an unfair teacher does, especially after he has already garnished a reputation for unfairness, can be devastating to that teacher's rapport in school—even to his career! You should control your urges to play favorites. Human nature will compel you to seek out and recruit teacher's pets, but for whatever you're worth, camouflage it.

2. You possess flexibility for extenuating circumstances.

Now, comes the most controversial argument of all, one over which there is much professional disagreement (as there is with much of the advice I offer to you in this text): Sometimes you must bend the rules to fit the situation. Students will respect you for it. Even the perpetual troublemakers, after screaming about "favorites!" for a while, are more likely to understand the moral principle and logistical necessity behind the concept of flexibility as a form of fairness.

At one time my high school had implemented a strict tardy policy; students arriving even one second late to class were written tickets for a thirty-minute school-wide detention. (I believe that upon their sixth tardy or something they were shot by a firing squad.) Of course, there were habitual offenders, and some students spent more time in their assigned detentions than they did in their regular classes; however, when a child who had previously never been late to any class or been in even a smidgen of trouble bashfully sauntered into class after the bell, I instinctively knew there was something weird about her specific situation.

After discussing late arrivals with students who do not normally breach the rules, I have found that more than 90 percent of the time they offer justified reasons for their tardies: detained by another teacher, bathroom business, not feeling well, legitimate car trouble, parent problem, etc. Even if kids don't have defensible excuses, after a period of time, certain children build up a "behavior bank account." Never been in trouble before? OK, we can let it slide *this* time (but only this time). In fact, occasions arise in which I don't even have to speak with the perennially good kids about their infractions; I simply overlook them.

This behavior bank account may look something like this: Muttering an inaudible comment, Maria turns to the boy sitting in the desk behind her; Kenneth responds, but his loud whisper can be heard by the teacher.

Kenneth: Yo! Turn around, bitch!

Teacher: (stops lecture and, much like a baseball umpire, throws an animated thumb) Kenneth, you're outta' here!

Kenneth: But she. . . .

Teacher: She shouldn't have been talking during my lecture, but I heard *you,* dude! You're gone!

Maria: I just asked him for a piece of paper, Mr. G.

The teacher heard Maria's defense of her own involvement in the fiasco, but he didn't respond to her; after all, she shouldn't have asked Kenneth for anything, given the fact that class had begun, and the teacher's lecture had been well under way. But the teacher proceeded to do what was absolutely required in order to eliminate the obnoxious, obscene, comment culprit from that day's class. Calling girls vulgar names is inappropriate, even when it doesn't interrupt the teacher; this time, however, the boy's vulgarity had been accentuated through his rudeness, and by virtue of his interruption.

Maria definitely had been wrong for eliciting anything from the boy behind her during the teacher's lecture; however, her actions were so discreet, the teacher had noticed nothing at all until Kenneth screamed the word *bitch* in her direction. Furthermore, Maria had exemplified model behavior in the past, never creating any trouble for this teacher. Kenneth, on the other hand, had been a constant source of classroom interruption and known to fly off the handle with even the slightest provocation. And now Kenneth's public outburst, one of the most repugnant, is also one of the most unforgivable.

Bottom line: Maria had built up her behavior bank account; Kenneth had not.

Perhaps, only a scrap of experience tells us exactly how this philosophy may be successfully implemented. All our lives we have been taught that *rules are rules; the law is the law!* Break our own rules, circumvent the enforcing of our standards of discipline, we are told by other educators, then all hell will break loose!

But even after vast amounts of experience in the classroom, we still have made mistakes, losing our patience and our understanding, and ignoring behavior bank accounts built up by deserving students. A colleague cautions us about patience and understanding—reminding us of the unfortunate circumstances some of our students have had to deal with—and we usually want to give this blubber-hearted coworker a "patience and understanding" knuckle sandwich. We derisively wonder if we should have tried harder to have "patience and understanding" with the terrorists who attacked New York City!

Yeah. Patience. Understanding.

Right.

Sometimes patience and understanding as a path to fairness are more easily discovered than Osama bin Laden's hiding place in the mountains of Pakistan.

3. Your patience and understanding pave the way for a secure, safe classroom environment, void of great fear and trepidation.

Perhaps, the smoothest vehicle for communicating these ideas would take the form of actual, specific teacher behaviors you can use to visibly demonstrate your patience and understanding with your students.

You may be aware of other teachers (maybe you had a few like these yourself) who are constantly yelling and screaming at their students. You know who these, uh, professionals are from what the kids have told you about them; and you actually hear them every day, as their loud, raging voices boom up and down the corridors of your school. They sound frightening. If you had to conjecture, someone in her classroom is being murdered; perhaps, the teacher herself is screaming for dear life.

Think back to when you were a small child—how, when Mom or Dad occasionally scolded you, you recoiled—sometimes you were severely frightened. Those of you who had parents who shouted and screamed and yelled at you constantly now can pinpoint when you had become non-responsive to them: Numbed by your parents' raging voice volume, you had gained immunity to it. What had happened for you to turn impervious to all that screaming and yelling? Simple: You heard it all the time. The sounds of loud, tumultuous voices soon went in one ear and out the other, or you blocked them out completely; you'd heard it too often.

The same is true with teachers. Instructors who constantly reprimand, yelling at their students—perennially nagging them—are quickly tuned out, turned away, and torched mentally by their pupils: "Oh, the jerk is going off on us again. Big deal." This soon escalates into a more tenuous situation, because the normal voice of a teacher is no longer effective in maintaining classroom authority; in fact, the teacher's voice has become an irritant. If students lose their responsiveness to the verbal commands and wishes of their teachers, these teachers have depleted their class control arsenals much too rapidly.

Don't sweat the small stuff; in fact, first discover what the small stuff *is*. Learn to nag and command only at the proper moments, in those precise cases you are sure there is a *reason* to harshly rake in your students' behavior; otherwise, you will surrender your effectiveness: as a teacher, disciplinarian, role model, and the guy they can go to for encouragement and advice. After examining *your* behavior, they'll chalk you up to being nothing but a wild lunatic.

4. Your model of pragmatism, honesty, and evenhandedness in dealing with the curriculum breeds an expectation of fairness and trust from your students.

My teenage nephew recently described a favorite teacher of his, who, on the first day of his English class, lifted the course's state-mandated textbook from his desk, waved it in front of his students, and proclaimed, "This is the book that we're *supposed* to use in this class."

And then he proceeded to heave the book against the wall, grumbling, "*That's* what *I* think of this book! What we're going to do in here is the stuff that's important, and we're going to throw away the junk we don't need. We don't need this book for us to learn!"

This teacher imparted fairness through a blatant honesty that defied not only the laws of standardized education policy and procedure, but the laws of inertia, as well. Some admirable audacity with his symbolism of the unnecessary (and then trashed) class textbook energized his students and possibly motivated them to back him up during any potential parent or administrator confrontation.

His students would bring him their extra banana nut muffins from Starbucks, too—that was a certainty!

Unnecessary regulations by those far removed from the classroom irritate students, teachers, and parents alike. Teachers who visibly buck the system illuminate a face for fairness that is difficult to defy. Some teachers vociferously criticize the mandated course curriculum in front of their classes. Other teachers carefully calculate what is a fair amount of homework to assign each night. Many teachers heartily announce that the information they are giving their students is wrong, might be wrong, or, at least has another (or several) other sides, aspects, or conclusions to consider.

One teacher I had in the eleventh grade—and I'll never forget this— told his English class, "You should know that the publishers of your book do not want to reveal to you that Walt Whitman was a homosexual. They are afraid of the consequences, if they conveyed this kind of truth to you. But I am willing to face these consequences, if they ensue;

you have a right to know this, because Whitman's sexual preference and
steaming sexuality significantly affected his poetry, some of his greatest
works. Whitman's passion came from his sexual desires, which were
unorthodox, yet, unrelenting."[3]

I'm still not sure why we needed to know this, but our teacher's apparent integrity really blew us away! And this kind of honesty seems
especially courageous; after all, we're talking about, like, 50 billion years
ago—well before *Brokeback Mountain*—when he informed us of the homosexuality of, arguably, the greatest American poet!

All this gleams of honesty. And our students love it; they see we are
treating them in a straightforward, candid fashion.

Only today, as a matter of fact, I had an anecdotal brush with the issue
of honesty. I explained to my students if they reviewed the film *Schindler's
List*, they would receive double credit for their paper. Since the students
knew they could not review a movie they had already seen, a pretty
blonde girl raised her hand, and the following exchange ensued:

Girl: I've already seen *Schindler's List*.[4]

Me: Okay.

Girl: Then can I get double-credit for it?

Me: No.

Girl: Why?

Me: Obviously, if you have already seen *Schindler's List*, you can't review it
for credit; that's the policy.

Girl: Then what can I get double credit for?

Me: You can't. No other movies on the list are worth double credit.

Girl: But other people can?

Me: Yes, if they haven't already seen that movie.

Girl: That doesn't seem fair.

Me: Right.

Girl: How is that fair?

Me: I don't know. It's not.

Girl: But . . .

Me: There are more than sixty movies on the list. Review an extra one. Also,
there are other ways to get extra credit . . . and—come on—*Schindler's List* is
long; it's like watching two movies anyway.

These students saw that (A) I admitted possible unfairness in the extra-credit policy, but only in relation to this particular girl's circumstance; and (B) though she was at a minor disadvantage, she could remedy her situation. When my students saw me shrug in agreement to her accusation, some ground rules for honesty had been established. And, yes—sometimes honesty compensates for what others deem a minor injustice. There's not a whole lot they can come back with—or feel frustrated about—when you *admit* to your lack of fairness and suggest ways to redeem yourself.

Most teachers calculate and issue grades fairly, even change a grade, if they find they have scored it incorrectly or marked the report card inaccurately. One of the greatest displays of professional decency from a teacher is the impression he will bend over backwards to reflect a true representation of what his students have learned in his class. Interestingly, most students want nothing more than that. Every now and then, they may tempt or nag their teachers for beneficial nudges in their grades; but when push comes to shove, the vast majority of teenagers admire a teacher who stays with an authentic accounting of their achievements.

In summary: We have examined four primary areas in which a teacher may strive for fairness. Here they are again—as they are worth repeating—followed by ten short demonstrations of how a teacher may apply these criteria for fairness to her everyday teaching world. Not all examples hone to your individual circumstances, but you will find some of them more personal, and, therefore, more important to your own success as a classroom teacher.

1. You promote clear, understandable policies for punishment and reward in your classroom.
2. You possess flexibility for adapting to extenuating circumstances.
3. Your patience and understanding pave the way for a secure, safe classroom environment, void of great fear and trepidation.
4. Your model of pragmatism, honesty, and evenhandedness in dealing with the curriculum breeds an expectation of fairness and trust from your students.

Mr. Tyner meets several times with David, a chronic truant, in order to solve his attendance problem. The teacher makes several attempts to discover what David is doing on the days he does not come to school, and he suggests solutions for David's diversions and distractions. (3)

Josie accidentally goes to the wrong room for an assembly, gets confused, and arrives at the right room well after the festivities had begun. Since she can't get into the auditorium, she walks to the park and rests for the hour under a shade tree. Her classroom teacher (and for the assembly) cautions her about being more diligent, and makes some jokes about her mess up. Josie has never been in trouble before, and was horrified when she found out what the repercussions could have been for her dalliance. (2)

Darla comes to Mr. Janson at lunch to explain why she has missed assignments for the past two weeks—and asks Mr. Janson for an extension on a huge novel review project. Darla's mother had recently been diagnosed with breast cancer and has been in the midst of several surgeries. As one may expect, Darla has been severely distracted for the past couple of weeks. Mr. Janson calmly tells her that she may be dismissed from the assignments and offers to help further, if she or her family can think of anything for him to do. "No," Darla smiles through her tears, "just be aware of the problem and give me some slack with the homework." Mr. Janson complies. (2 and 3)

Mrs. Walker offers her history students several opportunities for extra credit, based on their potential travels around the country—or world—during Easter break. She clearly delineates the number of points available, but she reminds her students that extra credit is not required to get an A grade for the term. However, she cautions them that students who fail to complete the required research paper—without any extra credit to their names—will automatically fail the class for the semester; she then suggests that they do begin the extra credit at home this week in the event they find themselves in a quandary later with their research project or another assignments. (1)

Ms. Crane tells her classes on the first day of school that any student who comes to school late to her class three times must face a one-hour detention after school. If they fail to come to the detention, she will recommend to the school administrators that those students serve an in-house suspension for one day. After a student acquires a second tardy, Ms. Crane sends a warning notice home to his parents. The notice is laden with anthrax. (That's an awful attempt at a tasteless joke. Sorry.) (1)

Mrs. Delltone tells her freshman English class that she is not going to assign the play *Romeo and Juliet* as part of the required curriculum. She states emphatically that she does not agree with the play's overt and covert sexual messages about lust, infatuation, and neediness—wanting her students to appreciate Shakespeare on a level at which he can be respected. Instead, she proposes her students read *A Midsummer Night's Dream*, also by William Shakespeare. "Not only is that play hilarious," says Mrs. Delltone, "its parody pokes fun at the shortcomings of *Romeo and Juliet*." (4)

Conrad has been suspended for five days by his guidance counselor. Fighting is the charge. Several witnesses had seen another boy approach Conrad from behind and then slam him in the back of the head with his forearm. Conrad turned around and defended himself by punching the attacking boy flush in the face, knocking him to the pavement. Although both boys were doled equal punishment by the counselor, it was abundantly clear that Conrad had assumed a defensive posture, by taking the other boy out—as a direct *response* to the assault.

Conrad's math teacher, Mr. Elroy, goes to the discipline counselor and complains about Conrad's unfair treatment: "After all," Mr. Elroy explains, "because of boys like Conrad—courageous lads who are willing to defend themselves against bullies—fewer bullies are willing to exert their influence."

But the discipline counselor tells Mr. Elroy that the school rules are clear: Fighting is punishable by mandatory suspension.

Mr. Elroy clenches his teeth and says, "That is asinine. I hope Conrad's parents come in here and threaten to sue you and the school district. Their son was *defending* himself! Trying to prevent boys from defending themselves by punishing them is not only ludicrous, it's dangerous, and it's downright immoral! And you know it! Conrad should receive a plaque, not a suspension—and when he returns to school, my class will throw a party in his honor!"[5] (2)

Mrs. Jackson, a veteran biology teacher, knows that dissecting frogs teaches her students very little about anatomy. She's been around long enough to understand the giggly classroom distractions motivated by an activity such as this one. She understands that the time, energy, and expense for this project could be better utilized elsewhere in the science department.

She tells her students, "You are not going to dissect frogs in here. I know they do it in Mr. Ginsberg's class; but students in this class will go on a field trip to a large hospital; at this hospital, you will be partitioned behind Plexiglas, and you'll be able to observe someone having major surgery. You'll sit in the same places reserved for university students who are studying to become doctors. You will learn more about the human body in one hour at that hospital than you would have learned in two weeks and thirty-five thousand dollars of animal dissections (and Mrs. Jackson might have added, "or in one one-hundred-dollar night spent in a hotel after the senior prom"). (4)

Benjamin, an honors student, doesn't turn in a required economics paper on the due date. He explains to his teacher that he went to the class's Internet site to check the date the paper was due, but the teacher hadn't posted the information. After calling a friend for the due date, he wrote the date down. But his friend had inadvertently given him the incorrect date for turning in the paper. Startled when he got to school, Benjamin went right to the teacher and pled his case. Right or wrong, Benjamin is an honors student with an impeccable record. His teacher merely shrugged in ambivalence and instructed Benjamin to turn the paper in tomorrow, which he finally does. (2)

Perhaps, after reading this, you will never look at the word *fairness* in the same light; or maybe you will shrug off my suggestions, definitions, and examples of fairness and trust your own judgment.

Which is fine.

Being fair may be the educator's biggest ongoing challenge (except for finding ways to have longer duty-free lunch periods); nobody likes dishonesty and injustice.

Not even the bad guys.

NOTES

1. I consistently enforce this rule. I tell my students, "If you are so tired that you must put your head down in my class, you shouldn't be coming to my class at all."—And then I give them the heave-ho.

2. An actual conversation, there have been countless others just like this one.

3. This teacher's conclusion about Whitman's sexuality is universal.

4. *Schindler's List* (DreamWorks, 1993).

5. Mr. Elroy (not his real name) was a teacher at my school, and this happened as he tells it here. I encouraged him to actually throw the party and award this boy that plaque, but he never did. At least, he confronted the administration for what had been—and still is—a blatantly stupid discipline policy about fighting.

9

Communicate with
Even the Ugly Parents

Sitting in the lunchroom, you may hear another teacher mutter sweetly, "Shoot! Dammit! I almost forgot; I have a parent conference this afternoon!" The teacher then pounds the nearest wall, kicks the closest chair, and swings his arms up in venomous frustration.

I may have slightly exaggerated this scenario, but meeting with parents—even pleasant parents—is one of the obligations teachers despise the most. It's not that teachers have to work harder by spending more of their valuable time in oral discourse with parents (well, yeah, it's that, too); teachers know that meeting with parents is part of the job description they signed up for when they volunteered to work with children. But when teachers chat with parents, those parents are judging them, holding them to task, evaluating how they have dealt with the most precious, vital people in their lives: their kids.[1]

The truth is, most of whether or not a child is going to be successful in school (or life, for that matter) has to do with the upbringing he receives at home. Today, with so many absentee fathers, mix-and-match families, and working parents who hardly ever see their own children, it's clear that too many kids face a gross lack of attention and a shortage of support for their schooling. Many of your students' parents (even if your students are fortunate enough to be living with Mom and Dad) are so busy, they rarely ask their children what's going on in school, which teachers they like the most, or if they can help them with their homework (or even whether they *have* any homework).

If you're a high school teacher, you have nearly two hundred students in your classes.[2] You would not be able to communicate with all their parents in five years, let alone a year—and much less a semester. So what do you do? Sometimes dilemmas get solved through compromise and sacrifice on the part of the person who has the most control.

My primary suggestion is that you readily—and often—contact the parents of your problem students or pending problem students. You do not wait until the situation becomes hopeless. You do not waste time sending nice letters home to the parents of your gifted and eager. That is a sweet idea, and in the name of "positive reinforcement" it has a lot of support in education circles; however, you'd be wiser if you played footsies with your best and brightest only after you have nicked the *problems* in the bud.

Within the constraints of your limited amount of time, you have a tough priority list to make. At the top of your parent contact priorities (in no particular order):

HIGH SCHOOL SENIORS

They won't graduate from high school if they don't pass your class. Is *that* enough pressure on you? Here's some advice: Throw the responsibility back on the adults—the parents. The most unpleasant meetings with parents usually transpire just before the graduation ceremony.

Mom comes into the office, her face already stained with tears; dad wears his intimidating tank top shirt, an image belied by a potbelly and sagging skin. What a sad scene this has become—and totally unnecessary, if you all had met only a few weeks earlier. Junior now won't walk down the aisle with the rest of his graduating class, and nothing his parents can do at this late date will change that fact. Contact parents of high school seniors *before* you must notify them that their child's graduation ceremony will occur after summer school in the middle of August—at a backyard family barbecue.

EIGHTH GRADERS

My cousin taught eighth grade for one year, and even *I* wanted to exterminate her students. By second semester the children were eating out of the palm of her hand, but only due to her amiable personality, unparalleled sincerity, continuous hard work, and numerous—and I mean *numerous*—meetings and phone calls to parents. Those were before the days of email. She called parents on the telephone or sent letters home, inviting them to meet with her at school.

Contacts with parents of eighth graders deflect the burden, once again, back to where it belongs and allows us to smile mischievously when no one else is looking; we have finally followed through on our threat to the little mutts that we would make their lives miserable by getting in touch with Mom and Dad.

KIDS WHO POSE A PHYSICAL THREAT TO OTHERS

This quaint, charming idea is to get Mom and Dad involved *before* their child murders someone else. Just a thought: An ounce of prevention is worth a pound of getting sued by an irate parent whose kid had been assaulted behind the gym.

If you hear a threat made by one student directly to another, get wind of a threat indirectly, sense a threat is in the offing (as your teacher intuition has been prickling inside your sensory receptors), or a student comes to you and confesses that he feels threatened by another kid, you have two options: one, you can redirect the problem to a discipline administrator; or, two, you can call the children's parents—of both the offending child and the one who potentially has been victimized. I like to differentiate between what I think may happen—remotely—because of my gut instinct, and what I believe has an almost certain chance of occurring, because I've heard the threat or seen the proverbial writing on the wall. The obvious ones always get referred to the mean guy in the plush office; the ambiguous ones—just to be on the safe side—get tossed to their parents.

And you can't always be sure what's true based on the way a kid looks. Last year a student who sat in the back row—I put him there because of his enormous height and weight—looked more threatening to other children in my classroom than Godzilla did to the people of Tokyo. But this child would have never harmed even the big spider that came down one morning from the light standards, causing every student to flee from their desks faster than teenage boys racing to catch a glimpse of Halle Berry parading in her lingerie on a community mall television screen. But much smaller boys—and yes, girls—have scared even me into believing they would cut the throats of their own mothers if the price was right.

And what do you tell a parent of a kid you think is a threat? Just that. Tell the parent that you have some concern Tommy has been bullying Billy at lunch—or that Billy is afraid of Tommy. You have no evidence to take to an administrator, but you want to advise the parent of the potential problem.

If you think a child is going to shoot up the school, you put it in writing and take any concerns or information to your principal—immediately:

"Dear Mr. Smith, I think Jimmy Jones is going to come to school with a gun and shoot all of us."

Or maybe you find something a bit more concrete, augmented by supporting examples for your concern. Don't balk on that one; history is replete with teachers who have stuck their heads in the sand after sensing catastrophe—and people wound up dying.

KIDS WHO CLEARLY IMPEDE THE EDUCATIONAL PROGRESS OF OTHERS

It's getting harder and harder to have disruptive students removed from your classrooms. Special education students today have more rights than any other protected-by-law entity in America—even suspected terrorists who supposedly are being tortured by having to listen to rap music in Guantánamo; it's almost impossible to get rid of these kids, even if they've been constantly obnoxious, irritating, and unruly. Many non–special ed kids push the envelope, too, and get away with it, as educators frequently wallow in their fear of being on the wrong end of an expensive lawsuit. But this is where parents can help.

An angry, frustrated high school teacher had the following conversation with the mother of a sixteen-year-old girl who would not stop chattering in his class, even after having been admonished countless times by her teacher. In addition to her offending garrulous personality, the girl never completed her homework and hardly ever worked on her classroom assignments—again, mainly because of her amorous, congenial social interaction with some of the other girls during their class:

Mr. Dickins: So, as you can see, Millie is in danger of failing—*and*—she's about to be referred to the A.P. for her constant verbal disruptions.

Millie's mother: I know, Mr. Dickins. But what can I do? I've tried everything.

Mr. Dickins: Well, not *everything*.

Millie's mother: Well, everything I know of.

Mr. Dickins: Here's my suggestion. Are you ready for it?

Millie's mother: (with some trepidation) Of course.

Mr. Dickins: Come to her class with her one morning. I'll provide you a desk right behind your daughter. Be sure to wear your bathrobe and have your hair in curlers. Every time Millie goes off task, tap her lightly on the back of her head. If you—*when* you—see aberrant behaviors like loud, obnoxious talking, using profanity, or just chattering about everything else but the task at hand, you can jot down what you saw and then have a friendly chat with Millie when she gets home from school.

Millie's mother: Are you *kidding* me?

Mr. Dickins: (a wry smile) That ought to work. Don't you think?

Millie's mother sat in silence on the other end of the phone line, her mouth agape. But eventually she did exactly what Mr. Dickins had suggested. Millie was mortified not just by the presence of her mother in her history class—but by the omnipresent bathrobe and curlers her mother wore that fateful morning.

Later—and only once—her mother quietly uttered to Millie that she would visit her daughter's classes again if she received another phone call from her history teacher. But Millie's behavior in all her classes changed; she had become a model citizen.

Some parents claim they are impotent when it comes to disciplining their own children; unfortunately, many who claim this are not fabricating their predicaments. But other times the only weapon we teachers have left for shaping up the disrupters and dumbbells is their parents. And they are only a telephone call or an email away!

YOUR STUDENTS WHO OPENLY SHOW DISDAIN OR DISRESPECT FOR YOU

Just a couple of years ago I had the misfortune of dealing with a student in my English class who was so unpleasant and disrespectful, I wished I could push a button and make him blow up. Probably for a myriad reasons, he loathed me. I espoused some ideas about life in general that he disagreed with strongly, so he smirked a lot and knew just how to get on my nerves. Making it worse, he refused to try the actual course work, preferring to sit there with his arms crossed, mumbling little wisecracks under his breath.

One day I asked Roger if he would speak with me after class; I expressed to him that he was one of the most unusual students I'd ever dealt with, because he liked absolutely *nothing* about me, the subject matter, or even the architecture of the classroom. He smiled—unpleasantly, of course—and said, "Coming from you, that's a compliment."[3]

Denying my underlying desire to whack this punk across the face, I dismissed him from class, went to the phone, and called his mother.[4] Completely sympathetic to my plight, she expressed horror about her son's behavior (naturally, a good sign).

The boy improved for a while but then went back to his old ways. I'd finally had it when he admonished me in front of the entire class for not teaching him *anything*. While it may have been true he had learned nothing in my class, I refused to take the responsibility for his academic failings and derelict character. Deciding not to call his mother again, this time I went directly to the discipline administrator, who removed him the next day. Had I not made contact with his mother first, the administrator would have only warned the little lad that he had better soon become the model citizen everyone could enthusiastically love, cherish, and admire.

There was, of course, a better chance he would become the next pope or president of the United States.

CHILDREN WHO HAVE FALLEN WAY BEHIND AND NEED TUTORING, COUNSELING

All public schools offer academic help for those who want it or need it; usually, this help is free. Once a student has missed too many assignments or messed up on a major test, it's a good idea to send a note home, advising his parents of his tenuous status. Most schools employ a structured warning system as a matter of policy: At a certain point, a teacher is required to send home a "failure notice" or "unsatisfactory progress report," or he may not assign a failing grade to a fading student at the end of the term.

What more and more schools are now doing—but not enough of them—is requiring academic tutoring for those who fall behind.[5] Sometimes kids simply need another person to prompt them with their homework (which, of course, parents should be doing); and they often require a fresher, more nimble brain that can help them with their algebraic equations (which most parents *can't* do; when my own kids begin adding fractions with different bottom numbers, I'm turning to an expert or a rocket scientist for help). A letter of recommendation to homework clinic or a reference to a local tutor—on campus or off—may meet the needs of students who would have otherwise struggled.

Some teachers believe that they actually will have betrayed a kid, if they contacted his parents. They call it *snitching. Snitching* is the word kids use on the playground. You are an adult, the teacher, and often your very best recourse for helping a child *is* to snitch on him to his parents.

Do it.

There are several effective ways to make contact with parents:

1. Call parents on the telephone.
   This is easy; just pick up and dial. Rather—sorry—take the phone out and punch the keypad. When parents leave work numbers, it means that they don't mind being interrupted there—or they prefer

it at work to no contact at all. If your school doesn't have easy access to a plentiful supply of telephones you can use free of charge, then talk to your union people. This is a major issue, and the union will go to hell and back over this one.

As I near the end of my teaching career in the "I hate cell phones mode," I should occasionally remind myself of the cell phone's practicality. Besides the various safety reasons to have this handy device, a teacher may relax on a plush recliner in the lounge (yeah, right!), as he shouts venomous four letter words into the phone's speaker system. Mind you, this makes very little headway with parents, but it certainly relieves some of those anxieties you may have otherwise taken out on your students.

2. Ask a counselor to set up a conference for you.

This way, you don't have to cope with the initial parental backlash. ("*What*? Why? What did he do? Why are you always picking on him?"); furthermore, having a counselor call and set up your appointment for you may cement in the mind of the parent a more serious attitude about the conference. True, parents should already take the meeting with you seriously, but let's face the reality: Much of the public today has no respect for our professional teacher status. If they did, they wouldn't come to our parent-teacher meetings wearing low-cut tank tops or fishnet stockings (and I'm referring to the *fathers*)!

Another advantage to having the counselor make the initial contact with a parent is the counselor can detect—and warn you of—a foul mood in the approaching parent; now you may defensively prepare your own foul mood, your foul mood antidote, or a beautiful foul mood sucker punch.

So much for, "our professional teacher status."

3. Send a letter home.

The purpose of a letter like this can be to set up a conference, or to report in writing a student's specific problems as per your professional evaluation—or both. Needless to say, a registered letter is even better; also, needless to say, you should make sure you don't have any grammar, spelling mistakes, or typos in that letter. The last thing you want is for a parent to hand a copy of your letter to your principal and quip, "It's no wonder my daughter doesn't know how to read or write. Look at how her teacher spelled *does! D-o-s-e!*"

What's *dose*?

4. Call from home.

This provides the same results as my other suggestions, but your calling from home impresses parents, because they will notice you are actively trying to help their children on your own time.

Before she had her first baby, my cousin was a middle school English teacher and preferred to call the parents of her eighth graders from her home. I often had the pleasure of hearing their conversations (at least, from my cousin's side of the exchange), and sometimes the candidness of what she said to parents startled me—though I still refer to this as a "pleasant surprise." Once, she called the home of a troubled student who had failed to show up for tutorial help after school. Although I couldn't hear the parent, I can only imagine what she was saying on the other end of the line!

My cousin: "Yes, well, it's good that your daughter is taking piano lessons, but she shouldn't take them after school; it's in conflict with my tutoring sessions. . . . Yes, she's behind. Uh-uh. Well, the thing is . . . let me put it to you this way: I've offered to help your daughter before school, and she says she can't get there early. She has piano lessons after school. Right. . . . Well, I've told you what *I'm* doing to help your daughter with English. Now, what are *you* doing to help your daughter with English?"[6]

Whew! My cousin is only five-two and 110 pounds, but now you know why she earned the nickname Mighty Mouse! Although she was only in her midtwenties when she stopped teaching to have a baby, she was an extraordinary teacher, and she will be again, when she resumes her career. She is certainly one of the best "parent contactors" I've ever known!

5. Attract parents to open houses and back-to-school nights.

Short of bribery, the only way to get a large turnout for these featured events is for the teacher to send letters home to each parent, personally inviting her to your classroom. You may also coax your students into getting their parents to attend back-to-school night; however, offering them extra credit for this has always struck me as being somewhat cheesy. Nevertheless, if it works, if it spurs good attendance, try it. Try anything. Keep in mind, however, threats of torture or other forms of violence are probably not very professional.

A back-to-school forum is one of the least effective for honest communication with parents. Typically, only parents of the "good kids" come; other parents in the room stand around listening to your miniconference. This is hardly the time you want to say to a parent, "Melissa has really been sloughing off in class lately; I suspect drug use or conflicts over oral sexual intimacy with her boyfriend. Can we look into those possibilities?"

Not a good idea.

You can use this opportunity to impress upon your targeted parents the need for a conference and either arrange it then, or implore

them to call the school to set up a specific day and time that are sat-
isfactory to both of you.

6. Email.

Never thought I'd say it; never thought I'd use it. Now I know it's
an amazingly effective way of messaging parents.

A huge advantage to email is that you have a record of the contact
on your hard drive, in case you ever have to prove that you made the
connection. You can send copies of student work home or transmit
data about their kids to parents from your hard drive—neat stuff
you certainly can't do over a telephone line.

7. Visit their homes.

Walk there and arrive unannounced the way Lucas Tanner did
on the TV show. Lucas always did his best work when he caught
parents off guard, causing them to shake and stammer and shiver
in his presence.

Just kidding.

One other characteristic of parents you should keep in mind: Some
of them are evil . . . or crazy. And many parents are never around or
don't answer your messages. Teachers should begin from the premise that parents of their students are going to be less than ideally
helpful (tactfully put, no?) in promoting their own kids' education.
It's about the glass being half empty. Assume that only one parent
lives with this child, her father is in prison, her mother has a das-
tardly temper, neither parent cares about her education, both parents
are impossible to get a hold of, one or both of her parents are drunks
or drug users. . . . Each one of these is a real possibility; presume one
or more of them apply to each of your students.

Take it from there!

In most cases you'll be pleasantly surprised by the caliber of your
students' parents: their willingness to help with your concerns and
problems; their efforts toward positive involvement in your classroom; their congeniality. Those pleasant surprises will generate
joy in your teaching and make you want to be a better teacher. But
disappointment in your students' parents is a numbing experience.
Escaping to Devils Island becomes an attractive option for a change
in lifestyle.

And this is never a good thing.

One final word about parent contacts: You need to be effective
around the parents. Look them in the eye. Assuming they have more
than one eye, look them in both eyes. Demonstrate passion for their
children; after all, *they* have passion for their children. They care
about what's happening in their lives. They desperately wish for
their children to succeed.

And they want you to have the same wishes and desires for their children as they do.

You have to impress them—with not only your teaching style and caring demeanor—but with *what* you are teaching their kids. Whenever you can, talk about what is presently happening in your classroom. Wow parents with all you will be doing with their children in the coming weeks and months: the fascinating projects their kids will complete; the meaningful assignments they will ask for help with at home; the lessons about life and love and goodness you will bring to their treasured children—those precious souls they have entrusted to *you*.[7]

NOTES

1. Nancy Gibbs, "Parents Behaving Badly," *Time*, February 13, 2005, 9–14.

2. This is the wild estimate almost every teacher uses, especially in times of great duress. The truth is the average high school teacher has many fewer than two hundred students at a time.

3. Temptation leers at me, as I fight not to reveal the real name of the kid here. Broadcasting his notoriety may be well worth a lawsuit.

4. Virginia R. Cassidy, *Academic Planning and Development*, Northern Illinois University, 2006, at ibhe.state.il.us/EffectivePractices/Featured/result.asp?Y=2006&F=001737&P=4&T=247&5=A.

5. Ibid.

6. Studying Mrs. Gevirtzman's comments to this parent should be mandatory for all education students in the free world.

7. *Data for Reform in Education* reported in 2007 that the numbers of parents visiting schools and their qualitative enthusiasm for involvement in the schools wane, as their children get older. By the time their kids reach high school, 17 percent of parents maintain regular contact with their children's schools, and only 35 percent have any contact at all.

10

✝

Immerse Yourself in the *Extra*, without Going Under

"My job is posh."

"What?"

"My job."

"Uh, yeah, well, what is it that you do?"

I tried feigning enthusiasm, but this guy's smugness really irritated me.

Leaning back on the weight rack, his soft paunch became more evident. But compared to some of the fatsos in the gym that day, he appeared to be in moderately good physical shape. He grinned—beamed, "I'm a teacher! I've had the same gig for ten years—teaching accounting."

"Oh!" I blurted out with less than obvious sincerity. "You're a teacher!"

Again the smugness: "Yup. Middle school. Same school—ten years."

Of course, for me at the time (six years ago) it had been same school— *thirty* years; but why intervene while we were having so much fun? I asked him, "So you get vacations and holidays and all that, huh?"

"Yes," he replied, "and I also get outta there at three o'clock in the afternoon, in case, you know, I want to catch a movie or something. . . . Now, if I wanted to teach summer school it would knock about a month off my summer vacation, but, hey, why do you think I wanted to become a teacher? So I could work summers? Hell, no!"

I wanted to stick my foot in this cocky guy's mouth; instead I shrugged, "That's pretty cool. I especially like how you can walk away at three o'clock in the afternoon; most people work a lot longer than that at their jobs."

"Well," he whispered, almost too softly for me to hear, "there are those suckers who work a lot longer than I do. They do all the extra stuff like coaching sports, drama, being club advisers, sitting on committees—but they're a bunch of morons; they hardly get any extra money for what they do, and they spend so much friggin' time doing it! Not for me!"

If this had been a teacher I wanted to get to know better, I would have asked him about the climate of his classroom, the success of his students, and the awesome—I'm *sure*—amount of respect he receives from his colleagues. However, from this brief encounter at the gym that one Saturday afternoon, I realized a short, frivolous discussion was about all I could tolerate with this guy.

This man was a teacher; it embarrassed me. His boasting about what most people disrespect about teachers and education had galled me enough; I didn't want to hear anymore. Besides, I already knew—without having any hardcore information—what kind of a teacher this guy was. Beyond his outer pomposity and bravado, he had told me he preferred to bolt from the school grounds as quickly as possible; that he didn't want to spend even an extra *minute* working with his students or other children on campus; that he met only the basic requirements of his contract and thought those who extended themselves to children above and beyond the call of duty were—as he put it—"a bunch of morons."

To be fair—and, once again, quite honest—my own situation besmirches what you have just read. I, too, spring from the campus faster than a streak of lightning; in fact, I'm probably driving my car out the parking lot well before the students even arrive at *their* cars (as they must stop by their lockers, meet friends, grab each others' bodies, and so forth). But here's my vindication: *I'm old!* I've been teaching high school since dinosaurs roamed the earth; actually, unbeknownst to anyone else, well *before* giant reptiles wandered on our planet, I had already been teaching school.

There were at least a billion days I arrived at school at six in the morning and didn't leave until ten or eleven o'clock at night. I don't know how many weekends I spent at speech tournaments, play rehearsals, or baseball games—probably hundreds. (The effect from the exhaustion of all these spent hours is that now I'm actually too tired to *count* anything—such as the total number of weekends I'd worked at speech tournaments).

I could have never written this book, offered advice, or been a role model for even the most awful of all teaching candidates if I didn't have quite an impressive track record for involvement in life at school *outside the classroom*. Getting involved makes teachers better inside their own classrooms, too.

Weirdly, even as busy, involved teachers moan and groan about their state of utter exhaustion—for example, from coaching a sport—their extra laboring hardly seems to lessen the quality of work they're doing with their classroom students. Unless these busy teachers have become distracted to the point of the ridiculous in their extra school activities—not getting enough sleep themselves—their extra energy, enthusiasm, and elation create better classroom teachers.[1]

Period.

John Reckenhouse said in a personal interview, "More and more we are finding teachers who motivate themselves by stepping outside the confines of their classroom and getting to know children and teachers with other kinds of experiences."[2]

So . . . ta-da!

ELEVEN PERSUASIVE REASONS FOR TEACHERS TO GET INVOLVED OUTSIDE THE CLASSROOM:

1. Teachers have a stake in the entire school.

The truth of the matter: Those who teach only a course or two and then promptly go home are being judged and evaluated by others solely on what they bring to their individual classes—and how they bring it. Why should they care about anything else? Belonging to an entire community may engross a teacher on a superficial level, but the reality of his belonging is legitimized only after a teacher believes he has earned an actual stake in that community.

2. Teachers become more familiar with a greater variety of adolescents.

What if—and I know this *never* happens—you are stuck all day, by happenstance, in a roomful of creatures like the ones who had mutated in the movie *The Faculty*?[3] In fact, the teacher victims in that film actually had an advantage over real-life teachers who inherit classes from the deepest bowels of society, because at least the movie's teachers had the fortune—or misfortune—to share their fates with other *adults*. Not so, of course, when you must stand alone with thirty or so gum-chewing, text-messaging, iPod-using, potty-mouthed teenagers.

It's only when your horizons become broadened and you venture out on the athletic fields, cheerleader courts, or theater stages that you begin to think, "Hmm . . . Maybe not *all* kids are like the transmutations I work with all day long in my classroom. Maybe there *is* teenage life out there that comes with a sense of decency, a little respect, and even a passion for something other than sex, drugs, and rap music."

As you coached Jimmy how to make contact with that curve ball, even after he had been absolutely positive the pitcher was going to throw up that fastball, all you thought about—hitting that curveball—was the immediate and beautiful task at hand.

3. Teachers find a professional balance.

Teachers are supposed to, well, teach. Does this mean they are relegated for their entire careers only to room number whatever and the same lousy whiteboard? Of course, it doesn't mean anything like this, but many teachers have a shrunken view of their jobs. Teaching needn't be tedious, redundant, and rote. Getting outside the formal classroom promotes a teacher's understanding of the plentiful and diverse opportunities available for expanding their teaching lives in ways that make them more professionally enthusiastic, and it compels them to perform their daily chores more effectively.

4. Teachers learn, too.

They learn about their students; they learn about others' students. And they also learn about the different components of a kid's life that make him whole. Children are more than just, "Brought your book? Have your materials? Now, sit down and answer the questions at the end of chapter 7!"

Our students are also, "Billy, during your campaign for student body president, you must appeal to the middle. Poll what it is that students at this school really want, find out how to make it happen, and then during your campaign, offer how you will do those things.

"Then you can go from there. Being a campaigner requires lots of hard work and enthusiasm. But I think you have potential; it's now up to you to rise to the occasion."

Life's offerings chime with a pleasant, inviting, soothing sound, especially when they foster experiences that are not being realized in a drab, monotonous environment.

5. Teachers break their own tedium.

And tedium often calibrates to a lack of concentration. A lack of concentration generates bad decisions, distracted teaching, and lifeless personalities. All these are bad for your classroom. Think about how much better you feel, how less stressed you are—more energetic and industrious—while you are trying something new.

Even after we have done the new and later gone back to the old, we have gathered a new lease on life; we have gotten the sense we explored our other options—and with that, comes a sense of relief. We can now more fully commit ourselves to those mundane tasks that have already begun to slip away from us; we no longer nag ourselves with those lingering doubts about our choices. For if the grass is truly greener on the other side, at least we have now experienced the other side. Yes, coaching a sport, leading a club, or chaperoning a dance has, at least temporarily, liberated us from the notion that we weren't doing enough for our students—*or* for ourselves.

And the truth is we probably *hadn't* been doing enough for either.

6. Teachers make a greater investment.

The more hours you work at most jobs, the more money you earn. And you also have a greater investment in seeing a higher quality in the products you're manufacturing. But even if, theoretically, you have taught in the same classroom every day for fifteen hours a day, the same four walls would be chiding you to beat your head up against the bulletin board while the backs of the pins are sticking out. Mathematically, two and two will always be four; and this objectiveness applies to nonmathematical problems, as well. If you spend eight hours in your classroom, and you require another two or three hours of work to hone your teaching talents, you'd be better off dancing with a variety of activities that expands your professional horizons.

For me it was coaching baseball. Baseball was—and still is to some extent—my life. What could be better, I wondered, than imparting my love and knowledge of baseball to a bunch of high school boys, while getting *paid* for it at the same time? Even if I hadn't been compensated the rather paltry amount of money they gave me, I would have done it for free. I came to know the kids; I got to teach. I immersed myself in the sport I adored.

And I made some kids' lives a little richer by doing so.

7. Teachers make their schools better.

You're already making your school better by being a star in your own classroom, right? Or maybe you will be doing this when you finally become a teacher. But think about how much more appreciative of you your students and administrators and parents will become, after you have branched out and taught in other areas of your expertise: sports, clubs, fine arts, student government, etc.

Remember when you were just a little lad and one of your parents patted you on the head because you did something they thought was really cute and good—like that time you made your own bed by haphazardly pulling the covers up and over the pillows? You felt like a star, didn't you? The theory goes, the more praise you receive for a job well done or for donating generous amounts of time to a worthy cause, the more desire you will generate for doing other projects that help shape the lives of others. It always comes back to you.

For some teachers, their special skills border on the unique. Mr. Dobbins, the woodshop teacher, can teach his students how to make baby-safe toys and build props for stage productions: two distinctly different—and rare commodities—offered by a man who would have been generally unknown, unappreciated, and unwanted had he not gone above and beyond the calling of his classroom.

Mr. Dobbins makes our school better.

8. Teachers stay at their jobs longer.

That's not an opinion; that's a fact. Assuming your working extra isn't going to kill you—a fair assumption that had *better* pan out—teachers who do more than just meet the same kids daily in order to instruct them in their regular courses last longer on the job.[4] There will be more pressure put on you by others not to retire. (Who wants to lose that wonderful band adviser?) You will put more pressure on yourself not to retire. ("I'm such a good band adviser—and the kids will really miss me." Or, "I'm having so much fun being a band adviser, I don't want to quit now!)" For a multitude of terrific reasons, teachers put off their retirements when they are involved in their schools.

And then they retire and die.

Sorry about the gallows humor.

9. Teachers become better all around.

The more you teach, the better you should become at teaching; at least, that's the theory. The more I work with my six year-old son at hitting a baseball, the worse I wind up pitching to him; but I think this has more to do with rickety, old bones breaking down, than it does with my inability to learn from my mistakes and benefit from the aspects of pitching I do well. Still, *he* learns to hit the ball farther, harder, and more consistently.

I know that every time I teach a poem, I get better at it; of course, if I teach the identical poem ten times in a row, I'm going to sag a bit in the enthusiasm department. And my approaches to literature pieces may evolve. I look back at some of the things I had said in the past about certain poems, and I cringe.

A book by Dalton Trumbo, *Johnny Got His Gun*,[5] used to be my personal bible. I loved its antiwar themes and its take-no-prisoners style in presenting its powerful themes. I assigned my students to read *Johnny Got His Gun*, we then thoroughly covered it in class, and in front of them I swore by the book's veracity—I'm sure now—to the point of the ludicrous. Thirty years ago I viewed the world differently; I also taught differently.

I still assign this novel to stress literary technique and theme development, but now I approach the book with a grain of salt; I also use it to contrast with the works of Thomas Paine, material I scoffed at *then* but revere today.[6] The bottom line: The more we teach, the more we grow as a teacher. It's not only "out with the old and in with the new"; it's "out with the *bad* old and in with the *good* new."

As we teach longer and harder, we tend to be more efficient discriminators about which materials we utilize and the manner we use those materials, theoretically, making us more communicative with our students. The experiences I gathered from coaching baseball, for example, offered me ammunition for dealing with kids in my classroom. Grounding into a double play with the bases loaded in the last inning of a tie ball game is akin to messing up on the latter section of a final exam—and then receiving a lower grade because of the mess up.

What can we teach our students about flubbing under pressure? And how, as teachers, do we help them to rectify it? The more we perform with these teenagers, the more we grow in our knowledge and skills for helping them lead their lives.

10. Teachers get on the good side of administrators, students, and other teachers.

The teachers who are jealous of you because of your students' expressions of gratitude for having you as a teacher, or for the accolades you have received—are the sorest lugs on the faculty; they are the pits. They see you spending so much time and making such an effort working with the kids at your school—while they sit back in their classrooms and sip diet soda. They watch the kids flocking to you during breaks and lunch. They watch you win popularity awards, teaching awards, and district/community awards, and they always have something snide to add to the milieu: "That Mr. Adams—that—that drama teacher. I'll bet he's schtooping his female students after school! That's why he spends so much time back stage with them!"

The teacher who made this comment would not even know what a backstage area of a theater looks like, let alone the truth of what Mr. Adams does—or why he does it. But by and large, everyone professionally connected with the school looks up to involved teachers; they respect them, and they appreciate them for what they have so generously given.

11. Teachers gain the respect and admiration of their students' parents.

Most parents start out with an inherent respect for teachers. Some adults, of course, largely due to their own miserable experiences while going to school, loathe all teachers, all schools, and anybody else associated with education. They are certain the education establishment is out to get them and, by extension, their loved ones; nothing stands a chance of changing their minds.

But for most parents, one quality in a teacher that has consistently earned their respect is hard work. Parents trust teachers who are not afraid to labor, involve themselves with their students, and project pride about what they do—and have already accomplished.

Parents never—I mean *never*—praised me for my knowledge of literature or my grasp of the English language (probably for legitimate reasons); but parents have shaken my hand for spending extra time with their children, for working those long hours with them at the theater, baseball field, or speech tournaments. Their appreciation is mired in their recognition of my involvement with their kids—not merely firing information and orders in their kids' direction.

OK, have you heard enough of the word "involvement"? I know I have. But what may be breeding frustration in some of you is that you have the following sense: *OK, Bruce. You talk a good talk, and on paper all this stuff about getting involved sounds great, but there are some questions—real concerns—I have about teachers spending all this extra time working with kids outside their classrooms.*

And this is *sooo* reasonable. I hear these qualms expressed all the time— I've had them—but allow me to relieve those understandable, unwarranted, and undesirable worries by letting you know . . . you are just plain *wrong*. (Gee, I wish I *could* do that; in truth, all I can do is present some arguments made by the other side and then respond to each of them.)

Concern # 1: When we spend so much time outside the classroom getting involved in extracurricular activities, we wind up spreading ourselves too thin.

In all honesty I have no idea what this means: "spreading ourselves too thin." Judging the girth of a great many of us teachers, the word "thin" hardly gets a lot of wordplay. When you volunteer for a job and take it on, you should *take it on*. If you do it well, you're not getting too thin. If you don't do it well, consider that you should not have taken the job to begin with. Of course, you should not immerse yourself in sizable situations you can't handle; if it does come to that, well, de-thin yourself. By the way, most teachers work effectively, doing more than they thought they were capable of doing, handling more than they could have imagined.

Concern #2: I have a family; no time will be left for them.

When my own family emerged, I gave up 90 percent of what I had been doing before; I cut down on the number of papers I graded at home, and I refused to volunteer for anything resembling spending time with other adults on committees, such as the safety committee or the attendance policy committee. I made time for a few random after-school involvements I figured I could handle, such as listening to competitive speakers before their big tournaments or helping to write debate cases. I tested the waters just enough to remind myself what it had been like for me in the past; yet, I still arrived home no later than 4:30 or 5:00 in the afternoon.

Even with a family, *some* extra involvement is not only possible—it's *healthy*. Most men and women who have normal jobs regularly arrive home in the late afternoons or early evenings—and sometimes even later. With more on your plate to do—to help bolster your classroom performance and improve your school—you soon may rival the get-home-just-in-time-for-a-late-dinner people with your own daily schedule.

Having looked at this before in a negative light, you should now reverse your thinking here. One day you may look back at the extra work you had done with children as some of the most important activities you had engaged in during your lifetime.

Concern #3: I'm already stressed and exhausted; this will push me over the edge.

The healthy glow we show from doing productive work and helping others can't be surpassed. If you worked in a coal mine, apprehensive about cave-ins, soot, and black lung disease—then yes—your extra work below the earth is certain to fatigue you even further.

My depressed friend Willie took on the assignment of assistant drama director and perked up over night. His eyes shone, his face suddenly had color, and his skin lost its pallor. He strode around the school with purpose, and even his students noticed the difference.

Willie told me, "I can't wait to work after school on the plays! I go through the day with purpose now. I feel like I got a new lease on [my teaching] life!" Of course, if you overdo it, don't get enough sleep, eat terribly, refuse to exercise, ignore your personal life, or go to a Dodger game (gag me), you wind up more exhausted than ever before. But it won't be because you are productive outside the classroom; it will be in spite of it.

Concern #4: We're working for peanuts! If they want teachers to do all that extra work, they should pay us what we're worth!

If "they" actually took us up on that, some of us would be in big trouble.

For those of you who are reading this book while considering whether or not you would like to become a teacher, I am sorry to report that, yes, there are teachers with this attitude; and, yes, sometimes they sour the climate of their schools. If you have begun your teaching quest with a similar attitude—and thereby ignored all the glorious benefits of teaching that pack this book—I suggest from this point forward, you pursue another line of work.

My father-in-law eventually must turn over his vending business to *somebody.*

Concern #5: It's not good to get too close to the kids; scandal can result.

Professionalism mandates that teachers separate themselves on certain levels from their students, and they preserve specific boundaries. But as long as you refrain from any of the following, you're safe, and your professional teacher-student relationship has not been breeched:

A. Don't approach students about their personal problems; if they wish to speak with you or vent, let *them* approach you. It may be wise to have a third party sit in on your conversations. It's mandatory to report to a school administrative authority any indications of drug or alcohol abuse, pending violence, threats of suicide, or child abuse; for example, California law requires immediate reporting.

B. Don't touch your students in an inappropriate manner. Quite obvious, of course, but now we have the idiots who don't want us to even hug our students. Ironically, I still hug my students—but only the males. Today I wouldn't dare touch in *any manner* a female student. Sad, sad, sad—but true.

C. Don't go to your students' homes. Friendly parents may meet you for a Coke, but it's a little weird when they invite you over for dinner.

D. Don't discuss private, sexual issues—especially with girls if you're a male—and censor inquiries about their sexual experiences, sexual orientation, and sexual attitudes. Don't discuss your own sex life either. (Duh!)

E. Eliminate most discussions about your personal life. Obviously, if you have a family, your students will want to share in your life with them; however, the serious—and very personal—issues of infidelity, sexual frequency, financial woes, poor habits, alcoholism, drug use, personal political views, religious convictions, and dogma are better eliminated in relationships between teachers and students.

I look back at some of my disclosures and discussions with students on the debate squads, baseball teams, and those in the many plays I directed—and I *cringe*. However, with age came wisdom—and the younger I was, the dumber I was; so I now impart to you some of my old geezer insight about intimacy between teachers and students. Don't do as I *did*; do as I *say* now. By becoming involved more with your students, you don't have to cross the lines I have drawn for you. The closeness is good; it's the overindulgent informality that ultimately reeks.

At the end of my first year of teaching in the school I currently work (thirty-six years ago), a soap opera drama rattled through our campus. The expansive cast of characters seemed never-ending: Fourteen teachers either were fired or pressured to resign. Among those . . .

- a male teacher who smoked marijuana behind the gym at lunch with the gifted and talented kids (not clear what they'd been "gifted" and "talented" in)
- a married male teacher who conducted a sexual affair with one of his own extracurricular stars
- a female teacher who frequently grabbed certain unmentionable parts of the anatomy of her male students
- a male teacher who took hordes of his students on ski trips amid rumors of alcohol use, smoking weed, and sexual romps
- a male teacher who had forsaken all his regular classroom furniture and replaced it with padded chairs, expensive sofas, comfortable throw carpets, Indian lamps, colored lightbulbs, and smoldering incense; he also turned off all classroom lighting and burned only bulbs he had bought specifically for his spruced up classroom environment
- a male athletic coach who constantly showed up at speech tournaments on the weekends for the sole purpose of sexually pursuing one of the debate team's star female speakers; whether he succeeded in his quest is mostly unknown.

Quite a group—and every single one of these examples is absolutely, 100 percent, verifiably true! To label these teachers as "unprofessional" is an enormous understatement; ironically—or not—each of these educators was among the finest, most popular, most reputable teachers in their school. But their abusive and—saying it directly—*stupid* behaviors had clearly done them in. It may be impossible for a teacher to *ever* recover from convenient overindulgences, poor choices, and despicable decisions.

For they all had gone way overboard.

But as with almost everything else in life, walking the middle ground provides rational attainment of goals and attracts respect from those who count the most. Most teachers who work beyond their classrooms aren't featured in a newspaper for their personality quirks or character guffaws. They don't wind up in prison or on those creepy afternoon talk shows that sometimes glimpse the freaks and outcasts of the education establishment. Their extra involvements in their students' lives are purely professional, related to their own career goals, and ultimately wind up in the best interests of the adolescents they have worked with.

Getting involved is one of the surest methods of making you a happier teacher.

But breeching boundaries winds up making you a discharged teacher. It's all in the mix.

NOTES

1. Karin Dienst, "Rewards of Teaching Inspire Students," *Princeton Weekly Bulletin* 90, 9 (November 13, 2000): 13.

2. Mr. Reckenhouse despised being a teacher until the year he assisted in the speech and debate program. His love for our school was augmented with each speech tournament he had attended.

3. *The Faculty* (Dimension Pictures, 1998).

4. Margaret Patton and William Alan Kristonis, "The Law of Increasing Returns: A Process for Retaining Teachers—National Recommendations," *National Journal for Publishing and Mentoring Doctorial Student Research* 3 (2006): 1, 8.

5. Dalton Trumbo, *Johnny Got His Gun*, New York: Citadel Paperback, 2007.

6. Thomas Paine's *Common Sense* presents ideas about war and the importance of fighting for liberty that are polar opposites of those espoused by Dalton Trumbo in *Johnny Got His Gun*. Studying both these books together has created a treat for students and a tremendous teaching experience for me.

11

Breathe, Pace, Chill

He walked in the front door.
Tentatively.

He knew it was his house, and his family would greet him.

But how?

His legs ached from standing on his feet all day; his bones were sore, too, since his joints had stiffened, and arthritis had begun taking its toll on his body. At only forty-five years old, he could no longer be classified as a youngster; but he was not an ancient mariner either. Perhaps this wouldn't bother him if it weren't for the stress that seemed to run through his system like a bucket of water seeping though a sponge mop. Sometimes he thought the back of his neck and his scalp were, literally, on fire. Of course, a cursory inspection in a mirror would not visually confirm that hypothesis; nonetheless, he feared the extent of damage mounting stress had brought to his body.

His wife emerged from the kitchen before he had the opportunity to set his briefcase on the floor.

"Hi," she managed to say, but with the usual lack of enthusiasm.

"Hi," he echoed tiredly, showing some disappointment at her ho-hum greeting. But he wasn't that surprised.

"You need to pick Jack up from karate class. Did you forget? He's waiting for you. Why are you late?"

"I'm sorry; I forgot. It's only 4:30, Mary," he reminded her.

"Jack's through with karate at 4:30."

"I had some business at school."

"Like what?"

"Like a couple of parents. Why are you being so belligerent?"

"You'd better get going; he's waiting for you," she ordered with a firm finality; then she stormed by him and walked toward their bedroom.

David had taught high school math for the past seven years, starting his teaching career at about the time his wife Mary had become pregnant with their son. Previously, he'd been involved in several business ventures that didn't pan out; when he married Mary, he went to work as an accountant for a small computer company. Their son's pending emergence into the world had inspired him—perhaps, compelled him—to seek a steady career. Only a few classes shy of earning his preliminary teaching credential as a math major, David knew he would have no trouble finding a job. Even if he attained early employment in a less-than-desirable school, he could always look later for greater job satisfaction.

As it happened, David's first seven years as a math teacher transpired in an upscale middle school in Vermont. He discovered his students to be rambunctious, rude, and rowdy; their parents breathed insolence. The administration at his school cowered in fear of possible parent reprisals for potentially unpopular decisions they would make. Support of teachers by administrators turned limp, mostly due to the parents' perception of administrative impotence.

David began to have hideous headaches. He even went through a battery of tests to detect whether or not there was something organically wrong with his brain. When these tests came up negative, his doctors diagnosed him with stress and prescribed anxiety pills. But David's problems mounted. While he was home one night watching a Red Sox game, debilitating intestinal cramps came out of nowhere. Figuring the pain had been in direct response to Big Poppy grounding into a game-ending double play with the bases loaded in the bottom of the ninth inning, David shrugged it off. But when the pains came back on his birthday a week later, he took them more seriously. Especially when the pains were accompanied by several choruses of diarrhea, a potential serious illness spoke to him in his head in hushed, solemn tones.

This time the doctor diagnosed David with IBS (irritable bowl syndrome) a benign—but brutally painful and messy—abdominal ailment, usually ignited by stress, work pressures, and major events or changes in lifestyle.

David, the forty-plus-year-old veteran eighth grade math teacher, was now officially a basket case; and unless he took strong measures to make major adjustments in his life, his prognosis would not be good.

Divulging David's fate, however, will have to wait until later.

Sorry.

In the past decade, many American businesses have wised up—at least in one regard: They have recognized the cumulative effects of everyday living and the growing burdens of the workplace—and how they continue to take a huge toll on their employees. More workers have been calling in sick, arriving at the job late, and resigning long before they would receive any significant employment benefits. The American Institute of Stress reported that 40 percent of job turnover is due to stress.[1]

Allstate and FedEx (among others) now offer their employees minimassage sessions right in the office.[2] Some employers have installed workout areas or small gymnasiums, with time built into the workday to partake of the facilities. Even a larger number of companies have set aside part of their employees' paychecks and directed the money (on a voluntary basis, of course, but with some financial incentives for compliance) toward gym memberships.[3] Some organizations have not only beefed up their health insurance packages, they pay their workers bonuses for seeing doctors for regular checkups and biannual health-screening exams.

The smartest among employers who wish to maintain a lucrative, productive network of businesses and company ownerships have accurately concluded that having *healthy* workers is an optimum strategy for obtaining better results: greater productivity, a bigger income, and a higher quality of products. A keen sense of how to maximize human potential has been their stalwart new direction—and it's mostly worked. Even the offering of in-house self-defense courses is intended to bring physical fitness and better health to the work environment.[4]

In the field of education, we have done very little to emulate this bottom-line oriented wisdom of private industry. If you want to get technical, you *could* point to examples of schools curtailing the amount of sugar they allow in soft drinks or groundbreaking, bold, innovative moves like disallowing the selling of candy for fundraisers on high school campuses.[5] (I hope to death that you caught the sarcasm.)

Ask any bigwig state official about this health policy, and he will tell you straight out: "It's a state law now. The state (of California) is in the business of looking out for your health. The state government is the food police." Other states have followed suit, making it a point to guide—and supposedly protect—the health of other parents' kids.[6]

Which means, in about three years, if a school security guard sees me standing in the center of campus chugging down a can of Pepsi, he will pull out a gun, shoot me between the eyes—and ask questions later. Coincidentally, as I type this, I am still reeling after being informed today by the staff in our school's cafeteria that teachers will no longer have access to purchasing diet cola drinks. The cafeteria lady told me point-blank, "The state is concerned about your health."

But don't get me wrong: I'm *glad* the people of our state give a bee's behind about my health; I just wish that they would allow *me* to decide what's best for *me*; I know the exact health issues *I* am dealing with—not the skinny guy wearing glasses at the state capitol building who wants everybody to switch to lightbulbs that would light up my face like a uranium explosion.

All in the name of looking out for my health, of course—as healthy teachers preside over better classrooms.

So why doesn't my school district give á hot patooti about the health tolls taken on teachers by raging amounts of stress and anxiety that are related to their work environment? With various performance standards, new mandates, in-service requirements, trendy (only *renamed*) movements, more stringent credentialing details, radical changes in teacher and student assessments, bilingual expectations, larger class sizes, cuts in funding—and salaries and benefits, layoff intimidation (and *actual* layoffs), threats to retirement pensions, soaring medical costs, parental pressures, recycled (excuse me—*new*) administrative directives, expanding meeting schedules, personal accusations, unrealistic testing expectations, unfocused parenting, counterproductive parenting, cultural diversity, crime, vandalism, gang infiltration, student rowdiness, lack of administrative support with discipline problems, public apathy, political finger-pointing . . . teacher stress levels and the consequences of that stress have risen dramatically.[7]

And upper-level educators—those who have the power to *do* something to allay these problems—have turned their backs.

Back to David:

"Did you speak with Jack's karate teacher about his advancement ceremony?" Mary asked him over dinner after their son had left the table.

David held a forkful of food, while contemplating her question. He had been shaken from his thoughts about a pressing problem at work: Declining enrollment had necessitated that his school would be losing a few teachers at the end of the semester, and David would inherit numerous students from other teachers who eventually would be dismissed entirely or transferred to another school in the district. Contemplating the disruptions and increases in his class sizes caused by juggling students in the middle of the school year helped to manufacture foreign intestinal acids not conducive to proper food digestion. "I—I'm sorry, Mary," he responded meekly. "I really don't—didn't remember what I was supposed to ask the karate teacher."

"About the *advancement* date, David," she opined. "We have a commitment to the Thermonds for dinner that night. We made it months ago. Surely, they can just give Jack his little yellow belt at a different time. What's the big deal?"

David sighed. "I don't imagine there's a big deal. But I'm not sure they want to do it that way."

"But you were supposed to *talk* with the instructor about it, David!" His wife persisted; she sounded to David like a whining duck—whatever that would sound like. No matter, he felt his skin beginning to crawl around on his body and a boiling, bubbling brew of blood right under his skin.

Dazed, he looked away from her. Apathy enveloped him; *nothing* mattered to him at that moment. His body went flaccid from head to toe. He had screwed up. So what? It hadn't been the first time, and it wouldn't be the last. "I messed up. I'm sorry," was all he managed to mutter.

"Can't you get *anything* right, David? All you care about is that—that damn school of yours! What about *us*!" she screeched.

"That 'damned school' is my *job*," David replied through clenched teeth. "It's what puts this food on our table."

"But your son was waiting for you! And you forgot to—"

"You know what?" David interrupted, as he stood in his place at the table. "From now on, *you* pick Jack up from karate! In fact, from now on, *you* pick him up from *everywhere* he goes! And you take him there, too!"

Agape, his wife stared at him; she barely flinched, as David turned and strode away from her, this time with a purposeful strut heretofore unseen in this little suburban household.

And there's more to David's story.

We'll tackle it later.

Here are some general facts you may have already expected about stress; they're worth rehashing: One of the greatest impediments to student learning is a stressed-out teacher. Some recent studies have linked higher levels of teacher stress with decreased pupil productivity;[8] however, since self-preservation and the possibility of an eventual extinction of teachers does pique my interest from time to time, it's important to point out that the effects of stress in the classroom are more than just job-connected. Physical illnesses, temper problems, general dissatisfaction (with depression) with employment, and severe emotional trauma are related to stress teachers suffer from working in our schools.[9]

So aside from the fact that your students won't do as well in your class (or adore you nearly as much), you might, like, drop dead at home as a residual effect from what happens at school.

Leave it to me to come up with something this primitive—stress reduction—as a whacky idea for a better classroom. In the comfortable confines of academia, colleges hardly ever mention certain problems—as unorthodox and gargantuan as they may be; so it's incumbent upon someone like me to tell you the truth. This book isn't entitled *Straight Talk to Teachers* for nothing. These ideas *would* succeed, if we implemented them. But here's the problem: There aren't enough educators like you *wanting* enough to see that these programs actually get off the ground.

We can do anything in education if enormous numbers of people buy into it. And that's usually the problem: the buy-in. People nod cordially and smile politely when we mention these ideas, but taking the next step—the action step—is essential. That's where we have fallen short. So as you consider the following methods for stress reduction, remember how unfair it is for you to tell yourself, "Come on! We'll *never* do that." Or, "Nobody would ever consider that at *my* school." Or, "Nice idea, but where are we going to get the money for that?" If we want better teachers, better classrooms, and better students we must find a way to make it happen!

WAYS ADMINISTRATORS CAN EASE TEACHER STRESS

1. Offer massage therapy on campus.

You now turn to anyone around you who is within shouting distance, and yell, "Hey! Get a load of what this weirdo writer has to say about helping teachers! He wants to reduce stress at schools—and the first thing he suggests is *massage therapy!* What a dork!"

Well, *someone* needed to say the truth about massage therapy.

Keep in mind, this therapy doesn't have to be elaborate. Maybe once or twice a month, a masseuse or masseur would set up shop in the faculty lounge and provide fifteen-minute massages before and after school—as well as during teachers' prep periods and lunch. Once massage has become a regular routine at your school, people who had previously despised the idea will be among the next to hop up on one of those tables, or—at their most passive—they'll simply avert their eyes. The massage, of course, would be paid for by the school district.

District officials should be convinced that it's much cheaper for them in the long run to keep their employees stress free. How much does it cost to pay a substitute teacher for one day of teaching? Around two hundred dollars![10] Add up the number of available massage days, figure out the costs, and notice that this method of stress relief is more than just slightly cost-effective; it saves money—big time! By the way, here's another nice auxiliary benefit: Providing massage therapy shows employees their bosses care about them for more than only their professional productivity.

2. Allow for more breaks and minutes between class sessions, (perhaps) extending the length of the school day.

If the school day lasts longer, teachers would have time to take breaks. Even though states mandate the number of actual minutes that must be taught during a regular day, they say nothing about how *consecutive* those minutes must be. With regular times to chill, teachers would feel much less stressed.

3. Have designated rest areas.

No, not like the kind with the smelly outhouses you find on the highways; but schools should provide quiet, darkened rooms where teachers can take their shoes off and lie down for a few moments during their workday.

Some studies have indicated that a simple "resting of the eyes" for twenty minutes sparks the human ignition system.[11] Imagine a soft cot, your head back, your eyes gently closed, and soft, soothing music, as you inhale long and deep and hard for a few moments—especially welcome after a particularly rigorous class or a conference with a couple of parents in need of an exorcism. If shortsighted administrators start barking about preferential treatment for teachers, remind them—nicely, of course—that *they* don't have to go nose-to-nose with the kids all day in classrooms full of human gas, pungent perfume, and rancid body odor.

True, the same unflattering characteristics may pertain to some of the parents who visit your administrators, but parents eventually *leave*; their children *stay!*

4. Establish an exercise area.

The school supplies free weights, modern machines, plenty of bottled water, and a stinky aroma (for authenticity). My daughter's elementary school has already built such a facility for its teachers. The kids are not allowed to step foot within ten yards of this room; it's for adults only.[12] And no television sets exist here. This room is for exercising only, not catching up on the morning news events—recounting how a balding, forty-year-old virgin who lives with his mother took a sawed-off shotgun into a local pet-supply office and blew away six people, two dogs, and a hamster. Hearing about this sort of thing while you're working out in a gym is not very soothing, if you ask me (but then, maybe the stress levels you're attaining in your classroom are actually higher than those of a bullet-peppered pet-supply store).

Again: the workout area is only for *exercise* and only for *staff*.

5. Permit access to a swimming pool.

No, I haven't flipped my lid. Not completely. Not yet.

Almost every high school in America is equipped with a swimming pool or has access to one, usually for student swimming competitions. Why, then, is there an unwritten rule like this one: *This swimming pool is for students only. Teachers who have health needs that may be met by using this pool need to find their own damn swimming pool!*

Water play is among the healthiest exercises imaginable; everyone already knows this. To be armed with this information and still refuse adult employees permission to partake of facilities that may extend their life spans is nothing short of criminal. And, yes, schedules may be worked out so students aren't using the pool at the same time teachers have the right of entry. Just take a look: Most of the day, the pool sits dormant; usually no one uses it in the evenings. What a pleasurable reason to remain after school or to return to school on the weekends! And bring your swimsuits for those moments of your workday you had set aside to fight for the Scantron machine. Take a dip (not another teacher) by plunging into the swimming pool instead!

6. Build or buy a hot tub.

You already have the swimming pool, but the therapeutic benefits of a hot tub or Jacuzzi are off the charts! Besides just feeling all around good, you may have some incredible epiphanies about life; amazing thoughts and ideas fly into our heads when we're relaxing in a bask of hot water, swirling bubbles and steam all around us, our back plastered against a forceful spray of stress-reduction liquid.

I've heard that Einstein figured out the formula for the atomic bomb while resting in a Jacuzzi. (Well, maybe I heard wrong.) But no matter: Hot tubs have a therapeutic effect on muscle aches, hideous forms of arthritis, gout, and back problems that not even chiropractors can cure.[13] In fact, after an extended period of resting in the hot tub in my gym, I found that I was once again able to bend over, lift a foot, and bite my toenails—something I hadn't been able to accomplish since I was eight years old and had fallen from the top of my next-door neighbor's tree house.

Frankly, if I weren't feeling particularly chipper in the morning, rather than lying in bed with an aching back from a too-soft mattress and aging box springs, I would somehow stumble to the school, falter through a class or two, and then waddle to the hot tub that has been provided for adult staff members at my school. Just a few moments of soothing relaxation—the heat, the bubbles, the pulsating, pounding waters—a quick shower, and I'm ready to take on the rest of the day! At the very least, I'm set to meet with, and explain to, Mrs. Barkus why her son is the primary reason I had to use a Jacuzzi in the first place.

7. Plan faculty functions.

On the surface this may seem as though it would actually *increase* anxiety among teachers, but getting to know other people in surroundings apart from their daily grind should benefit everyone.

You don't have to associate—even mingle—with people you don't like; and it's during get-togethers like these that teachers and administrators let down their hair and reveal parts of themselves that others on campus have never seen before. And assuming you've already gotten a glimpse of each other in the school's swimming pool, you're now better prepared for anything else that might add unnecessary stress to your life. I mean, next to seeing a fellow teacher in a bathing suit, any other shocking revelation pales in comparison! Naturally, it's not a good thing if your experiences turn tawdry or freakish, but parties, dinners, outings to ball games, etc., tend to lessen the tension later when those same people again come into contact with each other at school. Socialization can be a very good idea, indeed.[14]

8. Prepare entertaining faculty meetings.

Most staff meetings *are* somewhat entertaining, but usually not in a good way. The art teacher, chewing out the administrator in charge of building facilities in language dotted with sailors' obscenities, is not exactly the sort of entertainment that relieves stress. Mr. Pringle, our head custodian, publicly begging teachers not to allow students to trash their classrooms doesn't portend well for his future at a local comedy club. But there are men and women who have a niche for making others laugh, or for discussing vital school issues in ways usually not associated with the mundane, humdrum limitations of a faculty meeting.

Sometimes these gifted people are found within the personnel of the school; other times they are professionals who must be *paid* to perform. Running the school with a sense of humor is a rare skill not all possess; however, when people laugh, their stress levels dissipate, and they tend to do the one thing that will cause them to relax and enjoy their jobs more: They stop taking themselves so seriously.

9. Get rid of bells.

You would still stay on a schedule.
Students and teachers would be expected to arrive on time to class; consequences for being late would still exist. But the best thing about offing the bells: Annoying, juvenile, repetitious ringing or screeching or clanging would no longer be grudgingly anticipated seven thousand times a day. With the abandonment of this subconscious expectation comes relaxation of mind and evenness of emotion. Ask any teacher on a normal (huh?) high school campus that broadcasts the sounds of antiquated bells, sirens, or whistles, and she'll tell you how much she despises those sounds. A bell-less schedule would require a stringent, consistent enforcement of a strong tardy policy. And that's part of the point of relieving your school of its bells.

When administrative directives are applied evenhandedly and with consistency, teachers become less anxious; they know what to expect. Knowing what to expect—few unpleasant surprises—lowers stress.[15] Students take responsibility for looking at their watches or the digital clocks on their cell phones, forcing themselves to arrive on time at their destinations.

It's called *the way we do it in the real world.*

Imagine a school with no irritating, obnoxious, rattling bells.

Soothes the soul, doesn't it?

10. Demand lower class sizes.

And make sure you get them (an act that can be unduly stressful in itself), but eventually lower class sizes will pay off in the "being anxious all the time" department. The research on the impact of class sizes in student learning has not been definitive. Depending on the course, smaller class sizes can be hugely important to student outcomes; but in certain classes—those maintaining an effective teacher-centered, lecture format—the results are negligible.

One point, however, can be made with utter certainty: The fewer children that sit in your classroom at once during the run of a day, the less stress you will battle.[16] You'll come to know each child more intimately—eliminating most acute discipline problems—and field fewer diverting, distracting, annoying, and exhausting questions from your students. You'll have fewer papers to grade and record, and a smaller number of parents to deal with; you'll spend less of your own money on copying, supplies, and other supplementary materials.

Think of a big room full of noisy, chattering children—all nagging you for your attention—and contrast that image with one of a classroom housing a mere fraction of those children. These kids are much calmer, less verbose, and not nearly as demanding of your time and attention as those children in a classroom containing at least ten *more* students; you'll have the feeling of sipping a cocktail, while lying on the sands of Waikiki, the sun warming your gorgeous, tanned body.

That's the difference in stress levels.

Nice to imagine—no?

We expect our schools to provide safe, protective, pacifying environments for our children. But we also should make sure the same principles apply to the welfare of our teachers and other adults who work at our schools. When adults feel better and tend to their own health concerns, our kids wind up in a more pleasing setting. If adults are flying off the walls with anxieties worthy of a psychology book, students won't be too far behind in the nutcase department. And adults *do* need a place of safety, a sanctuary, a refuge, and shelter. Like children, they shouldn't be wrestling continuously with their most harrowing challenges, while trying valiantly to intervene in the troubled lives of children, hoping to assuage the effects of their students' problems, as well as their own—at the very same time.

But why not *home*? Shouldn't home be a place of safety—the sanctuary, the refuge, the shelter?

David's homelife didn't bring to mind words like "peaceful," "safe," or "protective."

Not exactly.

David's wife showed little understanding of what David had to contend with as a teacher, and her expectations of David as a father sometimes did not seem fair. She handled her dealings with her husband with less grace and dignity than one should expect from a loving spouse. David's homelife had been more stressful than his career life, and he actually *preferred* working at school to coming home to his family. As much as he adored his son—and "adored" is an accurate word to describe David's love for Jack—his wife facilitated in making their father-son relationship unbearable at times.

David's situation at home may sound awful, but there are countless other teachers who must contend with even worse: illnesses and deaths in the family, atrocious events revolving around their own children, personal mental and physical afflictions, and life's everyday disappointments we all face. Mired in a quagmire of distress and discontent, these teachers find no outlet or sanctuary—professional or personal—to help them get their lives in order.

David spent the next two years dealing with conflicts and challenges at school and more harangues at home from his less-than-tactful, uh, wife. So one afternoon in June of 1992, David left work and drove himself straight to a hospital emergency room; he had suffered a major heart attack.

After his recovery David stayed married (because of his commitment to his son) to his shrew of a wife, but he soon resigned from his teaching position. In order to pay the bills, both he and his wife were now forced to find jobs. (David landed employment with the U.S. Postal Service.) Today David argues eloquently in favor of most stress reduction on the job ideas presented in this book, and waxes on and on about how much they would have helped him, had he only been educated enough to see these suggestions through to their implementation.[17]

Yes, home is still a dandy place to begin a new life of relaxation and recovery.

Not everybody agrees a hot tub should be installed in the workplace.

NOTES

1. *American Institute of Stress*, "Job Stress," September 10, 2001, at stress.org/job.htm.

2. *Massage Magazine*, "Forbes Features Massage," February 28, 2006, 1.

3. Ann D. Clark, "The New Frontier of Wellness," *ACI: The Specialty Benefits Corporation*, April 2, 2008, at annclarkassociates.com/news_details.php?nidi.78.

4. *Corporate Wellness Training*, "Corporate Self-Defense Training," April 30, 2008, at company-wellness-program.com.

5. Darcia Harris Brown, "States Target School Vending Machines," *Education Week* 23, 5 (October 1, 2003):14–15.

6. Michael Pollar, "On the Table," *New York Times*, June 4, 2006, Opinion section, 1.

7. Cynthia Kopkowski, "The End of the Line" *NEA Today* (February 2007): 6.

8. C. Kyriacou, "Teacher Stress and Burnout: An International Review," *Education Research* 29, 2(1987): 146–152.

9. M. Kiui, "Surviving the Classroom, *The Teacher*, April and August 1998.

10. *Nearly* two hundred dollars, although not quite; from the pay scale of the Norwalk-La Mirada Unified School District, in Southern California.

11. *Zen to Fitness*, "The Simple, No-Nonsense Guide to Staying Fit While Living Life," October 6, 2008, several writers compilation, www.zenoffitmess.com/a-no-nonsense-guide-to-napping.

12. American companies are paying for gym memberships; some are providing work location exercise areas. These local workout spots are, seemingly, cheaper than membership dues and, in the long run, would save the taxpayers large amounts of money.

13. Julie Ann Amos, "The History and Health Benefits of Hot Tubs," *Ezine Articles*, 2005, at ezinearticles.com/?The-History-And-Health-Benefits-of-Hot-Tubs&id=108347, (summary of article).

14. Michael F. DiPaola and Wayne K. Hoy, *Improving Schools: Studies in Leadership and Culture.* (Charlotte, NC: Information Age Publishing, 2008) 33–44.

15. Jennifer Rothman, "A Letter from the Editor," *Insights* 10, 4 (Summer 2004): 2.

16. Christopher J. McCarthy, Richard G. Lambert, Megan O'Donnell, and Lauren T. Melendres. "The Relation of Elementary School Teachers' Experience, Stress, and Coping Resources to Burnout Symptoms," *The Elementary School Journal* 109, 3 (2009): 282.

17. David knows that the (good and bad) choices we make in our personal lives have a lot to do with the stresses we bring upon ourselves. His advice for getting married is parroted from the *Dr. Laura Radio Program*: "Choose well; treat kindly."

12

+

Nourish Thyself:
Keep Stuffing Your Face

Of all the books you have read (or not) about teaching, and of all the chapters you have plowed through with gusto (or skimmed with not so much gusto), this may be the strangest book chapter of all. The irony, however, is that of all the counsel in this book regarding the mental state of America's teachers, these recommendations may be the key—the basis—for reaching the goal of having good cerebral health and a hearty attitude about your teaching career. Arguably, the most bizarre chapter ever printed in a teacher improvement book (though the previous chapter gives it a run for its money), these pages should help you if you take them to heart.

We have known for decades the critical importance of getting enough sleep, eating well, and doing the proper kinds of exercises in the right amounts. Teachers have emphasized these healthy habits to their students, and parents have long established health and wellness ground rules with their children.

But teachers are people, too.

Or so they say.

Would these common sense ideas not apply to teachers, too?

I find it amazing—sometimes appalling—we teachers are constantly preaching behaviors we know will be helpful to others, but we ignore any application of these ideas to ourselves. What's good for the goose should be good enough for the goose's teacher. If eating properly—and often—brings us more energy, vitality, enthusiasm, and lucidity—why would we not want it for us, too?

So, yeah, this is a strange chapter, one in which we examine facets of science and medicine that have not been liberally advertised—what's nutritional—for our nation's schoolteachers.

And the bottom line: If these prove to be true, if the evidence does the talking, and you do the walking, your classroom will be rich in harmony, glow with vitality, and buzz with focus. As a teacher, you need your brain (among other things) to work optimally; food makes that more possible.

Mary Abbott Hess, RD, MS, suggested this: "[Eat right and eat often]. The key here is to eat as often as you can. And when you have three bites, make those bites something that really counts." Automobiles won't run on empty—and neither will teachers. Our brains require proper nourishment to keep us running optimally.[1]

Radical dieting, dieting fads, and dieting fanaticism may do a lot more harm than good. When a teacher's brain is hungry (not to mention the rest of her body), deprivation of certain kinds of food—in fact food, in general—is definitely not beneficial. Hess gives an example: "If you are on a low carbohydrate diet [the cool thing lately: "Carbs are the devil!"], your body has to break down protein to provide even the minimal carbohydrates necessary for your brain to function."[2]

Which means, those donuts don't look so bad for you now, do they? Okay, maybe *one* donut and a glass of milk—you won't die, and parts of you that had heretofore been so unhappy will be smiling like a toddler at the circus.

Nutrition analyst David Allen put it succinctly: "Our brains work best on the prehistoric diet that shaped their evolution . . . For generations, hunters and gatherers survived on wild game [that's *meat*, baby!], wild greens, fruits, berries, and roots."[3]

And if you're not eating much, you're probably not ingesting all these essential foods. It's very simple; unless you're one of those who has already deprived her brain of enough food, you are quite capable of figuring this out:

Energy.

Vigor.

Enthusiasm.

They gotta get fueled by *something!*

Allen goes further; he says, "The good news is that [even dark] chocolate can be good for you. . . . " It's all part of eating smart. "It appears that eating smart is not only good for the general health, but *can improve thinking, creativity, learning ability, and memory, while staving off long term mental deterioration* [italics added]."[4]

With the verdict in, the veracity of this wisdom should clobber us like a brick falling from a third story of a building during an earthquake (a little California humor there). Indeed, an examination of how to put into practice these nourishing manners is in order.

But first, I can't help but share with you—and I do mean this; I'm hopelessly compelled to stray for a moment to a frustrating story—a strange bit of irony when examining how the *real* world of public education, vis-à-vis nutrition, sometimes pans out.

My own school district has always been a paradigm of contradictions and paradoxes, making it extraordinarily difficult to figure out some of their policies regarding—*anything*. (Don't worry, if you're teaching now, your own school district probably offers up plenty of fodder ripe and ready for *your* future book about silly policies in education.)

Last June all employees of my district received a memo ordering them to remove all personal electrical equipment, such as refrigerators and microwaves, from their "work areas." Any appliances left in their classrooms on the last day of school would be confiscated (presumably, the parts removed and then sold to L.A. gang leaders). The district's justification? Going "green" (the exact certainty of what this means has always eluded me), but mostly, saving dollars on energy costs. After the new policy had been announced at a faculty meeting, our teachers rocked with some rather pointed and exasperated comments:

- "Fine. Now, I won't tutor anymore during lunch or after school. If I can't get a cold drink."
- "That takes care of meetings with students at lunch in my classroom!"
- "And they want to bolster achievement scores? Once again, the bosses downtown prove the true meaning of the saying, 'penny wise and pound foolish.'"
- "How stupid can they be? There are computers left on overnight in almost every classroom; air-conditioning stays on during weekends. Just who's not looking out to cut down on energy use?"
- "They [the school district's administrators] just spent—I don't know how many—thousands of dollars on that idiotic literacy program—that hasn't done anything to help anybody! And now they're telling me I can't microwave my ham sandwich in the classroom because of the cost? They sure know how to boost morale around here, don't they!"

OK, I had to get that out of my system. I so strongly believe in valuing all aspects of the teacher—not the least of which means embracing him as a whole human being—exposing those who would thwart the teacher's ability to nourish himself, exude enthusiasm, and remain healthy has become a major priority for me.

So here are those tips on teacher nourishment.
Brace yourself:

1. Eat plenty.

In the morning—and I mean *the first thing in the morning*—it's critical
that you begin your day by digesting *something*. Sometimes I like to stop
at Denny's for a full-course breakfast, but I'm not necessarily recom-
mending the likes of pancakes, eggs, and bacon every day at dawn; I'm
talking about just a glass of juice, a piece of toast—even a handful of
packaged chips. To those "everything-you-eat-will-kill-you-except-for-
organic-green-gunk" finger-waggers who have trouble sleeping at night
with the mere thought of their sister eating a bag of Fritos—I have news
for you: We reject your dogma; your incessant nagging has gotten old.
This is about the importance of eating *something*.

Of course, it's preferable to include all the food groups in a well-
balanced breakfast! Yes! Eating well, limiting your calories, lowering your
salt intake, and providing yourself everything you need for the absolutely
perfect diet would be nutritional nirvana. But it doesn't have to be either
the perfect mix—or nothing.[5] When all or nothing are the only choices, we
usually wind up with—nothing.

2. Invest in a small refrigerator and a cheap microwave.

Assuming your school district hasn't become a parody of itself when it
comes to common sense, they probably will allow you to stock up on
cool drinks, fruit, and other snacks. Keep the refrigerator full of liquid
nourishments; occasionally bring food you'll need to keep cold for one
day—such as sandwiches or frozen entrees. They will preserve well in the
refrigerator until lunchtime.

3. Store in your desk drawer a few nutritional breakfast bars.

My favorite is Slim-Fast Dutch Chocolate; they contain all the necessary
vitamins and nutrients for a full meal, *and* they taste delicious.[6] Have one
every morning as soon as you settle into your classroom. The back of the
box informs you these little delights compensate for a whole meal, but
don't count on that; use them only *after* you have already eaten something
else for breakfast.

4. Take a daily multivitamin.

Old geezers should dump down the vitamin pill that promises aging people will get what they need, such as extra magnesium.[7] There's no reason

to go with anything fancy here—just a capsule containing the minimum vitamins and minerals we should be ingesting daily.

Frankly—only my opinion, so you should definitely consult your doctor—I'm not a big believer in swallowing an extraordinary number of vitamin pills; most likely, it's overkill. A minimum dosage of vitamins and minerals is all we require; our immune systems should be preserved, and our energy levels enhanced by a single daily multivitamin tablet. Conflicting evidence about multivitamins hastening prostate cancer has caused some scares, but nothing provable is on the horizon.[8] Some companies offer all the benefits of a multivitamin in their natural concoctions, refuting the worries about free radicals and tumors.[9] Again, talk to your doctor if you're dubious. But you probably should be swallowing a daily vitamin supplement.

5. Eat a little bit every hour or two.

For high school teachers, this means between each of their classes; for middle school instructors, it means sneaking that occasional apple, Granola Bar, or cookie when no one is looking. In my ever-so-humble-never-like-to-be-expressed opinion, it's permissible for teachers to eat in front of their students. While teachers shouldn't pull out a roast beef sandwich and begin munching away in the middle of their lecture or during a student presentation, your eating a piece of fruit or a even Hostess Ding-Dong shouldn't set off an alarm warning officials of possible child abuse.

6. Make lunchtime something special.

If you're bringing lunch, have one you will relish eating—even fantasize about throughout the morning. When I start to ramble during classes—which happens often—it's almost always because I've been distracted by thoughts of food:

"What's wrong, Mr.G.? You look lost all of a sudden."

"Oh, I'm just thinking of potato soup from Black Angus."

"No way!"

"Yes, that's the truth; if you've ever eaten their potato soup, you can relate to what I just said: hot, creamy, chucked with bacon bits, and the perfect mixture of herbs and spices. . . . "

For me, lunch can be the largest meal of the day; this was certainly true during the time I had become deeply involved with students in hordes of extra after-school activities. Because of the busyness of my life, dinner was a much-maligned meal around my house. But even without all that bonus teaching I'd been doing, a hearty lunch made afternoon classes easier to plod through.

7. Have several bottles of water on hand.

And you may sip from them as you teach! *And* you may do it right in front of your students without any reservations, qualms, or guilt! Water is an item students may always have on hand at school, even in the strictest of places about eating and drinking in the classrooms. So don't worry about offending the kids; their refusal to bring drinking water to class is at their own peril. But no matter what your students do, *you* need to be drinking water.

8. Drink other fluids, too.

Water is a necessity; Gatorade, for example, tastes better. Sometimes we just need to drink liquids that taste good; they give us a lift. They encourage us to drink *more* fluids. They make us happy. And "A happy teacher . . ." It doesn't hurt to change it up a little.

For the first eight items, I have focused primarily on what you should be eating and drinking while working. But for these next two suggestions—and they're biggies—I offer some teacher-related nutritional/ nourishment advice of a more generic nature. Just remember, you are teachers (or eventually you will be teachers), and teachers can be weird ducks about a number of things. Sometimes in the nutritional realm, we are plain, well, weirder than a lot of other people—and much of the traditional thinking doesn't apply to us. Teacher nutrition may be jaded by expectations and demands way beyond the scope of human normalcy: our unique levels of stress related to children; our propensity for nonstop cerebral activity; our constant performing in the limelight; our propensity toward verbosity; our dissipated time at home—the consuming nature of grading papers, lesson planning, and reading supplementary materials for our courses.

9. Eat meat.

I'm citing experts here, but common sense is my most powerful argument.

Just think of the living, in-your-face visible testimonials of bodybuilders and other especially muscular athletes throughout the ages—and how enthusiastically they have endorsed the eating of chicken and red meat products.

And it's no wonder; in addition to the aesthetic benefits, researchers have found those who have adopted a meat-free diet are six times more likely to develop brain shrinkage than those who regularly gobble turkey, chicken, hamburger, or liver.[10]

Perhaps, it is brain shrinkage that prevents these people from under-standing the truth about meat products. But it gets even better. Meat is one of the most efficient ways of getting the protein we need into our diet. Unlike vegetarian foods, meat contains all the essential amino acids that our bodies (and brains) require for optimum performance. Also, red meat contains high amounts of iron, a real concern for those immersed in a vegetarian lifestyle.[11] Those celery sticks you've been warned to munch on, in lieu of enjoying some beef jerky, may be crunchy and delicious, but full of iron, they are not.

Meat should not be served at every meal; meat is not the cure-all for your aches, pains, anti-teen venom, and other ills. But meat, at least a few times a week, makes you stronger, preserves your bones, gives you muscle tone (very important for frightening kids who are intimidated by muscles), and in the long run, you'll be healthier.[12] Don't break off a sparerib and gnaw on it during class, but eating those beef ribs over the course of, oh, a month or so adds to your overall health, fitness, and energy levels. If you don't believe me, visually examine any (legitimate) vegetarian or vegan you know; she probably looks like she escaped from one of those underground dungeons from *Attack of the Mole People*.[13]

You shouldn't do comparisons with people who began eating beef (and trimmed absolutely no fat away) around 1960 and haven't come up for air since. But meat is a vital supplement to the perfect teacher diet, one that, unfortunately, too many do-gooders and anti-protein zealots have consciously—to their own detriment—ignored.

10. Regulate—don't eliminate—adequate amounts of caffeine intake.

Are you now gasping? Have you fallen off your chair, yet? Have you asked the professor of your education course to recall this book from your college bookstore and library?

Did that author really *encourage* teachers to digest a drug that has been known to cause—whatever—even bite-sized earlobes to grow under the rear bones of our jawlines?

To start with, here's the lowdown on caffeine: It gets a bad rap. And come on! Having almost *anything* in excess is bad for us, including power, money, fame, good looks, and dark chocolate. OK, maybe not dark chocolate—but to contend that caffeine is awful in small doses may cast aspersions on all other arguments a person makes about, well, *anything*. Also, the caffeine fear-monger is dead wrong. That's the worst part. Half-truths, innuendos, and study-regulated verdicts manipulated to fit al-ready established agendas are not science, and they offer little to augment the credibility of academia, especially in the research sciences.

The so-called experts not only disagree about the drawbacks of caffeine, they don't clearly delineate any of the particulars—doses, amounts,
weights—at which caffeine does bodily harm (and they are probably the
same people who warned us in the 1980s about the catastrophic effects of
buttered popcorn).

Consider what some nutritionists say about caffeine.

The Asian Food Information Center (of all organizations!) reported,

> "Over the last hundred years, cola drinks, ready-to-drink tea and coffee bev-
> erages and a new crop of 'energy drinks' have steadily gained in popularity.
> All these beverages have a common ingredient—caffeine. Although prod-
> ucts containing caffeine have been enjoyed all over the world for centuries,
> there are still many misperceptions about this common food component."[14]

Recent research has found some surprising health benefits associated
with caffeine consumption. Many caffeine-containing beverages, most
notably tea, and more recently coffee, have been found to contain antioxidants. Antioxidants may have health benefits in terms of heart health
and cancer prevention. Pretty cool, huh? Besides keeping us more alert
(while we're not bouncing off the whiteboards), caffeine helps our brains
to work better.[15]

Whereas the scientific community is conflicted about the side effects
and/or harms of caffeine, little (or no) disagreement exists about the benefits of caffeine: The main one, of course, is its ability to abruptly ignite
an energy flow—an awakening agent only found in prescribed pharma-
ceutical medicines (many of which we know have serious side effects and
harmful ingredients). Jean Tang wrote in the Woman's Health section of
Energy Fiend, "Researchers have been analyzing caffeine for years and have
not found substantial proof that it is bad for us. In fact, because it improves
alertness and function, small amounts can actually be good for us."[16]

My personal source for this energy stimulant is cola drinks; many
of you already receive adequate amounts of caffeine in your coffee. I
drink my cola in the morning and enjoy a Coke or Pepsi a couple more
times later in the day; by no stretch of the imagination am I overdoing it.
Clearly, one huge effect—at least, for me is—irrefutable: Caffeine helps
me to work with a spunk and energy flow I would not otherwise possess.
Again, *I am advocating caffeine only in moderate amounts—and only in your
favorite drink.* Here caffeine is already present and deemed safe in minor
quantities.[17]

You should now be thoroughly convinced of the importance of staying nourished and feeling physically strong and alert throughout your
teaching day. Still, we may be at variances as to the exact manner for our
achieving these goals, since each of us is different and possesses varying
requirements for meeting our nutritional quotas. And we are not alike

when it comes to food allergies, food tastes, and food digestion. What's right for you may not be right for me—and vice versa. See a physician to find out if these recommendations apply specifically to you and your own nutritional necessities.

Sometimes when I examine the eating habits of other people, I can't believe that we are from the same planet, let alone the same species; we are so different in those habits. Yet, none of these disparities or controversies around the topic of food consumption should detract from the overall theme of this text: *Eat well—and regularly—during your workday.*

Five teachers' comments, elaborating on the quintessence of nourishment for teachers, bring my thoughts about nutrition for teachers to a conclusion. These folks are all considered by their peers and site administrators to be better-than-average teachers; they are all medium weight to underweight—and adored by their students, who believe these teachers exude pep, energy, vim and vigor. (I never understood what vim has to do with vigor. But evidently these teachers are well stocked with both.)

- "I bring snacks from home. I put lots of celery, carrots, and sliced apples in a couple of Ziplocks and munch on them throughout the day. I usually finish before lunch, but I buy a good tray lunch in the cafeteria. They make a pretty good spread for our teachers."
- "I make three sandwiches: the same thing each and every day. I like peanut butter and strawberry jelly on wheat; bologna with mustard on a French roll; and my last sandwich of the teaching day—which I eat at lunch—is sliced turkey on white bread with a little mayonnaise, lettuce, and tomatoes."
- "I'm bad; I know it. But I like sweets, mainly candy—mainly dark chocolate. I mean, if I have to eat candy, which I guess I must, it may as well be dark chocolate. Isn't that supposed to be good for your heart and blood flow and the like? It's my favorite energy snack."
- "I drink bottled water all day, and occasionally I bring a couple of apples or other kinds of fruit. The main thing that works for me is a great breakfast in the morning. Can I say this? I stop at McDonald's every morning—almost every morning—for a sausage-and-eggs breakfast. It's fast, and it's good. I especially like their pancakes."
- "Popcorn. My wife tells me I'm going to turn into popcorn, the way I eat so much of it all the time. Unfortunately, I do eat way too much microwave popcorn at school; but with a microwave, it's easy to fix it there, obviously. It does keep me going, though. Isn't that what you asked about?"

Fortunately, that last teacher doesn't work in my school district; if he did, his microwave would have been confiscated by now, and he wouldn't be as likely to eat popcorn for his energy stimulator. The food police on campus would have tied him to his desk and inflicted a gruesome torture procedure, forcing him to watch his microwave be confiscated and then tossed into a large metal trashcan.

Eat right; eat often.

Stay healthy.

Nutrition spurs a dynamic teacher to even greater passion, and her classroom sings the benefits of her nourishing wisdom.

NOTES

1. Mary Albert Hess, "Eat Right for Two," *WebMD: Live Events, Transcript*, November 28, 2008, at medicinenet.com/script/main/art.asp?articlekey=54270.

2. Ibid.

3. David Allen, "How Eating Right Can Save Your Brain," *Buzzle* (Editorials), October 17, 2005, 2.

4. Ibid.

5. Lucy Danziger, "Pizza for Breakfast, Yes!" March 12, 2008, at health.yahoo .com/experts/healthieryou/1/pizza-for-breakfast-yes.

6. Slim-Fast also offers an instant nutritional breakfast of various flavors in the form of a milk shake.

7. Kathleen Fairfield and Robert H. Fletcher, "Vitamins For Chronic Disease Prevention in Adults," *The Journal of the American Medical Association* 287 (June 19, 2002): 3127–3129.

8. Sharon Lynn, "The Benefits of Taking Multivitamins," *AC/Associated Content*, August 13, 2008, at associatedcontent.com/article/927209.

9. Melaleuca: The Wellness Company brags about its natural formula that allegedly provides all the necessary daily ingredients, without the purported (so-called) risks of commercial one-a-day vitamin tablets.

10. Scott Reeves, "Eating Red Meat Beefs up the Brain," *Minyanville*, September 15, 2008, www.minyanville.com/articles/index.php?e=18965.

11. John Hawks, "Health Benefits of Eating Meat," November 7, 2008, at johnhawks.net:84/node/689.

12. Ibid (summary of article) 1–4.

13. *Attack of the Mole People* (Universal, 1956); Starring Hugh Beaumont, of *Leave it to Beaver* fame, still one of my most memorable films for showing really emaciated, pallid-looking people. They lived miles under the earth and probably had no meat to eat.

14. *Asian Food Information Center*, "Myths and Facts About Caffeine," January 1, 2000, at afic.org/2008/hydration.php?switchto=1&news_id=132.

15. Ibid.

16. Jean Tang, "Caffeine, More Good than Harm," *Energy Fiend*, July 14, 2006, at energyfiend.com/2006/07/caffeine-more-good-than-harm.

17. Don't spaz out, folks: Remember, *limited* quantities—*moderation* is the key.

13

Connect with Comrades-in-Arms

Insane.
Nuts.
Crazy.
Ludicrous.
Moronic.

These were the first words I thought of using in this chapter; I didn't even consult a thesaurus.

I used the word "insane" in the title of this work because lots of people are going to figure I'm plainly crazy for serving up these weird tips for better teaching. And I suppose when you look back at some of my advocacies in the last chapter or two (hot tubs? caffeine?), the word "insane" may have woven its way into a more acceptable framework in your thinking. But here I'm using that word—along with its various synonyms—in a pejorative context; and frankly, there are a few other words I would be delighted to write here instead . . . but won't, for reasons that should seem obvious.

Teachers often become frustrated with their jobs. It doesn't have to be this way, but a diversity of human components interacting, blending, opposing, contradicting, and competing is incredibly complex. Remembering that frustrations sometimes loom big in a teacher's life, this is a perfect time to reflect on the soul of the very first chapter: We should all have gratitude that we are teachers; there are so many powerful reasons to consider ourselves so fortunate. But even this optimistic approach can't obliterate the reality of divergent forces in teachers' lives—forces complicating their ability to buy fully into a philosophy of gratitude and appreciation.

In teaching, conflicts materialize, moments arrive, and memos appear, sometimes tempting us to seriously consider doing something totally rash and hopelessly impulsive, such as writing an evil anonymous note to our principal, sending off a disgruntled letter about our school to a Dear Abby column, or stuffing up the faculty toilets with paper towels.

And those moments perpetuate themselves; they never seem to stop.

So let's go back to those adjectives: "insane," "nuts," "crazy," "ludicrous," "moronic."

Where have these (especially selected) words been directed?

Consider just one scenario: Arriving at school on Monday morning, you find the usual clutter of papers in your mail cubicle in the faculty room. Pulling out a stack of those papers, you notice a note on the very top—which means it had to have been one of the most recent items slipped into your box—pleading with you for your immediate attention. The paper reads, "Attention! Assembly by grade levels in the gym today!" You wince; then you try to remember when you had previously been warned about the existence of a grade level assembly on the school calendar. It means that all your classes will receive today's prepared lesson on the Battle of Gettysburg—except for *one*: the class attending the grade level assembly during fourth period.

Now void of a chance to plead your case prior to the event's arrangement, but as a conscientious teacher and a human being of integrity, what should you do?

Here are your options:

You could . . . walk into the office of the administrator responsible for the last minute memo and tell him something like, "You unthinking, callous icon of stupidity! How dare you upset my teaching schedule this week—and on a moment's notice no less! What a moron!"

Or you could . . . Slip the culpable administrator a memo of your own, having written a simple two-word salutation. (I'll let you figure out what those two words are.)

You could even . . . Rant and rave in the corridors. Grab a random staff member, hold a knife blade to his windpipe, and threaten to kill him and set fire to the school, if the principal doesn't call off the grade level assembly.

Or you could just . . . Phone in an anonymous bomb scare.

You might conclude that you probably should . . . Boost your students up to parity; you're a professional, and professionals should have more flexibility than you're now showing. Just remember to bring the annoying scheduling conflict to the attention of your principal and suggest methods for disseminating the information next time in a style more compatible with an instruction-friendly atmosphere; perhaps, you can write up a more constructive, less-intrusive time schedule for having the assembly.

Which of these choices seems to be the most consistent with your transformation into a happy educator—for managing your stress levels, those furious waves of agitation that are magnified by other factors beyond your control?

Now may be a good time for you to return to chapter 11 and briefly review those methods for quelling your stresses, anxieties, and tensions. Unfortunately, the future may hold even more reasons for you to want to explode from the inside out and question yourself as to why on earth you even *dreamed* of becoming a stable, helpful, committed member of the teaching profession!

Consider these pain-in-the-neck (literally), stressful (a gross understatement) occurrences on school campuses. In case you're wondering, yup; they're real:

- A young teacher at your school shoots himself in the head after a tryst with one of his fourteen-year-old students at an underage drinking party.
- The school board demands the resignations of twelve teachers at your school, threatening to block any referrals or letters of recommendation for their next employment unless those teachers comply immediately.
- A third grade teacher is given a class mixture of three grade levels (second, third, and fourth grades), bringing the total number of her students to forty-two in a single classroom.
- An angry father of a fifteen-year-old girl accuses her teacher (a friend and colleague of yours) of inappropriately touching his daughter in front of the class, even though the teacher did not lay a finger on her, and every student in that class would be able to vouch for his innocence—but the father wants to meet with your friend privately in his classroom.
- Your district has just aligned the eleventh grade curriculum in your English class with that of the other four high schools in your district, making it impossible for you to teach what you have always taught—and love the most.
- Your district has just banned soda and other junk foods for *teachers*, thereby ordering the only vending machine (the one in the faculty lounge) removed from your campus.

- Your principal has just sent out a directive, mandating a mixture of specifically named teaching styles that must be utilized by all teachers, even though only one of those styles suits your own approach and personality.
- Your union's collective bargaining team has capitulated to a substantial pay cut, and the new contract has expelled your preferred health insurance provider.
- A student has directed some choice swear words in your direction, and your discipline vice principal has not taken—even after three days—any action on the written report you filed.
- Sixteen minutes have been added to the length of the school day.
- One of your students (who is known to have a heart ailment) has passed out in your classroom; you manage to revive him by administering CPR, but his parents seem unfazed by the whole incident, telling you calmly, "Well, you know, this happens to him all the time—we've gotten used to it."
- Your school has changed its attendance and tardy policies, making *you* more accountable for your students' absences and tardies, and the kids *less* accountable.
- A student refuses to look you in the eye right after you have reprimanded him for sleeping in class; he loses his temper and blurts out, "I can't stand this shit! I can't stand you, and I can't stand this class!"
- Valuable time is wasted at a special faculty in-service chasing huge helium balloons around the room; the balloons supposedly represent those students who have somehow gotten away from teachers (failed their courses). Running after the balloons like a bunch of circus clowns supposedly demonstrates to teachers how difficult it is to catch your lost students—and heal them.
- An administrator, *after only twenty minutes of watching you teach,* writes up a critical formal observation report for your annual evaluation
- After an aggregate salary slash, an increase in class sizes, and a curtailment of custodial help, you find in your mailbox a grape lollipop taped to a photocopied thank-you note from your superintendent—for "Teacher Appreciation Day."
- The guy who teaches down the corridor hasn't shown up for his morning classes—very strange, because he's never been late before; later in the day, an announcement that Mr. Jackman suddenly died from a heart attack is made on the speaker system.
- You've been ordered to attend another one of those "bright new ideas on the horizon" types of education seminars, supposedly with the notion you will be caught up with new times in the latest teaching modalities. You have been at your school for thirty years; you

have been through "The Golden Reader," "Second to None," "Above and Beyond," "No Child Left Behind," cooperative grouping, interpersonal dynamics, aligned curriculum, pattern maps, phonics, whole reader, literature-based curriculum, the Whole Child, the Half Child (kidding), creative spelling, literacy initiatives, blah—blah—blah—come and go, go and come. . . .

Good riddance!

Other than desiring to sneak home and drown your head in a bathtub, how do you deal with these bogus events, wasteful programs, and quirky reforms? *You* know better. You know what works and what doesn't work—what has worked before, but what won't work now. You've been there, done that.

You are in a foxhole with the kids, not the bean heads downtown who wouldn't know a chalkboard from a whiteboard. You've sat in those oppressive rooms for after-school presentations, summer workshops, and Saturday seminars—and listened to perfume-laden, middle-aged women in pants suits ranting and raving with their alleged insights into the causes of bottomed-out SAT scores—and what should be done about them.

You've listened to that short guy with the shiny bald head tell you— right to your face—about racism, sexism, classism, homophobia, prejudice, and the general all-around bigotry that have permeated our education system, including, probably, the leadership in *your* classroom ("But don't take this personally. . . . "), and you wanted to sock the guy right in his glossy, well-oiled nose.

I know about these scenarios; I've experienced them. These secrets you harbor may be kept from *some* people—but not from me. I'm with you on this; I know what it feels like to be frustrated and confused and anxious about my job, the manner I'm performing my job, and how others perceive my performance. After all, we teachers have pride; and it's this pride—or a lack of it—that either propels us to success or drags us backwards in our careers.

So when we began this chapter with those "crazy" adjectives, it was for good reason: Almost every teacher who has ever strode into a classroom or crusaded for what she knew was right and true and good has used these words to describe the programs, dicta, or curricula she's had to cope with throughout her career. If you're a young teacher, you, unfortunately, have these ongoing debacles lurking in your future. This is why in previous chapters I provided you with some weird coping mechanisms; this is also why I am going to give you some advice you will value only after you have already begun experiencing the following helpful benefits of having "comrades-in-arms."

Comrades-in arms are other adults in education you can go to with your problems, questions, complaints—or to exchange some old-fashioned gossip. Comrades-in-arms suit you perfectly, because they possess generous amounts of empathy, sympathy, pathos, and ethos (who was that other Musketeer?), simply because they have also "been there, done that"—or they are doing that right now. Comrades-in-arms can be found in different capacities for a variety of functions, but the foremost reason for their existence in *your* life is that they help to make your role as a teacher easier; they *connect* with you.

WAYS TO FIND COMRADES-IN-ARMS

1. Become active in a teachers' union.

Disregard the fact that teachers' unions in America have become immensely unpopular over the last several years; there are numerous reasons for this—some justified, some unjustified. But one reason you should get involved in a union is, a teachers' union—with varying measures of strength and degrees of intensity—will be supportive of you in your times of crises.[1]

2. Organize—or join—social functions for the *teachers* at your school.

Teachers from other schools are permitted, of course. But upper-level or local administrators should be excluded. No hard feelings for the big shots, but teachers need to let their hair down, too; and their gig may soon be up if they strut their social self around people who are paid to judge them—professionally—as they behave in ways that are not intended for education administrators to view them. The embarrassment this may cause would be palpable.

3. Find chums at work.

And this means at your school. The necessity of socializing with your friends from work, while *at* work, is for your own judgment; however, do remember hibernation is for bears, not social studies teachers. One teacher at my school, Mr. Gifford, had not been seen for such a lengthy period of time, he was presumed dead by most of the staff. When his smiling face finally emerged at a faculty meeting one Thursday morning, the throngs present gasped; they were shocked. Mr. Gifford was not lying in the basement of the science building, his body encased in a block of dry ice. His consciously manipulated antisocial behavior—

which he labeled as "self-preservation"—had removed any remnants of his existence from our campus.

I asked Mr. Gifford about his peculiar habit of ostracizing himself, and he responded, "I get here at six o'clock in the morning; I leave here at three-thirty in the afternoon. I eat lunch in my classroom, where I keep a refrigerator and a microwave (ah, the good old days)! What I do with my time otherwise—and why I do it—is really no one else's damn business!"

Geez, Mr. Gifford! Be nice. I'm writing a book here!

If Mr. Gifford ever needs help, someone to stand beside him for moral support—another human being to sympathize with his decision to flee from a wife who runs around the house chasing him with a rolling pin, he's going to have a difficult time finding sympathy among our staff members. Naturally, he's not required to play the part of Little Mr. Gregarious; on the other hand, he ought not emulate the reclusive life of J.D. Salinger either.[2]

My own favorite workplace chum—and best friend for the past twenty-seven years—has been a teacher who also happened to be the president of our local union branch for several terms.[3]

I'm no dummy.

4. Volunteer to be a mentor—or to be mentored.

These professional pairs tend to look out for each other, to cover each other's backs. If you're mentoring someone, you wouldn't want him to entrench himself in the abusive quagmires of education crapola (is that a word), only to be dumped on by a powerful establishment feasting on the weak, the needy, and the inexperienced. If someone is mentoring you, you don't want him writhing in misery, tempted to surrender his mentoring position to some Bozo who wouldn't appreciate a new teacher the likes of you. You *need* your mentor to be happy, secure, and enthusiastic about everything he does—and this includes mentoring *you*.

So you help each other; you stick up for each other. And if need be, you may have to protect each other by kicking a little tush every now and then.

5. Have a shtick. *Do* a shtick.

Compel others on campus to like and respect you. You already find that other people—in or out of education—are easier to deal with and more pleasant to be around if they don't think you're a bonehead. Figure out some ways that others on campus—not including students—will find your presence impossible to be without. Why? You're known as the helpful guy, the compassionate woman, the fixer, the doer, the funny dude, the award winner, the diplomat, the listener, the builder, the arranger, the organizer, the mastermind—you get the idea. When you need others to help you or simply to vent with you, they will come.

6. Be your students' teacher.

This doesn't necessarily mean their *best* or *favorite* teacher, although that would be nice, too. But as long as your students respect you, as long as they think you're letting it all hang on the line for them, they will let it all hang on the line for you.

No, you won't scurry over to a student who's munching from a package of Cheetos at lunch and land a high-five, "Hey, dude, what's up?"; but you will attract the confidence, trust, and faith of all those kids who sit in your classroom day in and day out. And your closeness to the children you work with after school or during lunch or in the wee hours of the morning at the swimming pool will motivate them to go to the ends of the earth for you, even if specifically not called upon to do so.

7. Be kind to your administrators.

Your bosses are not your enemies.

If you follow the directives and edicts presented to you by your site administrators, your life will be much easier. No one is telling you to perform in ways that are antithetical to your good sense, your perception of right and wrong, and what's good for kids. And most of the time, administrators want to do what's right; they have the best interests of the children in mind, too. During those moments you are at odds with an administrator, rather than charging into an office looking as though you do not intend to take any hostages, try one of these approaches:

- Set up a meeting. Most administrators have open-door policies. Come prepared to your meeting with an administrator, present your case, and then wait for a response. Don't freak out if the poor shmuck wants some time to chew on what you've told him, or would like to respond to you in writing. You've already started the ball rolling. Unless the administrator is blatantly wrong about a policy significantly detrimental to teachers or kids, don't argue.
- Be polite. In your conversations with administrators, refrain from saying words like those used in most Clint Eastwood films. Call your administrators by *Mr.* or *Mrs.* or *Ms.* with their last names, until they have initiated permission for you to do otherwise. Also, using "please," "thank you," and "I'm sorry" has never made anyone's relationships with other people worse.

- Stay up-front. Before you gripe through school-wide emails about site policies or administrators' personalities, go directly to the offending party and try to repair it with her first. I've never known an administrator who wanted her teachers to complain to the district superintendent *before* they spoke to her about the difficulty prior to the complaint. I've known administrators who have been bent out of shape by teachers who went behind their backs to try and fix problems that could have been alleviated by drawing the administrator's immediate attention to the situation through direct communication.

Make friends, garnish respect, and enlist the cooperation of your school's administrators.

Your comrades-in-arms who have the most power to help you sometimes come from the most unexpected sources.

8. Join an entertaining lunch group and meet with them regularly.

Remember that eating with your students who love you should happen only once in a blue moon (or whatever color a rare moon happens to be).

However, I recently asked a few questions to a group of incredibly old teachers who have eaten together at the same table in the faculty dining room for the past two thousand years. I'm quoting their responses here practically verbatim. What they actually said is far too entertaining for me to mess with. Of the seven teachers who religiously had eaten lunch together at this table, one is dead, and two are retired—which now leaves four. The cast: John (shop), Jeff (English), Jerry (science), and Craig (science)—along with yours truly, who was actually more nervous about doing this interview than any other I had ever done.

Me: So, why do you guys like to eat together?

Jeff: What kind of a stupid question is that to start off with? Who's gonna buy your book with that kinda fluff it?

See what I mean.

Me: (smiling as I clear my throat) Okay, what are some things you four have in common that make you so attractive to each other?

I discovered immediately—a very lousy way to ask that question.

John: You're looking at *us* four, and the word *attractive* comes to mind?

Jerry: (lifting his upper lip) Look at these teeth; yellow as they come. That's *attractive* to you?

Me: (now forcing a grin) OK, let me ask it one more time. Funny, because I've conducted so many interviews in the past few years—with the books and all—you'd think I'd do better with you guys. So—

Jeff: (interrupting) You're nervous, Bruce; we make you nervous. You know the kind of royalty you're dealing with at this table.

He gestured with his head toward the tabletop, which was covered with ground soda crackers, smidgens of bread crust, and several sprinkles of liquid from a variety of dripping beverage cups. Jeff caught my sense of irony.

Jeff: That *is* the trademark of royalty: four old guys who've eaten lunch together for years, and now know each other's doctors and fiber regimens well enough to fix their own constipation problems.

Of course, Jeff had to be the English teacher in the bunch.

Me: That's what you guys talk about at lunch—fiber? Constipation? Last time that I ate with you, you almost took my head off because of our differences about the war in Iraq! There was no mention of bodily functions then.

On cue, John passed gas. Loudly.
We all laughed. Even John.

Me: So, that's it, huh? You harangue and badger and cajole and coax and berate—and in the end you love and support each other?

Jerry: Well, I'd put it another way: First, except for one of those words you just used, I have no idea what they mean; but, second, yeah, we do all that stuff, I think, but we do it to others, too—to folks who don't eat at this table. And that's where the real fun comes in.

Me: People around here refer to you as the "Grumpy Old Men."

Craig: Uh, that's one way of looking at it. But when we get all these stupid directives and all that New Beginnings crap, it's very nice to just sit here, tell each other off, and talk about the idiots in education who don't know their rectum from their prostrate.

The mental health of teachers magnifies exponentially based on the number of supporters and cohorts they have; these supporters and cohorts, through a variety of methods, clear teachers' heads, provide teachers vehicles for venting, and allow teachers access to some less-traveled roads that often lead to healthy mental equilibrium.[4]

Bringing this concept down to its most basic philosophical component: When we need help because we're going crazy, when we must have someone to talk to because we're confused, when we require a good listener as an antidote to our most current emotional crisis—comrades-in-arms rush in and go right to the front lines with their first aid kits. Comrades-in-arms know what we're going through.

They're just like we are.

NOTES

1. Diane Ravitch, "Why Teachers Unions Are Good for Teachers and the Public," *AFT: A Union of Professionals* (Winter 2006–2007): 1.

2. As of November 2008, J.D. Salinger was still alive; he was eighty-nine years old. He has not given an interview in twenty-eight years.

3. Eric Jordan put teachers first. Following through with this philosophy as the head of the union, Eric, through helping teachers, caused our *students* to become the ultimate winners.

4. Allen Richter, "Teacher Stress Rising, But Venting Helps," *BNET Business Network* (December, 2003): 14.

14

Enroll Yourself Back in (Yikes!) School

Knowing full well your body posture at the moment is that of a cowering fool, you silently pray inside for a vision of yourself that is very different from the one you now possess. Your eardrums pound with the impact of a bass drum thumping out a hip-hop song, and you worry that your skin has transmogrified from its pale flesh tone into the remnants of a red skin color left behind by the searing sun on a hot afternoon at the beach. You are absolutely certain all other eyes are riveted upon you, reveling in your personal embarrassment. Secretly, you wish for a sudden, enormous earthquake or a terrorist attack—a direct hit on the classroom in which you now sit.

As you sit in your middle school classroom, reeling from a confrontation with your eighth grade English teacher, you look around for a hole to lower yourself or a wall to embed yourself; perhaps, impaling your body on a sheathed fireplace iron would suffice. But no matter, time crawls like water running through a residential street gutter, as you silently suffer the indignity of being shown up by your teacher.

And you would love to see this teacher suddenly drop dead in front of your entire class.

An innocent recreation of the dynamics of this episode would go like this:

"So," Mr. Jimenez sighs as he addresses his English class, "why hasn't anyone finished their homework? This was not exactly rocket science stuff; mere rote copying of material is not going to jar any makeshift bolts that are holding in your brains."

You look around briefly and notice that the other kids are shrinking violets under Mr. Jimenez's triumphant stare. He is a huge man, one you would like on your side in a dark alley, but not one you'd like to come across in that alley if he were a stranger to you.

The other students' cowardice has prickled your vocal chords, encouraged by that foot you are about to thrust in your adolescent mouth. You say, "If rocket science was as boring as this class, we never would have had a space program. Nobody would have been able to stay awake."

The class laughs in unison; they're on your side. You have said what they would only dream of saying. Score one for you!

But Mr. Jimenez is now moving in your direction; you notice that his already large body seems to be getting even larger as he comes toward you.

"I suppose [your name], you are the catch-all, end-all when it comes to the science principles inherent in producing space rockets?"

You remain silent. What can you say to that? You don't have even a clue what he just said.

Hovering, he continues, "You just proudly proclaimed, 'If rocket science *was* as boring as this class, we never would have had a space program.' I surmise you didn't do the assignment last night on the use of the subjunctive mood?"

Your heart falls to your ankles. You don't remember anything about an assignment about "subjunctive mood"—or whatever. You have no idea what that *means!* Subjunctive mood! Who *cares?*

And then Mr. Jimenez makes a speech for which you silently wish he would be hauled off (in a very large truck) to the California death chamber and executed by lethal injection—or preferably other, even *more* painful ways of dying: "And you call what *I* teach you in this class *boring*, Mr. [mentions your last name with disdain]? And since when have *you* been known around here as the rockin'-out, party-hearty, socially advanced neophyte of Excitement City? Hmm? Just a thought—although, as you already know, I wouldn't want to be judgmental—but did you ever consider, Mr. [grumbles your name again], that you refer to all that we learn in here as *tedium* because *you* are the one who is boring?"

Again, what are you supposed to say? This guy's got you on several levels: He has a master's degree, a silver tongue, a teaching credential, and twenty-inch biceps; he's very mean and can *destroy* you with one brush of his heavily calloused hand. He's also a favored employee of the school district, and with a flick of his pen can relegate you to hard labor in Outer Mongolia. You can't stand up to him; everybody in your class knows this, and they all feast on the way Mr. Jimenez gloats in his power.

So now the only recourse you have is a slow, painful death at your desk, praying you are taken quickly, don't suffer much, and are spared further humiliation. But you will probably survive; no official deaths have been recorded due to a student mortification malaise, although you shelter some lingering doubts about the absence of *any* deaths that can be even indirectly associated with the pain of being a student, son/daughter, and teenager—all at the very same time.

Teachers, have you forgotten what that was like? Have you pushed from your minds the drudgeries, anguishes, indignities, and embarrassments of being an adolescent who is struggling to get through school? Why—even the simple things, such as standing up on the first day of class and introducing yourself, reignite painful memories for some people. When I was a student, I always despised that first day, because I dreaded the recurring scene of my new teacher reading through her roll sheet for the initial time and then stammering through my last name.

I always cringed with embarrassment—not for the teacher—for myself, because I had such a difficult name to pronounce. "Gevirtzman" might as well have been a name used by the leader of the first extraterrestrials to land on earth. I always believed all eyes were watching me just before the teacher came to my name on her list; and now all the other kids would reel with enjoyment when she tried to say it.

"How is she going to mispronounce his name *this* time?"

"Ha! Ha! What a dorky name!"

"Why did Bruce get stuck with a name all the teachers would hate to say? Can't he just change his name—finally, and for once?"

Do you remember something similar happening to you?

As I prepared my list of the *terribles* of being a student in a high school or middle school, I became overwhelmed with a sense that I would never be able to mention *all* of them—let alone discuss each of them separately. Life, after all, is short, and who wants to spend so much time reliving some of our biggest nightmares, let alone writing about them! Ultimately, I came to the conclusion that mentioning the Top five advantages to teachers becoming students again—at least, temporarily—would have to suffice; and I would revisit some of those awful moments again by working them into a discussion of a few satisfying disclosures that may prompt you to go back to school—at least, for a little while.

TEACHERS WHO BECOME STUDENTS AGAIN . . .

1. will develop more empathy for their own students.

By putting yourself in the place of that humble eighth grader who has Genghis Khan for a teacher, you can readily comprehend a necessity for more empathy. The humiliation of being chastised in front of a bunch of your peers competes with the humiliation of being caught with your zipper down in a public place. Countless opportunities for mortification exist in the daily life of almost any teenager on this earth, and perhaps you have forgotten most of them.

And what are a few other areas you can learn to reconnect with your past, thereby building up an arsenal of sensitive understanding, rivaling Walt Whitman's empathy for fallen soldiers on a battlefield, for your current students?

- forgetting to do an assignment
- doing an assignment incorrectly
- having to prioritize school, when there are 8 billion other events and people in your life requiring your time and attention
- shelling out money for books and supplies, at a time you desperately need to earmark that money to 42 million other places
- getting up especially early or going to bed especially late
- putting up with a teacher duller than your father's tax accountant
- worrying about being called upon to perform in class, which is far worse than being called upon to perform in the back seat of an old jalopy (depending, of course, on the natural talents of the guy in the old jalopy)
- not being able to go to the bathroom when you really must, but having to ask permission to relieve yourself at someone *else's* convenience (disregarding that teachers *can't* leave for the bathroom during class, because there is never a convenient time for them to desert their students)
- dealing with erratic and unreasonable time schedules and deadlines over which you have no control and no say-so
- buying clothes to wear around people you have to put up with and wouldn't have otherwise associated, unless your mutual families were the lone survivors of a thermonuclear attack
- trying to stay awake while someone else is talking—someone who could bore the britches off seventeen thousand people at a Rolling Stones revival concert, while the Stones are singing
- spending money on gas in order to drive to school (even though most of your students don't drive; they, do, however, have to come up with *some* method of getting to school, and griping about filling up the gas tank has recently become very cool)
- forfeiting opportunities to watch television, going to the movies, and having any fun
- stressing out about difficult assignments and exams (and pulling all-nighters)

- figuring out ways to impress the teacher, providing yourself a slight edge when it comes to the subjective part of his determination of your course grade

This list could go on forever. You should have some idea by now—if you hadn't already—that going back to school allows you to live your life as your students do each and every day they sit in *your* classroom, under your jurisdiction, the recipient of the use or abuse of tremendous power *you* hold over them.

Teachers who become students again . . .

2. will learn more about their subject matter.

You think you know everything there is to know about computers and designing web pages.

But you don't.

Perhaps, you do know enough to teach technology to sixteen-year-olds who haven't the faintest clue about Web design, although some teenagers know more about computers than even seasoned adult computer geeks; but your schooling will make you once again eager to discover even more about new technologies—and how can that be a bad thing? Your thirst for knowledge may lead to finding out quirky things about your subject that will jettison you back to your classroom with an enthusiasm and energy you haven't seen in yourself since you won that raffle at work and took home four box seats to the seventh game of the 2002 World Series.[1]

New information, refreshing ways to teach it, and endless minds to absorb it will make learning a heck of a lot different—better, more meaningful—for you than it was forty years ago, when the only reason you had gone to college in the first place was to dodge the military draft.

Teachers who become students again . . .

3. will work toward earning a higher degree or an advancement on the pay scale.

What does this have to do with creating a better learning environment for your students? Teachers who have a master's degree make an average of ten thousand dollars a year more on the regular pay scale than teachers who have earned only a bachelor's degree. The bottom line is teachers earn higher salaries by having advanced degrees.[2] The logic here is so obvious, turning to so-called "expert" analysis would be, literally, a mere academic exercise and a tad condescending.

But here's the lowdown anyway: Teachers with more money have greater flexibility in their lives; teachers with more choices and flexibility are, generally, happier human beings. Teachers who are happier human beings, *generally*, are better teachers and produce better students.[3]

Getting another academic degree bolsters teachers' effectiveness on many levels, and going back to school puts teachers on a path that leads to success.

Teachers who become students again . . .

4. will connect to another positive social network.

Virtual communities such as Facebook and MySpace encourage social interactions among multigenerational groups of people—and for every imaginable purpose. In order to promote my books, I've recently connected on these networks with several people I haven't seen or spoken with in over forty years. It's safe; it's quiet; But most of all, it's a rather dull way of interacting and communicating with people.

When you *physically* return to the classroom, you have *physical* contact with people you can see—sometimes up close and personal. You can *see*, for example, that the sixty-five-year-old school teacher from another school district is, well, a rather elderly-looking sixty-five-year-old school teacher from another school district—and not a curvaceous, twenty-year-old blonde you have been fantasizing about for the last four months while punching the keys on your computer and staring at the images (real or forged) on Facebook.

Darn it!

But on the other hand, your social and academic networking helps to develop a more comfortable you—perhaps, a revitalized appreciation for teaching, tutoring, and teens—and you may go back to your classroom with a greater sense of support and camaraderie. You see firsthand that others are also struggling to be better teachers and have the same fears you do about the snake pits of the job; perhaps, this commonality portends well for your own more extended understanding of what you do on a daily basis while on the job, and how you may do it better.

Teachers who go back to school . . .

5. will sense that your students appreciate your commitment and effort to better yourself.

We're constantly expecting our students to go the extra mile, to extend themselves, to visibly demonstrate a desire to learn more while exuding an appreciation for academia. Now it's our turn to model for our students that we are doing likewise; that we revere education and the knowledge that comes with it; that we, too, have a desire to better ourselves in order to help us make *them* better.

Desiree, a seventeen-year-old eleventh grader, expressed her thoughts about teachers who, concurrent to their teaching assignments, also were attending college: "You kind of expect the younger teachers to still be going to school. But when you find out that some teachers are going to school because they *want* to, it's, like, oh, wow! I mean, not too many kids would go to school if they really didn't have to. So I have a lot of respect for teachers like that."

Going back to school can come in all sizes, shapes, and forms (listed in a very subjective ascending order of complexity):

Number 10: Correspondence courses

I thought these were obsolete, until I recently saw them advertised in a large metropolitan newspaper. Students seldom see the teacher; they communicate with the teacher only by email, but even that method is not required. With correspondence courses, students never have to be in direct contact with the teacher. These courses will, however, apply some of the familiar pressures of being a student again, and for that reason alone, they are probably better than nothing; plus, they're fairly inexpensive.

Number 9: Cyber classes

Unfortunately, you lose out on the primary benefits of going back to school, such as connecting to actual *people*. Most of the challenges and stresses that would hand you parallel misfortunes to your own students are lost in this poor excuse for an authentic classroom. Yes, you receive college credits; and, yes, you set and reach professional goals. But no, you do not face the wrath of a teacher's disappointment in your performance; and, no, you will not be forced to contain your bathroom needs until more, uh, appropriate times. These voids in your schooling structure separate you from most of your students' everyday realities.

A special friend who actually teaches one of these courses in cyberspace (for the purpose of his students' procuring cleared credentials) told me: "It's very difficult for me to assign a grade. I can't tell if these people will be—or are—good teachers just by what they type on their computers. I don't know what they look like, sound like—I have no idea how they would perform in front of children."[4]

Number 8: Saturday workshops

They rarely offer you a grade, but they may give you college credits; and, alas, there are actual humans teaching you—in person! And the elements of growing more empathy for your own students remain in tact, such as benign humiliation, unrelenting boredom, and loss of self-respect. But on these early Saturday mornings, don't forget to brush your teeth; if you do forget, you'll make it a lot harder on your classmates.

Number 7: Vocational schools

Now you can work on skills that provide you true skills and advantages in the real world, such as being able to repair a car or change a lightbulb. Your own teachers will yell at you occasionally, providing the necessary requisites for motivating you to improve your own classroom climate. I should have enrolled in a vocational school of some kind a long time ago; perhaps, I could have learned a few things about automobiles, such as what happens when I turn the ignition key. All I have ever known about this is the car goes after I turn the key—if I'm lucky.

Number 6: Commnity College (one class)

Enroll for *one* class at a community college. A huge benefit of community colleges is that these schools hire instructors who actually teach their own classes. They don't turn over the workload to their graduate students, while they're spending time (and now with the advent of the Internet, much *more* time) doing so-called academic research and writing books. Teachers at community colleges are usually highly trained, intensely focused educators with a mission to help young people transition into four-year universities, earn a lower-level degree, and meet their students' special, individual, compartmentalized needs. This is where *you* come in. *Your* special, individual, compartmentalized need is to take only *one* class in order to know what it again feels like to be at the other end of the bullet. With your renewed empathy may come skills or knowledge you would not have otherwise gained; plus, you might be inspired to further your education by finishing your full teaching credential or shooting for a master's degree or Ph.D.

The rather economical tuition and minimum accessory costs make this an attractive option to many—especially cheapskates.

Number 5: Community college (several classes)

As a full-time community college student, you receive all the perks of being only a one-class community college student—and much more: You'll finish your degree more quickly, learn further material in your subject expertise, and have the requisite dread and trepidation—five or six times more intense than you would have had by taking only one course—already possessed by your own high school students.

Number 4: Finish your credential

You'll need to attend a four-year college (even if you choose to school yourself online), but the rewards of having that teaching certificate finally authenticated are awesome! Just for starters, you won't lose your job. That alone sounds like a pretty good reason to finish the proper credentialing. Pay close attention to the various timelines, deadlines, and guidelines; they differ from state to state.

Number 3: Shore up your specialties

Are you in special education? Finish your certification. You'll also receive updated advice and the latest know-how for aiding these needy children you have so nobly chosen to teach. Laws, regulations, and special statutes for special education are constantly changing.

One maximally beneficial way of keeping up is going back to school. The feeling you receive from being a student in these college courses, and the adrenalin that starts pumping after you learn about such bizarre territories in education, will send you into your classroom with an entirely different outlook: For one thing, you'll have sensed greater power, the awesomeness of possessing more control; for another thing, you'll have cultivated a broader understanding of your special ed students and a greater sensitivity for their unusual problems.

Number 2: Classes of supreme interest (four-year college)

These do not have to be courses that steer you in any particular direction—toward a degree or specific credential. Take classes for fun. Audit the courses, if you don't wish to take exams. The point of going back to school is learning, and it's also about returning to a routine of following a particular regimen, regulating your time, organizing your raw materials in the most efficient manner, disciplining yourself to follow orders, obeying rules, and adhering to regulations.

Four-year colleges offer an environment more aligned with your own goals, perceptions, and expectations of higher learning. You're a personality that may be more satisfied—a better fit—in a traditional college or university setting and, therefore, more likely to produce results that will be helpful to you and your students.

The upshot of all this is that you will have killed three birds with one stone: felt what it's like to be a student again; learned about material especially interesting to you, and worked toward another steppingstone in your personal career—while you will have had a wonderful time studying that which you love the most.

Number 1: Change your teaching focus

At various intervals in our existence, a reevaluation of what we're doing and why we're doing it is in order. It's not reasonable for us to decide at the dawn of our lives what we're going to be doing sixty or seventy years down the road. Goals change. Interests change. Ideas change. *People change.* So for some of you, it would be prudent—not to do over what you have already done—to take steps forward, making changes that become extensions of what you have already accomplished.

Here is a suggested sequence of questions you should be asking yourself at lengthy intervals. But start *immediately*, if you have never posed these questions to yourself before:

- Overall, do I like my job? If the answer here is *no*, you have some important work to do. The amount of that work or its complexity may depend on your answers to each of the questions below; in fact, you may decide to forfeit your career as a teacher altogether and latch on to another job. When my wife goes back to teaching full-time, we're going to need a domestic servant to help keep our house clean. Are you interested?
- Do you still enjoy the subject you are teaching?
- Are there other areas of interest or subjects that could replace those you are teaching now?
- Are your financial resources such that you could temporarily quit teaching and go back to school fulltime?
- Do you have family and other commitments that would make going back to school now infeasible?
- Are you mentally ready to take on a load of classes—or even one class?
- Is your spouse in accord with the changes you have decided to make?
- Are your employment prospects hot enough that your returning to the job market in four of five years would not create an undo burden on you and/or your family?
- Would it be practical for you to make a change now—effective immediately?
- Do you have a specific school in mind?
- Can you afford the school you have selected?

- Have you organized a timeline and schedule for applying to college, completing your course work, capturing the appropriate credentials, scoping out the job market, and landing a new teaching position?

Some teachers, of course, wish to move up in the administrative ranks; they think it's a step forward. Is it? I'll leave that verdict up to each individual. But do know that a change does not have to mean more money or a "higher" rank on the pecking order.

Moving *on* means going on to something you'd desire doing even more, are better doing, and would consider doing for the rest of your life.

The most basic concept is, during this long, arduous process, you will have wisely paid attention to your own teachers. And from having gone through the drudgery of being a student again, you can finally understand what most of *your* students are feeling every day they sit in your classroom.

You now have a fresh recollection of what it's like to be on the other side of the teacher's desk.

NOTES

1. Besides my wife, two children, and teaching, baseball has brought the greatest rewards to my life. I have known several other male teachers in the vicinity of my age who reap the same emotional benefits from baseball as I do.

2. Emily Alpert, "In Tough Times a Bold Bid by a Teachers' Union," *Voice of San Diego*, August 6, 2008, at voiceofsandiego.org/articles/2008/08/06/news/+unionproposal080608.txt.

3. Molly Bloom, "Happy Teachers Tied to Good Students," (summary of article), *Statesman.com*, November 12, 2008, at statesman.com/news/content/news/stories/local/11/12/1112surveys.html.

4. Bob Pacilio teaches in San Diego County; much more about this talented teacher comes in Chapter 17.

15

Plan According to
Specifications: Your *Own*

Ms. Herzer began her day at 5:30 A.M. A veteran high school economics teacher, she knew that one major component to staying sane in
the world of education was to establish a routine for herself: Every morning as she climbed out of bed, her mind, heart, and body led her to an
identical series of events: tending to her bathroom needs, scarfing down a
muffin—usually banana-nut—chugging down a cup of black coffee, and
chomping on a breakfast energy chocolate bar. Her drive to school took
around thirty minutes—more when traffic clogged the streets—and she
always arrived at her classroom (after a short visit to her school mailbox)
between 6:40 and 6:50 A.M.

Ms. Herzer's first class of the day would begin filing into her room at
around 6:55 A.M. for a 7:00 A.M. start.

Do your own math: This gave Ms. Herzer approximately five to ten
minutes to plan her economics lesson for the day and also prepare her
room environment (whiteboards, seating arrangements, posted bulletins,
etc.) for over thirty sleepyheaded high school seniors.

Unless, of course, she had already planned her lesson the previous
night while she had been at home, and tended to her room environment
before she had left school yesterday.

No, Ms. Herzer had not worked on her lessons the night before either;
her approach to planning was quite different from the strategies outlined
in textbooks studied by education majors in colleges, or by the human
Muppets (in the tight plaid pants) who ran those monotonous in-service
workshops.

The lesson plan: Almost every workshop, seminar, class, or other formal presentation teachers attend has a segment on the preparation of a lesson plan. Every college education department assesses teachers and would-be teachers on their lesson plans for a particular subject, with a prototype of that plan usually furnished by the instructor. Fairly recently I finished a supplementary credential so I would be, uh, qualified to teach English-as-a-second-language learners (whom, I guess, I'd been *unqualified* to teach during my previous thirty-five-some years of service); and a big part of the final exam for this course dealt with a bunch of *prescribed* cockamamie lesson plans.

Having been a teacher for a thousand decades or so, I've had lesson plans running out my ears!

Actually, that isn't true.

For the most part—except in situations like I described above, I have ignored the use of a formal lesson plan as a tool for my daily teaching practices, unless you count what follows as a lesson plan. For this shot of unadulterated brilliance, I simply typed up my notes that I had written for today on a small ninety-nine-cent pad of paper:

Monday, December 8:

Poem, "Attitude" by Charles Swindell

Vocabulary, #17 misogyny—the hatred of women

Reminders: sentence comb. Test-T; extra credit due Wed., no school T.

Recap of yester.

Introduce Patrick Henry, pages 42–44 "Give Me Liberty . . . " stuff

Ask students about Paine

Paine quotations—"The Crisis Number 1" Go over, make fun of British, etc.

If you'd prefer to call the above a lesson plan—whatever warms the cockles of your heart—be my guest.

All teachers have to do *something* to get ready for class the next day. The key is to . . . *get ready for class the next day.* Teachers must do whatever it takes. Unfortunately, most colleges and education moguls have forced upon teachers a notion that only certain prescribed methods to get ready for school have merit—*and that's all.* But there are problems with these preconceived, old standby conceptions of what—and when and where—teachers should do to prepare their lessons.

A RUDIMENTARY ANALYSIS OF A FEW WELL-KNOWN
OBJECTIONS TO TRADITIONAL LESSON PLANNING:

1. They detract from what a teacher *really* needs to do.

If you must look up the latest information about genetic engineering, so you don't wind up sounding like a derelict for departing the wrong "facts" to your science students, you may balk at frittering away your valuable time. If your precious moments are spent—instead of looking up those facts—struggling a tightly structured, textbook-ordered, district-mandated, roll-back-your-eyeballs-into-their-sockets lesson plan your college professor brainwashed you into believing you *had* to design before you could so much as open your mouth in your classroom, in all likelihood you are wasting your treasured time.

You should have been doing that research—not that busywork.

2. Lesson planning sap a teacher's strength.

At its very best, regimented, cookie-cutter lesson planning gives us a framework for knowing what we're going to teach on a given day, during a full week, or beyond. But at their worst, required lesson plans straightjacket teachers, ultimately becoming a counter-productive dictate from faceless entities that usually deny any responsibility for their pronouncements.

Sadly, lots of teachers, even after valiantly attempting to wrestle with mandated, trendy lesson planning and other pseudoeducation mumbo jumbo, fight *themselves* to keep from throwing up their hands and surrendering to the demons of pompous, overstuffed, out-of-touch, think-tank weirdoes, many of whom have placed nary a single foot inside a real live classroom.

3. Lesson planning discourages the best the brightest from becoming teachers.

Have you ever sat in an education class and heard what they're telling prospective teachers about planning? About how you should great ready to teach your entire course—or how you should prepare yourself for even a single day of teaching? If you have taken education classes—and most of you have—there's no need to belabor this point: But people—good people—*quit*. And they quit all the time.[1] Oh, I'm sure lesson planning is not the sole reason for teacher rebellion or future educators rejecting their once well-laid plans and selecting a different itinerary for their lives.

Education student Maureen shared an experience:

> My worst encounter with writing up formal lesson plans came from a col-
> lege class that may have been my overall worst experience in school, so it
> didn't surprise me how ridiculous it was. I took an upper-level inclusion
> class; the part of the course dealing with cultural diversity had been the most
> difficult to contend with, but when the dust finally settled by the end of the
> semester, I thought somehow I had done enough, sufficiently bitten down
> on my tongue to make it through. But I was wrong. When it came to the end,
> the teacher asked us to write in *Spanish* a sample lesson plan for "slow and
> diverse learners"!

Before anyone waves an angry finger at me, of *course* I know that many
teachers have had positive, valuable experiences in learning how to
plan—and also in utilizing those plans. Without prior consideration and
organization for teaching a class, this job would be practically impossible.
This is very clear; however, many teachers have—with some degree of
justification—complained about regimented, cookie-cutter, can't-see-the-
forest-from-the-trees approaches to lesson planning, a system in which
form surpasses substance. And the negative results accrued from these
dictates have earned forced, regimented lesson planning a well-deserved
reputation for being at best, irksome, and at worst, counterproductive.

Here is an example of a lesson plan format—albeit simplified—that you
may find in a typical textbook for teachers or an in-service guidebook
(you know: the kind fastened together with a shoddy staple gun):

- date
- course
- term objective
- lesson objective(s)
- preferred outcomes
- behavior objective(s)
- required materials
- teacher focus
- student focus
- modalities
- assessment(s)
- long-term assessment(s)
- potential follow-ups

Beyond getting used to these strange terminologies, various renditions
of different sections to a daily lesson plan vary from college teacher to
college teacher, from in-service provider to in-service provider, and from
principal to principal. These ideas having been organized and reorga-

nized at least 14 trillion different ways, while the mundane chore for each teacher or education student has been to doodle *something* next to the required terms, posing as acceptable daily planning for a real-world classroom full of actual school children.

Let's examine the net worth of each idea.

date	This suggests that the lesson can be completed in one day, and meaningful short-term objectives with their accompanying lessons will follow suit. All good educators know the importance of flexibility here; perhaps, this may be the actual day the lesson is *begun*.
course	I suppose that we do teach multiple subjects, but *really . . . !*
term objective	This may be a reference to mandated state standards, but why must a teacher write this down each day for every lesson? Just how will this help to get him more focused? Even the science teacher who has a reputation for sounding at least semi-intelligent depends on securing some time for a bit of last-minute preparation before her genetic engineering lesson. At face value, *this* easily appears more important than writing on the whiteboard before class, "Standard 2C: genetic biology, human growth hormone technology/historical outline, subheaded in three layers—demonstrating mastery of the aging process." To what end must she keep repeating before deaf ears and blind eyes those state standards?
lesson objective	This may sound something like, "by the end of class all students will have learned five new words in French," or the names of five additional wars in which the French retreated and/or surrendered.
preferred outcomes	Want to clue me in? I prefer an outcome that shows my students learned something in my class to an outcome that shows they didn't learn anything. I prefer an outcome that shows I am alive by the end of class to an outcome that shows I am dead.
behavior objectives	These apply to the students, not the teacher—I *think*. Then again, I'm not in the know as to what this really does mean. If a teacher asks her class to—let's see—paint a mural with lots of pretty

colors, and by the end of class they have painted a mural with lots of pretty colors, I suppose the teacher has achieved his *objectives* in regard to his students' *behavior*. Go figure.

necessary materials You had better make sure you have enough of those materials—you know—because you might come up short, and then what would you do? If you want your students to put together a small wooden cabinet, just be sure you have enough, uh, wood in your supply closet. These days lots of teachers purchase supplies with their own hard-earned cash. Sometimes it's necessary to take to heart an old adage: "If you want something done right, you just gotta do it yourself." That goes for stocking up on self-bought pencils, crayons, paper, etc., because, frankly, nobody is going to knock on your classroom door and beg you to accept plenty of these commodities for free.

teacher focus I'm not sure what this means either, but just make sure you're thinking about what your *students* are doing at any given moment, instead of that glossy photo of Jessica Alba you found last night on the Internet.

student focus Ditto the above analysis on teacher focus.

modalities These may get confused with various ugly instruments medical doctors use for certain invasive procedures or surgeries, especially those involving sensitive private parts of the human body; however, *modalities* is just another piece of fancy-schmancy jargon for indicating which teaching methods you will be using today: Lecture? Cooperative grouping? Kinesthetic activities (which is a highfalutin way of saying you'll make the kids get out of their seats and run around a lot)? Peer teaching? Pairs? Nonproductive gossip mongering?

assessment(s) Are you going to give an exam to the little buggers, or have them turn their work in to you for your evaluation? Maybe you're planning on hearing them deliver an oral project, while you sit tensely in the back of the classroom, anticipating the first obnoxious moment one of your students quotes a few vulgar words from the lyrics of another rap recording by Snoopy-Doggy-Do-Do. You reveal here just how you're going to know if the kids learned—*on this day*—about what you were *supposed* to teach them.

long-term assessment(s)   In about, say, two hundred years from now, how will you know that this lesson and the ones that followed actually *taught* your students anything worthwhile (as per state standards, school standards, dictates of the federal government, administrative directives, workshop brainstorming, the students themselves, your own goals, and those ornery criticisms and suggestions from feisty Uncle Carl); and just how much of it have they retained? On the bright side: By that time, you'll be dead and buried.

follow-up(s)   OK, you taught a totally boss lesson today. But tomorrow how are you planning to make it "bosser"—even more meaningful?

Embrace whatever you prefer from these examples, but it appears that two core, fundamental truths exist here: (1) Teachers *do* need to plan for their upcoming classes; and (2) rote, formal lesson planning can be counterproductive. What most teachers *really* require are methods of planning that suit them individually—their *own* personalities, time constraints, teaching styles, and levels of experience. The old "one size fits all" approach works out well infrequently in education, and never has this been truer than in the business of teacher planning.

So how do I plan thee?

Let me count the ways (on second thought, I'm not going to count them).

But for the Grace of God

You don't plan anything. You walk into the classroom in the morning, and—bam!—you're ready to go. The only "planning" you *may* have done is making sure you have enough copies of your handouts, or reminding your students the day before to bring their textbooks. But that's about it for your planning strategies.

Teachers for whom this type of planning would be a success: Those who have taught the same course for a minimum of 105 years and still have stores of confidence, clarity of mind, and a brain that works. These teachers are fairly rare.

By the tip of your marking pen:

You plan; you just don't use much strategy in your preparation for classes. You care; you just don't express it evidentially. You may succeed as a teacher; you just don't maximize your potential to break through to all your students. At the end of your workday, you prepare your whiteboard in your classroom for the next day's activities (if it's before a weekend, you do this Friday afternoon); you put up your agenda, reminders, homework assignments, lesson instructions, announcements, and any other information your students will require for the next day's activities.

Teachers for whom this type of planning would be a success: Those few who have excellent control of their methods, knowledge of their subject, and the strongest desire to get the hell out of the classroom as soon as possible.

By the Light of the Moon

Do this: Come home from work; take a thirty-minute nap. Eat dinner (preferably at your favorite restaurant). Take a walk. Watch a little television or read a good book or listen to some inspiring music or engage in your favorite board game with a friend or family member. Connect to your hobby. Mess around on the Internet for about thirty minutes—visiting your favorite websites, writing email, or joining chat rooms. Make love to your spouse.

Stop! Wait!

Knowing ahead of time not *one* of us leads a life reflective of this utopian lifestyle makes it much easier for us to dismiss the notion that most teachers—let alone all teachers—live in an environment conducive to at-home lesson planning, grading papers, or a life free of insanities, inanities, regimentation, and strife.

Much more likely: Family conflicts, responsibilities to children, commanding in-laws, marital squabbles, second jobs, blaring technology, financial woes, illness setbacks, demands of friends, religious commitments—and the like—impact our lives.

So allow me to simplify:

Take a short nap—of almost any duration—and you will be refreshed and ready to go for the gusto later on. Dr. Mark R. Rosekind, Ph.D., studied the effects of therapeutic napping and came to this conclusion: "One of the most effective strategies to improve alertness is a short nap."[2]

Pretty simple, no?

After your nap, have dinner, play with the kids—just cope with the aspects of your life mentioned above that you need to cope with. In no particular order of events, lead your life; don't sweat it. As with anyone else, there will be setbacks, drawbacks, and Outback Steakhouses.

But what about *lesson planning* for Pete's sake!

Ah! You see, in that comes the significance of this chapter inheriting its own, specific title: "By the Light of the Moon." You will do your planning at night—after everyone else is in bed, asleep—after all phone calls have been concluded, after all TV programs have been viewed, and after all arguments, disagreements, conflicts, and disputes have been resolved, worked on, or appeased. The time ahead is set aside especially for *you*, to help make your students brighter and more knowledgeable—and you more efficient and, perhaps, more healthy.

You work by the light of the moon (not *literally*, but you knew that, didn't you?), and you plan for the next day's work—and only the next day—at school with your students.

That which you are permitted to do under this system:

- grade papers . . . but that's not lesson planning, so . . .
- type or write up or otherwise prepare materials you will use the next day
- make to-do lists
- think about, jot down, or discuss with others short-term lesson objectives
- watch an inspirational movie about a teacher (I know; those movie teachers can be bogus, but sometimes they—or the screenwriters— offer ideas that accidentally inspire me to emulate them. Such an occurrence took place after I saw *Stand and Deliver*[3] for the first time. Jaime Escalante took me to the next level of enthusiasm for my job with his mastery of a directed teaching approach.)[4]

All these activities help to get us ready, and we do them by the light of the moon. (I'd better clarify again: This means *just before bedtime*.)

Teachers for whom this type of planning would be successful: Night owls and those who lack great clarity of thought when under duress; also those who can absolutely—for certain—take a nap as prescribed.

By the Seat of Your Pants

Most of you have probably figured out this has something to do with *sitting* down. But it's a tad weirder than that. Here's what you do to inaugurate this fourth tip for lesson planning: You sit (already confirmed).

But you're not allowed to get up until you have completed your planning for the next day's sessions with your students.

I used to insist that teachers should not allow themselves the luxury of using the bathroom, but this came off to many as being a little *too* odd, so I gave that one up. But the premise remains: You remain stationary (with emergency bathroom breaks) until you're finished.

As a writer, I discovered this technique a long time ago; it cured those cases of an inevitable writer's block: I'd sit at the word processor for an hour (or until I had completed X number of pages), and didn't move for *any* reason. I found incidences of lapses in my thought process during this time to shrink, and the actual number of pages I wrote to grow.

Those teachers who would find this kind of planning successful: tenacious ones; teachers with a large bladder and excellent bladder control. Sitting in one place until the task is through requires great self-discipline (and, perhaps, a nicely padded buttocks).

By the Hair of Your Chinny-Chin-Chin

And when do most of us (male types) pay attention to our, uh, chin—and other aspects of our face? That's right: when we *shave!* And just when do we usually shave? Correct: in the *morning!* Unless you are an Italian woman, shaving does not apply to the ladies, but the symbolic nature of the time frame in focus here is still relevant. Which is to say—utterly offensive metaphorical intent and cuteness of technique aside—we wait . . . and then do our lesson planning in the morning, perhaps, a few moments to an hour or so before we leave for work.

Two key factors here, however: (1) We work at home (adding to the uniqueness to this format); and (2) we leave enough time to complete our task. The disadvantage of trying to plan lessons while actually driving to work probably requires no elaboration. The bottom line: We relish the comforts of planning our daily schedule while working in the *morning—*writing to our heart's content, reading to allay fears of any last minute ignorance about our topic, and maybe practicing our lecture in order to avoid sounding like a bumbling idiot while those brazen fourteen-year-olds are sizing us up.

Teachers for whom this kind of planning would be successful: morning people—and procrastinators; some folks can't get going unless they have gotten a good night's sleep—or don't get going until their backs are braced up against a wall.

By a Yearning for Instant Gratification

Most teachers get their job satisfaction only when they acknowledge the fruits of their labors.

Just how do we know whether or not we have produced any, uh, *fruit*? We can't just say to ourselves, "Boy, that was a really good class today! Turned out some pretty tasty fruit!" I mean, we *can* just say this, but its meaningfulness pales next to, "Wow! I accomplished just what I wanted to today!" Which is to say, "I decided what I wanted to do, what I wanted the kids to do—and guess what? All of us done-did what I had planned!"

Mr. Palladin is one of the most respected teachers in his school. He participates in several adult, staff-related committees; he works with students outside his classroom. He has won several teaching awards; his administrators do not nag him, even though he constantly strays from a well-laundered format administrators expect all teachers in their school to follow. Students always have good things to say about Mr. Palladin. He is not as young as most teachers; he is not old as I am. He's *just right* (although, frankly, a *little* on the old side).

Technically, Mr. Palladin has never turned in a formal lesson plan in his life, for (in *those* days) he had not been required to do so, even for his college education courses. But here's a recreated conversation I had with Mr. Palladin (the tone I recall), with Mr. Palladin's views on teacher planning and similarly related topics:

Me: You're known as a bit of a rebel around these parts—a maverick.

Mr. P.: Yeah. Me and John McCain.

Me: Does your administration give you a hassle?

Mr. P.: Come on, Bruce! I've been here longer than all the administrators at my school have been here—combined! What's the shelf life of a high school administrator—five years?

Me: (settling him down with a smile) Right. But you must admit, you like to do things your own way.

Mr. P.: (with a scoffing chuckle) I'm always going to do what's best for kids. Sometimes the powers that sit up in their ivory towers don't really get that; they have other agendas. Does this qualify as planning? Every day before I arrive here [at school], I've figured out what it is I wanted my students to know by the end of a particular class period. In my *head* I've decided how I'm going do that. The really cool thing is when I know they learned what I wanted them to learn. But you already know that, Bruce.

Me: Nice, but how do you assess their learning for that day?

Mr. P.: I might test them at the end of the period. I might have them make a brief oral presentation. But mostly, I just know.

Me: Can you provide us an example?

Mr. Palladin sighs, leans back in his chair, and provides a verbal example of what had been a recent lesson plan. Most teachers will have to jot down their objectives, but it really doesn't have to be too radical:

LESSON:	muscles in the human body
DURATION:	Three days
ACTIVITY: (day one):	Post-it notes kinesthetic labeling
MATERIALS:	five hundred Post-it notes, fifty pencils, textbooks
ASSESSMENTS:	brief quiz, observation

The beauty here comes in its proclivity for immediate results, something a teacher can genuinely grin about each day during his ride home.

Teachers for whom this kind of planning would be successful: veteran teachers who rebuke change, invoke their own form of rebellion, and resist instructions (also a *bad* ass whose wry grin is infused with the knowledge of a veteran teacher who has planned to retire six months from the day of his interview for this book).

By Setting Up a Checkmate

Zach had wanted to become a teacher ever since his tenth grade year. Impediment after impediment, however, followed him around: poor grades, a messy divorce by his mother and father, mononucleosis taking him our of school for over a month, a girlfriend who wound up caring more about boozing at parties than she did about caring for Zach, and diversions in football, football, and more football.

Finally, after six years of floundering around as an accountant for a small chain of mini-mall laundry franchises, Zach decided to go back to school as a math major and earn his teaching credential.

He began teaching junior high school in 1996, and has never regretted his decision to leave the business world for a universe of adolescent boys who engage in farting contests, grabbing each other's rear ends, and besting one another with a plethora of rap music profanities.

"The fact that I can help do something in these kids' lives that will help them with their problems," Zach told me, "makes me glad I became a teacher. And besides," he grinned, "I *love* numbers! Now I work with numbers every day with the special joy of trying to get America's kids turned on to numbers, too!"[5]

To each his own of course; but Zach brought with him to the teaching sphere his numbers personality: an orderliness, a systematic, organized, cut-and-dried slant on teacher preparation.

In his lesson planning, Zach took no prisoners; he had a mission.

My son is a competitive chess player—even at the tender age of six; for him, everything has to be constantly organized and analyzed and processed in his young mind. He also—and I don't think coincidentally—loves numbers, which is quite unlike his mother and father—who love words much more than numbers; in fact, my wife and I don't like working with numbers at all.

Exploring a mind like Zach's—or my son's, for that matter—is helpful in the lesson-planning analysis in this context; for a chess player must be able to see simultaneously a broader range of the landscape *and* the immediate picture; for example, the chess player searches for what he must do his very next move in order to set up—or escape—a checkmate. But he also looks several moves ahead in order to gleam where his current trend of play will inevitably lead him.

In the wonderful film, *Searching for Bobby Fischer*, the twelve-year-old chess master finishes off his opponent in a championship tournament by projecting *fourteen* moves ahead of their current play![6] He had immediate goals; he also had set long-range goals that would eventually come into fruition *by reaching his immediate goals* in a proficient, expedient manner.

You can't cheat while you're playing chess—and you shouldn't; you shouldn't cheat while you're using this method of lesson planning either. It's convenient; it's practical, and it's efficient. But frankly, it requires a certain kind of mind to make it work—a mind like that of Zach, who has already mastered this method of planning.

Here is a groovy example:

- Topic: practical algebra
- Immediate goal(s): understanding equations and identifying situations in the real world in which knowing how to work equations is advantageous and important
- Long-term goals: efficiency, efficacy, and accuracy in computing equations
- Teaching methodologies: lecture, peer pairings, individual practice, peer review, class discussion

Note that Zach would have skipped the last step. Since he already had embedded it in his head, he probably wouldn't have written anything down on paper. Forced to turn it in to his desk-glued principal, he would have jotted down as little as he could have gotten away with. "Why spend all that time writing this stuff down?" he might have asked in exasperation. "I know it; I *do* it. If anyone wants to look at it, fine. But otherwise, please don't bug me."

This fairly well also sums up the philosophy of most chess champions, as well: calculation, processing, courage, and good old-fashioned common sense (and a lack of patience for us plebeians).

Those teachers for whom this sort of planning would be successful: really smart ones—teachers who see the whole picture and aren't stuck on the minutia; teachers who exasperate those who are jealous of others' patience, intelligence, and organizational skills.

Checkmate.

By the Book

And there are hundreds of books about teacher lesson planning. Pick one. Pick several. Scores of America's mostly widely accepted education experts have already provided us with their ideas for how and when to do lesson plans.

Administrators remain persistent in asking for lesson plans, especially on the elementary school level; and college educators continue to instruct students how to do them. These plans may be even more tedious than any of the examples provided in this chapter, or they may be as simple, as, well, flying by the seat of your pants.

Teachers for whom this type of planning is successful: usually beginning teachers—but by the time they have wised up to the value of the old-time approach, they probably have decided they don't want to be teachers anymore.

Here are a few sources for finding (ho-hum, hum-drum) lesson plan templates. They can run anywhere from so simple as can be, to so arduous and boring they push you in the direction of wanting to quit teaching and take a job filling cat litter boxes at the local pet shop. Check out (if you must) these book titles in the endnotes, as you may need them: *Am I Teaching Well?*[7] and *Writing Effective Lesson Plans: a 5-Star Approach;*[8] and *Lesson Plans That Wow!*[9]

Seriously, check them out. You'll come crying on your knees right back to this very chapter!

Finally, I would plead five quick reasons for *some* kind of lesson planning (in case you have come away from these suggestions with a notion that it's better for a teacher to walk totally unprepared into her classroom):

1. You increase your efficiency.
2. You maximize your effectiveness
3. You relieve your stress.
4. You have at your disposal a strong, a well-documented defense—just in case your administrators begin to pester you about your methods of preparation.

5. You obliterate any self-doubts you may have harbored about taking your career as a teacher seriously, (and forget about that plot brewing in your mind to gather up the family, move to Alaska, and start up your own school—free from mandated lesson planning).

Frankly, some of us plan very little—not because we are so good, but because we are so lazy. My theory is that teachers who don't plan wisely last only a very tiny amount of time in this profession. And it isn't because they get canned; it's because they become so unsettled by their own ineptness, they despise showing up for school. In their heart of hearts, they know darn well their students are jumping at the bit, just waiting to eat them alive.

NOTES

1. Shannon Griffin, "Why New Teachers Quit," *Creative Loafing*, July 19, 2007, at charlotte.creative loafingloafing.com.gyrobase/content?oid=oid%3a3284.
2. Mark R. Rosekind, "The Cost of Fatigue Is Great," *Sleep and Dreams Magazine*, October 30, 2007, 2.
3. *Stand and Deliver*, Warner Bros., 1988; What teacher *hasn't* been inspired by that film?
4. *Directed Teaching* is the term often used to describe an approach used by a teacher who leads his classroom in a learning activity, as the entire class participates at once. The teacher lectures, asks and answers questions, assigns drills, and provides almost immediate oral feedback.
5. Zach does sound insane. He really does believe that his students turn on to *numbers* rather than the actual money a mastery of these numbers often promises.
6. *Searching for Bobby Fisher* (Miramax Films, 1993); The chess player in real life is John Waitzkin.
7. Hanna Cabaj and Vesna Nikolic, *Am I Teaching Well?* (Toronto: Pippin Publishing, 2000).
8. Peter Serdyukov and Mark Ryan, *Writing Effective Lesson Plans: The 5-Star Approach* (Upper Saddle River, NJ: Allyn & Bacon, 2007).
9. Stephanie Dyke, Ed McCormick, and Jon Weiman, *Lesson Plans That Wow! Twelve Standards Based Lessons* (Summit, NJ: Teaching Press, 2007).

16

Strategize under
a Core Umbrella

When Mike Scioscia took over the helm of the Los Angeles Angels (then Anaheim Angels) in 1999, he brought with him several of his former teammates from the Los Angeles Dodgers; these Dodgers of yesteryear became the club's prized coaches, all working diligently to instill a philosophy for how to play baseball, strategies that work best for a team to win, and proper ways for professional ballplayers to present themselves to others on and off the diamond.

Something must have clicked. Scioscia's teams became progressively more successful; they eventually won the World Series in 2002, and have been crowned champions of the Western Division of the American League five out of the last six years. In 2008 the Los Angeles Angels—though a loser to Boston in the playoffs—racked up the best record in all of baseball, having clinched the division title sooner than any other team in baseball history—September 10—a full three weeks before the end of the regular season.

Looking at Scioscia, you don't really notice anything too impressive; in fact, he could be your Uncle Mike from Philadelphia—the guy who visits you every year around Christmastime with plenty of presents. Mike Scioscia seems to be a quiet, unassuming, humble man; he never tries to steal the limelight from his players, and his earthly modesty sometimes gets on peoples' nerves. Yet, Scioscia has been considered by many baseball aficionados to be one of the best managers in baseball today—a prime fillet cut among others who would qualify comparably, at best, as decent hamburger or ground round. Many have predicted Scioscia to become a future Hall of Famer—not from his prowess as an everyday catcher—but as *the* manager of the Los Angeles Angels.[1]

Jon Heyman of *Sports Illustrated* had this to say about Mike Scioscia: "Scioscia, who may be baseball's best manager, was the main man in the team's turnaround at the top of the century."[2] (Later in the article, Heyman pegged Scioscia to top the writer's personal list of baseball's best managers.)

For Scioscia's Angels, these fifteen mandates conglomerated to form the organization's core philosophy(ies), with Mike Scioscia (the teacher) at the rudder, and his players, coaches, and even clubhouse boys (his students) absorbing them and then implementing them to reach plateaus in their Los Angeles Angels baseball lives:

1. Play harder, but play *fair*.
2. Run the bases with abandonment, but don't be stupid.
3. Character counts—a *lot*.
4. They'll still remember us fifty years from now. What would you like for them to think of us?
5. We're thinking of the long term, even if the short term hands us challenges and setbacks.
6. Baseball is *not* life; it's *about* life.
7. Stand up to those who would get in our way; if we're wrong, have the honor to admit it, apologize, make restitution, and move on.
8. Develop our farm system; the young players are our future.
9. The home run is nice, but given a choice, several base hits and a few walks in an inning are even better.
10. It's about our fans. Without our fans, we wouldn't even have jobs.
11. Baseball is about a team, not about a bunch of individuals.
12. Sacrifice: bunts, fly balls—giving yourself up to advance the runner.
13. No scoreboard watching during the game; concentrate on the task at hand.
14. Tradition matters.
15. Dazzled by the numbers—the statistics and the percentages—don't lose sight of the fact that each one of us is an actual *human being*.

If we can narrow this myriad of mandates into one core philosophy that has governed the Los Angeles Angels for the past several years; it may go something like this:

Winning baseball games is clearly—without a doubt—our primary goal, but we will do it with grace, dignity and fairness. Baseball is a splice of humanity, but without graceful, principled interactions with each other and those who respect and admire us, the ring of winning baseball games is a hollow one, indeed. With maximum effort, a style of play that relies on scoring runs in smaller numbers, and a group of close-knit, like-minded players, we fully intend to develop ourselves into the elite of Major League Baseball.

OK, what's this, you ask? What does all of this have to do with teaching? This is a *teachers'* book, Bruce—and a book for would-be teachers; why are you torturing us with your nutty passion for baseball? What a waste of your publisher's maximum-word-count boundaries!

Sorry—or maybe glad—to disappoint you; it all depends on the way you view education (and baseball). But there is a terrific, fascinating parallel between teachers and the L.A. Angels—and Mike Scioscia. Yeah, you heard that right. Mandates and core philosophies all add up to one thing: becoming superior (at least *better*) at what you do. A core philosophy is like the setup for the manned space program. At space central sit the decision makers and gurus for the mission, while all activity around them emanates from their positions of authority. What the astronauts ultimately do, and how they conduct their activities rely almost exclusively on the orders that flow from space central, whether that hub resides in Washington D.C., Miami, or Houston.

So now that you have a definition of *core philosophy*, let's take a look at the fifteen mandates for a Major League Baseball team, and then we'll reach a core philosophy—not for baseball—for *teaching* that flows from those mandates; remember, unless we begin with mandates, arriving at a core philosophy is nothing more than a mere shot in the dark.

FIFTEEN MANDATES FOR A MAJOR LEAGUE BASEBALL TEAM:

1. Play harder, but play fair.

The emphasis in this one is on the word *harder*. The presumption is that we have already been working hard at what we do; and if we're already teachers, that we've been teaching hard. Now the mandate is a tad different: Dig down deep, suck it up, and give a little extra.

As for playing fair: Don't step on other people's toes. If you're going up the ladder, give some consideration about climbing up those rungs, over whom you're stepping over to get to the top. Don't hammer someone when's he's down. Wait your turn in line; sometimes this means in a line for promotions, special recognitions, or steps up the salary scale.

2. Run the bases with abandonment, but don't be stupid.

I was stupid.

And depending upon whom you talk to, I may be stupid now.

Early in my career I did very, very dumb stuff. I had originally been hired as a speech and debate coach with the possibility of dabbling in the drama department, and this left me susceptible to various opportunities for dumbness that could never have been measured on a stupidity scale, they were so incredibly brainless. It's not that I conducted myself in a manner that had been blatantly immoral, but I certainly crossed the line of the inappropriate. After all, I had been told to work hard, plow forward, and take no prisoners when it came to thrusting myself into my job.

Teaching was challenging, I had been warned; the kids will walk all over you, if you don't show them by your actions that you are in control, you are the master, you are absorbed by your dedication and commitment to your work. So that's exactly what I tried to do; unfortunately, too much unsupervised time (meaning the hours I spent with the students outside the classroom) absorbed *me*, permitting me on certain occasions to lose my sense of good judgment. I was also young and immature, which didn't augur well for a guy who wanted to accelerate to the top of his profession before any practical measure of time and experience would allow him to do so.

I know. You'd like to hear what in the heck I mean here. Some examples, please!

Without any of the ugly specifics, let it suffice to say that I had done one, some, or all of the following during the first ten years I taught high school. I offer these as a warning to you. How I managed to survive in my career for thirty-eight years should be a topic for a book written about this phenomenon by someone else:

- took my students to 'R' rated films in Hollywood;
- attended my students' parties;
- drove students to various events—even paid for them—sometimes without signed parental permission slips;
- shielded their personal tales of sex, pregnancy, and abortion without going to my students' parents to tell them about their own child;
- used profanity—some real zingers;
- fought counselors and administrators in order to stand up for my students, even though my students had been *wrong*.

By the grace of—whomever—I managed to escape the history of my inane activity and poor, unprofessional choices. Time cured all ills—except for the kids now grown into adults who mock me every chance they get. I suppose complacency and maturity overcame desperation and immaturity. I survived my assault on good sense, and life has gone on. I'm still employed, fairly well respected (until people read this anyway), and brimming with wisdom that should be passed on to others.

Whew! Did I luck out—or what!

Yes, go hard, work hard, play hard.

But don't be stupid.

3. Character counts. A lot.

Here's the kind of teacher you can choose to become: one who considers doing the right thing at the top of his list of life's priorities, and who spends every morsel of his energy instilling this ideal in his students—the same ones who rip off soda at McDonald's by requesting water cups and then filling them with Coca-Cola. Life is short, unpredictable, and you want your students to know this well, so that they may live up to the virtues decent people expect from other human beings . . . before it is too late to make other choices in lifestyle.

The problem is many of your students gag at your rhetoric; they don't believe *any* human being can live up to your descriptions and expectations. They think only men and women over the age of 150 would even *think* about taking your approach to humanity, let alone your philosophy as a teacher. They give you high marks for teaching, but low marks for honesty, simply because they don't think you can possibly be the real deal. It will now be *your* task to convince them that a man or woman like you actually exists—and the best way for you to do this is through your ongoing behavior.

At funerals we talk about a man's faithfulness or his compassion; we're silent about the amount of money he has left in the bank or the beautiful suits he wore to work. Ripping two hundred base hits in a single season on seven different occasions may be an astonishing achievement.[3]

But Pete Rose will probably never get into baseball's Hall of Fame.

4. They'll still remember us a hundred years from now; what would you like for them to think of us?

Baseball is a peculiar game in that its history thrives forever, much like American history which lives for all eternity. Great players of the past are not forgotten, and many of those who made only a temporary appearance on the game's stage are usually the butt of jokes many years after their tenure in the game had been over (maintaining a type of unenviable immortality).

Teachers, too, can go either way. We have all had teachers we remember still—and will remember until the day we, too, exit our stage. We recall some of our teachers as being energetic, brilliant, and inspirational; others we recollect as listless, ignorant, and dull. In fact, some of our teachers invoke horrible memories for us, better forgotten than brought back in any form.

Which teacher are you planning to be?

It's *now*—not later—that seeds the fruit of your students' memories.

And what we actually teach our students stays with them for a long, long time.

Or not.

5. We're thinking of the long term, even if the short term hands us challenges and setbacks.

John Litham began his teaching career in 1987. After having attended four different colleges to earn his credential, he journeyed into the market to land his first teaching position. It took him two weeks to be called for an interview at the school of his dreams. John said to me, "After I received a call from the personnel department from [name of that district], I began dancing around the house—literally. My roommate, who worked as a finance manager at a loan company, just sat there shaking his head.

And then John Litham found out he had throat cancer.

"I had this feeling I could never completely swallow anything," he said. "I decided to get it checked out before school began in September. Actually, I didn't get the diagnosis until the second day of the school year. Imagine, you begin a new life, and one day into that new life, you find out you have a disease that has a very good chance of killing you."

After having opened the first two days of the school year with his new science students, John was forced by his fate to miss the next three weeks. Surgery had taken its toll, and John's doctors set up a regimen for radiation treatments.

When John returned to his classroom, his students barely recognized the former robust, handsome young instructor who had stood before them only a few weeks before. But John never lost his enthusiasm; in fact, as he lay in the hospital, weakened and racked with pain, he had clung dearly to his yearning to return to teaching. He had already gotten a taste of it; he needed to get back. All sorts of self-destructive, melancholy ideas rattled his brain; but somehow Mr. Litham would use this awful experience determined to become the best teacher in the science department at his new school, even though the totality of his professional experience had ranged somewhere in the neighborhood of ten hours.

But those nagging thoughts about his mortality wouldn't go away. All his grandiose plans for the future may never materialize; after all, he had cancer—and a deadly form of cancer. Perhaps fate had handed him a kick in the groin he would never recover from. Maybe the full extent of his illustrious teaching career would take place only in his mind and soul.

Twenty-one years later, and John Litham still stands before his students in room 45C at the same high school he had begun teaching so many years before (different students, by the way, in case you were wondering about that). Mr. Litham's cancer had gone into remission, he passed the crucial five-year period without its return, and now he works as though it had never happened—except for one thing: His mental outlook on life, on teaching, and on his future had been forever changed.

If there were ever a human being who would have been forced to think only about the short term in his life, it should have been John Litham. The old adages about taking life each day as it comes, about living only for the moment, should have reigned supreme.

But John possessed a different point of view. He explained, "The possibilities of doing wonderful things with my life, of making a difference in the world, never left me. Even through all those horrors, I knew I had a choice—a very simple choice: live to live, or live to die. I had to survive the current day—and then the next, and then the next. But for me to do that, I also had to look far into the future; I had to know what it was I wanted to achieve, just where I wanted to be in my life thirty years from now. Of course, I took each day as it came, and I relished those days like I never would have done before my illness. But my dreams and goals kept me functioning and able to get through some very tough times."

For John, this meant also having a wife and a family. He has been happily married for fourteen years and is the beaming father of a twelve-year-old daughter he adores more than life itself.

For John, long-term planning also meant getting an advanced degree in his field. John received his master's degree in 1993; in fact, while working on this degree he met his beautiful wife-to-be, then a secretary in the college's finance office.

The future for John also meant something else: Every lesson he taught his students—nay—every *day* he planned with his students would have an *end*, a *goal*, that would make that day special. Lecturing to his kids about the anatomy of a frog may have seemed ludicrous to his students at the time, but their ultimate understanding of the human body, it's organs, and how they work could not have happened as quickly and as successfully without an appreciation for the temporary—and even the mundane.

6. Baseball is *not* life, but it's *about* life; it's not only about baseball.

Teaching is not life—not for most people. Although parents teach their children and employers teach their employees, when it comes right down to it, during most of our lives, we teach at our own speed and at our own pace; we're not burdened with clocks, bells, and nagging parents and administrators. But here's the caveat: Teachers—to be effective and respected—must teach *about* life's real issues.

Those of us who have managed to let the world slip out of our classrooms have probably allowed our students' minds to slip out of our classrooms, as well. Their minds no longer focused, and their emotions no longer vested in what we are giving them every day, they might as well have never come to class at all. Somewhere along the line they have uttered to themselves, "This sucks. Why do I need to learn this?"

Some teachers have looked at their profession as life itself, an *end* rather than a means to an end; their goals have engulfed their desire to be the best teacher they can be. Why? They want exactly that: to become the best teacher they can be. Everything in their existence lives and dies inside their classrooms, their lesson plans, and their assessments of their students. Their administrators' evaluations are always held in a cynical light because, after all, what can a school administrator really know about what goes on in a teacher's life, in her classroom—in her psyche?

Not being able to see the forest from the trees is a real problem for these teachers. Their goals are obscured by the obsessive/compulsive approach they take to teaching. Whereas the vast majority of us would admit it is a positive trait for a teacher to care about the quality of his teaching, to care about his students, and to care about advancing himself professionally, hardly anyone would give a stamp of approval to those teachers who throw themselves into their jobs with an abandonment that others would find rather eccentric.

And these teachers die early.[4]

And wouldn't that be a bummer?

But—and here's the good news—when teachers make their careers about *teaching about life,* they are, in fact, taking their students to the top of the learning mountain.

If teachers can incorporate real life into their lessons, students will have a clearer understanding of:

- why they need to compute numbers
- why they need to understand what they read
- why they need to know the process of how life sustains itself
- why they need to be able to synthesize and organize their thoughts and ideas
- why they need to know the reasons we study history
- why they need to know the functions of the three branches of government
- why they need to know how to give a speech
- why they need to know how to locate Iran on a map
- why they need to write a clear, concise, well-supported paragraph

Teachers must take the peak ideas and concepts in their course curriculum and ask themselves whether or not these ideas and concepts are about real life. If they aren't, they ought to consider depositing their planning books in a trashcan.

7. Stand up to those who would get in our way; if we're wrong, have the honor to admit it, apologize, and move on.

"You know what I can't stand about men?" a former girlfriend confided in me after one of our patented arguments about the differences between men and women. "Men never-ever apologize for their mistakes and bad judgments. They go right to the *edge* of doing it, but they never do it!"

I should point out here that she hurled her hasty accusations at me immediately after I had apologized to her for one of my mistakes and bad judgments. Never mind, that despite my contriteness, she flew at me with the wrath of that evil-queen stepmother chick in the movie *Enchanted*.[5] Still, the gist of what she said held its own veracity. She was right; men in general do not apologize often or well, and women are not accomplished at getting them to really mean it when they do apologize.

A teacher friend of mine gave the wrong standardized test to his math students. He simply took the incorrect stack from the testing room and distributed them without checking—probably without looking at them at all. After recognizing his error, and with all his students sitting in his classroom, he hurled insults about the incompetent fools who had placed all the test booklets in an unorganized disarray about the testing room, and then he dug into the school's administrators for permitting such a tight, inflexible schedule, one that would not allow for screwups like his (not his words) to correct themselves.

When the teacher in charge of testing heard about my friend's tirade, he walked over to his classroom, and the following after-school exchange ensued:

Test Teacher: Hey, [Eddie], what in the hell have you been telling people? That it's *my* fault that you were stupid enough to give your students the wrong test? That it was *my* fault?

My Friend: Who put the tests out there without labeling them properly—and so close together? Not me!

Test Teacher: You're really wrong about this one, [Eddie]. You ought to take responsibility for muffing it—and not try to pin it on everyone else. And that's as clear as day.

Sometimes simply doing what Test Teacher admonished my friend to do—to take responsibility for your mess ups, inadequacies, or bad decisions—has such a soothing effect on those around you. It also does wonders for your reputation; once you have said, "I'm sorry," who can legitimately be angry with you anymore? Most people—even professionals—are forgiving and understanding about the frailties of other human beings. This is also true in the teaching community, a place in which a few other human beings actually have been known to exist.

Students need to hear you take responsibility. When you apologize for not returning their papers in a timely manner, for losing their work, having no answers to their inquiries after you had promised them you would find those answers for them, making an error in judgment when it came to a reward or punishment issue, forgetting to call their parents, not showing up for a tutoring session, failing to explain a concept clearly, goofing up in a grade computation—and so on and so on—when you apologize to them, it's safe to say they not only will forgive you, they will know that you, too, are a human being.

And a decent human being at that.

8. Develop our farm system; the young players are our future.

Old teachers never die; they just fade away.

Actually, they sometimes just drop dead.

Our schools always have their sights set on the future (sometimes to the detriment of the present). How teachers are trained, recruited, and mentored has more to do with the success of our schools than almost anything else we regulate within the education system. Many great teachers are born teachers; they already know what to do, and their personalities are suitable for planting themselves in their classrooms and just going at it. True: Tips, workshops, textbooks, and friendly reminders (such as those you read here) have their places, and they do impact what kids learn—or don't learn—in the final analysis. But natural talent and spirited personalities make it possible for some teachers to reign supreme before students.

In the meantime, while the establishment is searching for *you*—school boards are forced to hang on to veteran teachers, a nonsolvent proposition, because they have to pay them twice as much in salary as they do beginning teachers. A first year teacher in my district makes about forty-six thousand dollars; a guy who's been lingering around perched on his tush for the last six thousand years years makes close to ninety-two thousand dollars.[6] So . . . having *which* teacher in the classroom is to the financial benefit of the school board? Unless veterans retire on their own recognizance, they return to their classrooms year after year after year, even though the taxpayers can get two new teachers for the price of one old fart. The employment of which teachers is the better financial bargain? Hmmm?

Administrators know that seasoned teachers, despite their age and Geritol energy spans, are generally better teachers than the young whippersnappers just exiting from education colleges. Remember, the veterans—the *proven* ballplayers—make the real dough; they have repeatedly demonstrated their effectiveness and ability to perform under pressure. But these are also the players who have a greater propensity to bankrupt the franchise.

9. The home run is nice, but given a choice, several base hits and a few walks in an inning are even better.

Hitting home runs has made a lot of men rich. But other men have become wealthy because of their high batting averages. You achieve high batting averages by getting lots of hits—singles—which look just as good as home runs when it comes to figuring out a batting average for the season; in fact, if you hit even a ground ball single only 30 percent of the times you batted during your baseball career, you would wind up a multimillionaire and eventually be inducted into the Hall of Fame.[7]

What's the equivalent of hitting a homerun for a teacher? I put that question to a whole bunch of teachers, and when they came to understand what I meant (which is a pretty neat trick, because *I* wasn't sure what I meant), they gave me the following comments:

- getting through to someone: "My student finally got the concept! Sometimes they even smile, and that makes it better, too."
- telling me that I did a good job: "I ask my students to fill out evaluations and comment forms at the end of each semester, and they mostly energize me; some students are actually glad I was their teacher."
- running smoothly: "Things go well on a given day—fewer obstacles and challenges for some reason—and you just know that you did an especially jazzy job that day."
- doing well on a test: "I love it when tests come in showing a semblance of student achievement. It can be a standardized test or one designed by me for my course; I know they learned!"
- returning to give thanks: "Students sometimes come to back to school after they've left my class or after they've graduated, and they praise me for what I've taught them; or they just talk about what a valuable, worthwhile experience they've had. At a recent back-to-school night, I met a former student, a smiling older woman I had taught thirty-six years ago; her daughter had also been in my class—and now I am teaching her granddaughter. And she told me she was quite happy about the whole lineage!"

- applying a life's lesson: "Students sometimes give me examples of how what I taught them made a difference in their lives; they actually applied what they learned through our literature. Once a troubled girl told me that she dumped her abusive boyfriend because of a newspaper article we had read in class about handling abusive males. She worked up the courage to get rid of the creep; and when she let me know about it, I was stoked."

Memories of home runs in the past chill me with excitement; but most of us get through our days—not with home runs, for they are few and far between—with singles, doubles, and triples: Your students show up on time; your own attendance has been splendid; you explain a concept with unusual clarity; you crack a good joke; a kid who never reads enjoys a book; a kid who never passes a test scores above 70 percent on a test; your students put their books neatly away; you handle a discipline problem particularly well; you develop a special lesson plan that actually works; you eat a good lunch; you have constructive engagement with a parent; you assist a student in finding her own solution to settling the drama in her life; you go through an entire class session without yelling at anyone, writing a discipline referral, or becoming particularly agitated inside. . . .

If you rely mostly on home runs, your batting average is going to reek. But if you factor in all the base hits—even minus home runs—your average still will rock. And what's more, you're on your way to winning a lot more games.

10. It's about our fans. Without our fans, we wouldn't even have jobs.

"I hate the kids."

"What?"

"I *hate* them!"

"Kind of extreme."

"What's extreme? I'm just letting you know how I feel."

"Yeah, but a teacher hating kids? What would their parents say if they knew you said something like that?"

"I don't care. I hate the parents, too."

In this exchange a hateful teacher may have forgotten a basic concept about the whole arena of education in the United States: If it weren't for the kids, he wouldn't have a job; in fact, no one who works in education would have a job.

What would *you* do if you weren't a teacher? And for those budding teachers, what's your next choice of profession—because I guarantee you, next to teaching, your second choice comes up a weak second in a lot of categories (salary, working conditions, holidays off, summer vacation, retirement plan, prestige) when that second choice is matched up with teaching.

So let's hear it from our greatest fans—and critics: the kids and their parents. Without them—to quote Willy Loman in *Death of a Salesman*: "I'm nothing, Biff! I'm nothing! I'm a dime a dozen! I'm nothing!"[8]

It's perfectly normal for you to claim you don't like *some* of the kids, but boasting you hate *all* the kids reflects mostly on *you*. It would be akin to working in a chocolate factory while despising the candy—and making it obnoxiously obvious to everyone else who works in that factory how much you loathe the chocolates.

Only in a chocolate factory, the workers don't have to eat the candy.

11. Baseball is about a *team*, not a bunch of individuals.

A school should work like a well-oiled machine. The teacher turns the crank (shows my age again), and that machine starts up its motor; the rotation of that machine's internal device fuels the nearly two hundred children he faces each day. Without the teacher, the wheel doesn't turn at all.

And what about the folks downtown? They lend their support to the guys in the trenches with the kids (or since I just conveniently broke from the original metaphor, to the guys who turn the wheel).

Occasionally—or, perhaps, nearly all the time—managers in the front office bark orders, release directives, and do inspections. United, these workers develop products they are proud of. The credit goes to the company as a whole—not usually singling out one individual or even a group of individuals.

This past season Ichiro Susuki had two hundred hits for the Seattle Mariners baseball team; the Mariners lost over one hundred games.[9]

There's not a whole lot Susuki could boast about, if the goal of the Seattle ball club had been to make it to the playoffs. He contributed nothing tangible toward meeting that goal, despite his impressive individual statistics. The net worth of your contribution is zero, if the desired result never materializes.

Maverick, rebellious teachers, administrators, and even school secretaries brew success stories by doing their own thing; but they often do not succeed in making a much more attractive product by themselves. And when it comes right down to it, they wouldn't even exist in their positions, if not for those peons (everyday folks, such as custodians, maintenance men, P.E. aids, gardeners, etc.) who labor endlessly around them.

12. Sacrifice: bunts, fly balls—give yourself up to move the runner.

Three types of sacrifices exist in baseball: A batter bunts the ball in order to move the runner from first to second or second to third base, even from third base to home plate; a batter hits a fly ball deep enough to the outfield in order to score a runner from third (or move other runners up a base); a batter intentionally hits a ground ball to the second baseman in order to advance a runner from second to third. He makes an out, but the runner now stands in a much more advantageous situation; for in any of these scenarios, the batter has been told by his manager—or has decided himself—to do what is best for the whole team, which is to move runners around the bases.

This kind of play doesn't necessarily help the batter to advance his individual statistics, and won't stand out during the off-season when it comes time for salary negotiations, but every member of the team—including the managers and players—knows his contributions for making the team better and moving them toward their eventual goal of winning a championship.

Teachers sacrifice all the time. Unlike players in a ballgame, however, their sacrifices too often go unheeded or unnoticed. Sometimes we teachers feel like standing atop a hill, screaming as loudly as we can about all we have done to give ourselves up for the good of our students.

Just a few examples:

- spending your own money on books and supplies and field trips and prizes/gifts and certificates and trophies for students
- giving up a movie—a date, the TV show, the gym, a good book, a walk in the park, a wedding, a peep show club in order to grade papers or (gasp) do lesson plans
- refraining from drinking, eating too much, gambling, or dressing like a slob within the borders of your own community—which, of course—is all good for you in the long run but quite boring and inhibiting, especially if you have an, uh, expressive personality
- losing sleep to do school work or to worry about school—whichever comes first
- going out of your mind with workshops, mentoring, seminars, inservices, and crusty, old presenters

The list of sacrifices is endless. But you know it's a means to an end. If teaching were not your priority, you would not have structured your goals to help you become a great teacher.

By nature—or a command from God—teachers are nurturers, givers, and the yeomen of our nation. If you constantly ask, "What's in it for me?" or grumble about doing your duties when others call out to you for help, at the end of the inning—or worse, just after the ballgame is over—you will see the runner, alone and forlorn, quietly stranded on third base.

13. No scoreboard-watching during the game; concentrate on the task at hand.

One of the most difficult tasks for teachers is to leave their baggage at home. Married teachers may have sick children or ornery spouses. Single teachers may have oppressive, demanding boyfriends. All teachers face challenges with their finances, relationships with friends, aches and pains in their body, annoying pets, leaky roofs, serious doubts about their self-worth, nosey neighbors, deaths in the family, insomnia, late night acid reflux, iron poor blood—or *all* the above.

During the slower moments of a baseball game, it's extraordinarily difficult for the fans in the stands, and even the players, not to watch the scoreboard—the line scores of other games being played around the nation. Before, during, and after a contest, this distraction commands our attention. The activities around us are sometimes a lot more interesting than the tasks in front of us. And usually the pressures we voluntarily invite into our lives, or those *forced* upon us—often *out* of our control—become major detractors, too. They are internal demons that require extrication in order for us to go on living and teaching.

The other day I picked up my six-year-old son from his martial arts class; I routinely asked him what he had learned today, and he replied triumphantly, "Focus!"

"Focus," I repeated, somewhat distantly.

"Yeah, Daddy, are you okay?" he asked, internally noting my lack of concentration.

"Fine," I answered. "I'm just looking at the car. It's getting old. Maybe we need to do something. And look how dirty it is! Maybe tomorrow we can take it to the car wash. Or maybe we can just take the hose out at home. Yeah, the car is getting old. I think it's safe. You think it's safe? [What a dumb question to ask a six-year-old!] So what was it you said you learned today in karate?"

"Focus," my son told me again, this time a bit miffed with my *unfocused* presence.

Focus.

Ironic, huh?

14. Tradition matters.

Because of its designation as the national pastime, baseball stands apart from all other sports.[10] Each sport also boasts of history, but only baseball can safely claim a very long, deep, rich tradition that comes from its very American roots. Slow to change, baseball has been intelligent enough to recognize that change (especially for the sake of change—or merely out of a panicky expediency) is not always good; in fact, in the cases of those projects already working successfully, change is hardly *ever* good. With change must come benefits that could not have been accrued under an umbrella of traditional circumstances; *change must imply progression—not regression.*

Education in the United States also has its traditions, but somehow they have imploded in the guise of progress. Obviously, as our student population metamorphoses and technology surges, attention must be paid to new ideas. Clearly, much of what we've tried and done in years gone by has already had its day, and now it's time to move forward.

But is *new* necessarily *forward?*

And, yes, certain traditions in teaching, schools, and education in general have not lost their luster, relevance, or importance.

Some traditions should always be treated with dignity and respect; for despite some of the doomsday prognosticators and liberal-minded do-gooders, these traditions have maintained their places in the annals of education accolades:

1. *Reading is first.* And this means learning how to read in English. Students can't learn if they can't read the textbooks, and the textbooks are written in English.
2. *Math computes.* Kids still need to know their multiplication tables; it's frightening to see those who don't. Many students are still counting on their fingers in the eleventh grade or using calculators to add double-digit numbers. Never mind the huge numbers of middle school kids who don't know the product of 6×7. (Uh, 42—right?)[11]
3. *Teachers teach; kids learn.* While students have much to contribute in the classroom, the teacher is the final authority. (See how much responsibility still weights on *your* shoulders?) I've never liked the theory of teacher as a *facilitator*. It sounds as though a computer can do that chore—and I don't like that idea either.
4. *America comes first.* If you don't teach in an American school, forget this one; but if you do, then it should be obvious. Unfortunately, it isn't. Too many educators want to internationalize our schools. Of course, we need to adapt to those who have come here and wish to integrate themselves into the culture of this country. But in the final analysis, this is the United States. Our kids need to know our history, our government, and how to read and write English. Even though many native citizens can't do any of these, ideas for assimilation are not from a wish list; they are an imperative. Later we can add to our ever-busy curriculum the study of cultures different from ours—that contribute to ours, nevertheless. Flag Day on June 14 means displaying the *American flag*; it doesn't mean parading flags

of 120 countries around the schools (as happened in Los Angeles several years ago).[12]

5. *Students dress appropriately for a special place called school.* Less than that, it's less special. If it's less special, then our kids will learn less.

6. *Teachers are backed up in their discipline policies.* First, teachers must establish those policies clearly; second, administrators must back teachers up. This means, home suspensions, in-house suspensions, deportations to Jupiter, detentions, work details, trash clean-up groups, and good old-fashioned public floggings. And then we can begin to think about discipline enforcement for the *students* in the school.

7. *Teachers command public respect.* Students refer to them as *Mr.* or *Mrs.*, unless, of course, they aren't quite sure (which, these days, is a distinct possibility).

8. *A division of labor in the school exists.* All these integrated decision-making boards and committees often muddle the issues, confuse the hierarchy of leadership, and generally tick people off. The principal is the head guy (or chick). He's the boss. What he ultimately decides *goes.*

9. *Schools are run from a local level of administration.* The closer to the action the leaders are, the better; this means, more local funding of our schools, more local control, and more leftover chocolate chip cookies from local bake sales.

10. *Parents get involved, but they don't rule the roost.* Teachers desire more parent influence and involvement in what happens at their school, but we don't like parents meddling. Seemingly—and I know this happens to be a very weird concept for some people to latch onto—*teachers* and other educators know best about how to educate our children: the methodologies, styles, and supplies necessary for student learning. But parents may know best what works for *their* individual children. These should mesh.

15. Overriding the numbers—the statistics and percentages—don't lose sight of the fact that each one of us is an actual *human being.*

Ludicrous philosophies about standardized testing and assessment have permeated the education community. Some schools are now called 800 schools[13]—and that's good; if a school is a 600 school, send your kids to Siberia before sending them to that school. Students are now 430 in reading—and that's good. But if they're a 200, send those kids to a dunce farm (which, really, I don't know where that is, but that's where my father often threatened to send my sister).

You know, and I know, and the kids know, heck, even my dead mother knew (when she was alive, of course) that schools are much, much more than a bunch of numbers. The only people who seemed to have not caught on to this reality are the policy makers and politicians, many of whom have influenced communities into changing their zoning so as to not be influenced in real estate values by some random testing number assigned to a neighborhood school. "The heck if I'm going to send my kids to Podunk High!"

"Why? Bad football team? Unqualified teachers? Dangerous school environment?"

"Nah. None of that. I'm just not sending my kids to no 650 school!"[14]

Even ballplayers are human beings, their numbers an artificial representation of who they really are. They may hit for a 220 average, but on life's stage of living and dying and loving and healing, they may be slugging around 350—in the scheme of things, a much more revealing rating for the worth of their existence.

Those were a lot of philosophical complexities coming at you all at once; let's stop here to summarize the truth: These are fifteen mandates for the Los Angeles Angels (based on my best guess and synthesis of the ball club's latest management directives) applied to teachers and schools as part of a parallel universe. But the task isn't for you to adopt all these ideas as your own (for that would be a preposterous and wasteful chore); your task is to sit with them, blend them together, and then ask yourself this all-important, significant, *crucial* question—perhaps, the most important question you will ever ask yourself as a teacher—or as a budding teacher: As a teacher, *what am I all about?*

Finally—and *briefly*—here are five core philosophies I have found stimulating, invigorating, and enriching. In my ever so humble, never-like-to-be-expressed opinion, these cores help to drive teachers to reaching their students and to elevating their own personal lives:

1. Students are a work in progress. My calling is to help complete that work in a way that allows students their own dignity, self-respect—and *eventual* autonomy.
2. Every day that I teach I give it my all; my focus is on the job I must do and the goals I must reach for that day, that term, that year. If I fail in my endeavors, I will maintain my dignity and decorum. I have, after all, given it my absolute best effort.
3. American values and traditions are sacred. I have been afforded astoundingly good fortune to be able to impart American values and age-tested wisdom to a new generation of Americans. I see a whole person in each child; I don't see a computation. Every child whose path crosses with mine will have an opportunity to develop

as a learned student, extraordinary human being, and committed American.

4. I am the leader; I am in charge. These children have been blessed with the good fortune to learn from me—my knowledge, my wisdom, and my goodness.

5. All I do—every move I make—comes down to what is best for children. Although I care about—and identify with—adults, my ultimate mission in life and in my teaching career, is to do what is best for children. Adults come second; even if I have to face adversarial situations and risk losing my position as a teacher—the academic, moral, and physical health of children comes first.

Pick one.

Combine them.

Embrace them all.

Make up your own.

You have chosen one of the toughest—yet, most rewarding—careers of all. You have been entrusted to protect the minds, bodies, and souls of other peoples' children. The parents of these children look to you with apprehension, but they also trust you and have high expectations. You have the power to be worthy of their trust and to meet their expectations. Through an abundance of hard work, clarity of mind, and a flagrant demonstration of passion, you can help to make everyone's dreams come true.

Your insanity has already driven you to be a teacher.

Or, perhaps, the teacher already in you has driven you to insanity.

NOTES

1. Scott Long, *The Juice Blog*, October 28, 2007, at thejuice.baseballtoaster.com/ archives/853276.html. As of now, there is not a whole lot in print on this topic, but writer Long seems to concur with my prognostication about Scioscia's future.

2. Jon Heyman, "Why Mike Scioscia Is the Best Manager in Baseball," *Sports Illustrated*, April 30, 2008.

3. From Wikipedia: The Online Encyclopedia, at wikipedia.com.

4. *NCEA Workload Health and Safety Survey*, 2007. www.geocites.com/conteach/ OSH_survey.htm.

5. *Enchanted* (Disney Pictures, 2008); Academy Award–winning actress Susan Sarandon played the evil queen all too well.

6. Salary scale for the Norwalk-La Mirada Unified School district in 2009.

7. This is based on the assumption that the vast majority of lifetime 300 hitters in Major League Baseball make millions of dollars a year and eventually get to the Baseball Hall of Fame.

8. Arthur Miller, *Death of a Salesman* (New York: Samuel French, Inc., 1948), Willy Loman, Act II.

9. *Yahoo Sports,* "Seattle Mariners 2008," at sports.yahoo.com/mlb/players/6615.

10. Ross Douthat, "The Best of All Possible Games," *The Atlantic,* March 11, 2008, 3–4.

11. If the bottom numbers in two fractions are the same, I can add them together. If the bottom numbers are different, I have absolutely no idea what to do with them.

12. This occurred a few years ago in a Los Angeles Unified School District, June 14th Flag Day Ceremony. Most schools in the district participated, and officials were proud of the huge number of diverse flags paraded that day around its schools.

13. An "800 School" means higher property values for homes in the surrounding neighborhoods that feed the school. Sometimes these amounts increase thousands of dollars, depending on the total score assigned to a particular school.

14. Joseph Serna, "Adams' Parents: Kids Aren't Shortchanged," *Daily Pilot,* January 23, 2008, 1, 3, at dailypilot.com/articles/2008/01/29/education/dpt-board meeting23.txt.

17

Observe—and Then Take It with a Grain of Salt

Jackson Axel (not his real name, thank goodness, but close enough, unfortunately) had wanted to become a teacher since he said his very first words ("money," "beer"), at the age of sixteen months; the little tyke then tried unsuccessfully to inspire his infant sister to verbalize these very same words. Frustrated that the newborn could do nothing but gurgle, poop, and cry, Jackson had an idea: When he was certain his mother and father were not looking, he knelt down in the infant's face and chortled those words over and over: "money," "beer." Not that a sixteen–month-old toddler inspires an accumulation of new words in an infant, but amazingly, his baby sister began uttering sounds that were strangely like the words Jackson Axel had been teaching her.

Well, not entirely, and in all probability, not at all, but to hear Jackson recall this story almost forty years later, you would swear that it bore a semblance of truth. "It was ingrained in my childhood psyche," he said four decades hence. "I was a teacher then—though I'm sure most people would consider I used questionable methods, even for a boy not yet two years old—and I'm a teacher now!"

Judging from what many of Mr. Axel's students and peers have said about him, he is a *superior* teacher now. Mr. Axel is known around his school as "the teacher to observe" for the younguns who have yet to be embraced by the sky above as aged enough or experienced enough to be labeled a full-fledged master teacher themselves. But by comparison—at least, to *Mr. Axel's* reputation—*nobody* else is qualified to be a full-fledged master teacher.

Teachers on Mr. Axel's campus have been known to step inside his classroom for a few moments for the sole purpose of discovering what this wonderful teacher might be doing with his American government students at any time of the day. Most teachers despise observing other teachers, especially teachers out of their own subject area; but those who take a look at Mr. Axel claim he is an exception.

As one advanced placement calculus instructor commented, "Exemplary teaching is exemplary teaching; I don't care what course it is. When I take a few moments from my day to watch Jackson in his classroom, it inspires me. I know full well that I could never pull off what he does with any degree of success, but that doesn't matter. After being with him, I feel encouraged to use my own methods and my own personality to teach my students calculus."

Good teachers breed other good teachers. All prospective teachers undergo extensive training during their internship or student teaching phase, but few young teachers have the good fortune of watching a plethora of excellent teachers in action. Although the observing teacher may go in with high hopes, excellent role modeling is not a certainty. Styles, genders, curriculums—even attitudes and core philosophies—should match up for the optimum growth of a young teacher.

Even longtime veteran teachers occasionally leave their abodes and wander into other teachers' classrooms, not only to learn what they *should* do, but to reinforce what they already are doing right. Often this is a confidence booster; so-called great teachers—those with top-notch reputations—inspire and stimulate others to emulate them in a manner the observing teachers can adapt to their own styles and skill levels.[1]

I used to detest watching other teachers teach; that is, until I had an opportunity to observe one of my own former students who later became a teacher instruct a high school freshman English class. While I always thought this guy would make a great teacher, I had never figured he would have been ready to *star* so early in his career.

On the day I visited his San Diego, California, classroom (before I saw his principal for a job interview), Bob Pacilio had been teaching only *four years*. Although getting hired for that teaching position never panned out for me, what I saw in Bob's classroom that day—his boundless energy, his contagious enthusiasm, his caustic sense of humor, his passion for the literature he was discussing, his quick, yet patient, pacing—proved to be an inspiration. The quality of my own performance as a classroom teacher was later bolstered, augmented by a mere one-hour observation of Mr. Pacilio—something I have never revealed to Bob.

I do hope he reads it here.

Pacilio has since gone on to become one of the most well known and highly regarded—and awarded—teachers in all of Southern California. In

1999 he captured the Teacher of the Year trophy—not just for his school or his school district—but for all of San Diego County.

I take absolute credit for Bob's success, since he had worked so closely with me when he was my student; and I'm sure he observed—and eventually emulated—every move I made in the classroom. By the way, if you believe this, you probably have not understood any of the other sarcasm in this book either. Bob Pacilio has become accomplished through his own hard work and dedication to teaching. He now has the honor, privilege, and good fortune to model his teaching style for hundreds of other teachers.[2]

Briefly, here are five important reasons for observing other teachers—in or out of your own subject area.

1. An enormous body of evidence suggests that observation is one of the most helpful ways of preparing teachers to do a better job—or even to become teachers in the first place.[3]
2. You pick up good habits. A lot of what you observe rubs off, even if you try and fight it tooth and nail—and many teachers have done just that: fought observing other good teachers tooth and nail.

    Actually, I never understood what is so powerful about a "tooth and nail."
3. You notice and learn what you should *not* be doing. Lots of teachers sit in classrooms and watch in introverted horror, as supposedly tremendous teachers demonstrate teaching styles and philosophies that don't have a *chance* of helping anyone else. As these veteran teachers are clearly embarrassing themselves, you say to yourself, "Well, now I know why I never tried *that* before."
4. You can do a hands-on, academically enriching study of the classroom. It's very tough to be objective about education at the very moment you are working in your own classroom with a bunch of hard-to-reach thugs. That's why it's so darn enlightening to sit back, glance at your notes and checklists, and *study* what's happening to *another* teacher. Much of your subjectivity slides into remote corners of your cerebral cortex, as you fill out check boxes and write analyses of what you have just witnessed. You can call on your notes and memory bank later on, when you need them the most.
5. You may now silence your administrators (or your professors) who claimed you have never done anything to improve your wretched results and miserable teaching style (or maybe not, but I meant that last point in jest, didn't I?).

So here's yet another example of why this book is different from other teacher books you may have skimmed—er—carefully studied: a unique observation scorecard! But first, a *typical* checklist for observing another teacher may have these items—or items like them:

- adheres to state-mandated content standards
- acts as a facilitator in order to meet students' needs
- promotes cooperative efforts in learning and in probing the curriculum
- provides an understanding of content objectives and long-term goals
- maintains order and discipline and in a continuous manner

First of all: Ha! Ha! Ha! Ha! Ha! Ha! Ha! Ha! Ha! Ha! Ha! Ha!
Sorry. That was very inappropriate and exceedingly unprofessional.

But: Ha! Ha! Ha! Ha! Ha! Ha!—anyway—because I can't react in the even *more* inappropriate and unprofessional manner that happens to be tempting me at this particular moment.

Come on! How do educators at any level keep a straight face while looking at this observation form? Keep in mind this is a sampling of only five items from a form; there are probably thirty to fifty other nebulous, unclear, vague, imprecise, unformulated check boxes on this same paper. If I had posted those, too, I would have typed "Ha!" for three or four more pages. But let's very quickly—and I mean that, because *quickly* is all it deserves—void the checklist items printed on these pages; it won't be difficult at all:

adheres to state-mandated content standards: A moron can do this—or make the observers *think* he's doing this. It's only when those health teachers are showing students how to unwrap condoms, or social studies teachers are vilifying our American military forces that we should start to become a bit dubious about teachers adhering to state standards.

acts as a facilitator in order to meet students' needs: Did you attend school all those years to get a license to become a *facilitator*? I didn't. And what does this mean anyway? That you don't have to work as hard as a real teacher?

promotes cooperative efforts in learning and in probing the curriculum: And what if you happen to be observing a teacher who—at a particular moment of his instruction—is *not* promoting cooperative grouping? Does not "promoting cooperative grouping" make him a bad teacher, one not worth emulating? Oh. Maybe he's just being a facilitator.

provides an understanding of content objectives and long-term goals: Yeah, like the gang-banger in the corner is going to stop daydreaming about the drug run later in the evening because you have made it clear to him that six months from now he will understand all punctuation rules and thereby eliminate comma splices from his text messaging. Uh-huh.

maintains order and discipline and in a continuous manner: Some schools have developed formal observation plans. In one school all teachers are required to observe during their conference period (one period per day) at least twice a month, once within their own subject discipline and once outside it.[4] Regular, standard evaluations forms or checklists are provided, and at the end of each month they are distributed to teachers.

As with the typical partial checklist offered above, who really knows what these observation criteria are all about? Even if teachers do claim to know what they're all about, they still need to consider the worth or relevance of the whole project, especially in light of the specific details— utter minutia—on the observation form.

What young—and work-in-progress— teachers *should* be doing is watching for traits that stand out, teachers who offer a refreshing mix of both traditional and less-than-traditional (though currently acceptable) styles and methodologies of teaching.

Thus, the new teacher observation form is born. Enjoy these, although I do expect you to take them more seriously than you probably took my idea about installing Jacuzzis in the faculty lounge (chapter 11). My new observation form would have the following ten areas listed, with nothing more than a check box next to each. If a teacher modeled the specific skill or demonstrated the required attitude *clearly* and *forcefully*, he would receive a check from the observing teacher or college student.

That's it.

This activity has much less to do with an observer rendering a nebulous check in a box (Check-in-a-Box? Isn't that a fast-food franchise?), than it does with that observer keeping her eyes acute, looking for a sampling of a particular skill or general attitude on the part of the teacher. So much of any judgment is subjective; one observer may conclude that a category should be checked off, while another observer doesn't find the evidence she's looking for in order for her to check a particular box. But the bottom line: All observers are at least *looking* for the same qualities. What they ultimately conclude individually means far less than the process that brought them to their conclusions.

I have put all ten categories in a simple format, easy for Xeroxing and distributing; and the procedure is so incredibly fast and simple, most teachers and would-be teachers would never balk at having to do this very minimum amount of required paperwork.

TEACHER OBSERVATION CHECKLIST

___ 1. This teacher role models professionalism: in attire, demeanor, and attitude.

___ 2. This teacher is commanding of the students' attention.

___ 3. This teacher demonstrates observable knowledge about the subject being taught.

___ 4. This teacher gleams with energy and enthusiasm throughout the class period.

___ 5. This teacher is definitely passionate about teaching his subject matter.

___ 6. This teacher generates a positive atmosphere of warmth and security throughout the classroom.

___ 7. This teacher handles—or appears capable of handling—major disciplinary problems fairly, effectively, and in a timely manner.

___ 8. This teacher appears to be organized.

___ 9. This teacher is likeable.

__ 10. This teacher reminds her students (without literally telling them) that they are very fortunate to have her for a teacher.

WHAT YOU LIKED ABOUT THIS TEACHER AND/OR STUFF ABOUT THIS TEACHER YOU WISH TO CRITICIZE:

_____

_____

During various stages of this book, each of these categories has been covered in detail. But if you are observing a teacher and need evidence or proof of these skills and attitudes, perhaps, we should briefly mention what it is you are looking for. Remember, all these are _subjective_—though observable—qualities; your verdict for each of them is, perhaps, less important than your specific _search_ for those isolated teaching characteristics during your observation.

Which means, by then some of these positive traits of great teachers could have rubbed off on _you_.

And, yes, they can be contagious, depending, of course, on each observer's personality type, willingness to absorb, or old grump factor.

1. The teacher role models professionalism: in attire, demeanor, and attitude.

As a personal preference, I don't prefer teachers who work without an air of professionalism. They undermine our authority; they diminish the quality of our profession. Nobody admires a doctor who does not act professionally. Why would the same not be true for a teacher?

2. The teacher commands the students' attention.

As you observe the teacher, make sure *your* attention is occasionally diverted to the eyes and body language of his students; after all, a receiver in a football game captures everyone's attention only after the quarterback has thrown him a pass. And nobody really cares anymore about the quarterback once he has thrown that pass. The kids will let you know how the teacher is doing. Visuals, unusual sounds, and weird movements and faces and gestures by the teacher all help to keep students interested. But in the final analysis, if they're not watching and listening, not much of what's taught is going to stay with the kids. It's the teacher's duty to capture—and keep—the children's attention.

3. The teacher demonstrates observable knowledge about the subject being taught.

I'll be one of the first to admit it: I'm very good at talking about things that I know absolutely nothing about—and then making it seem as though I do. At the same time, I'm also very good at detecting when other teachers are trying the same maneuver. Acting, as I indicated in chapter 6, is a beneficial talent for teachers to acquire, but fabrications of facts, statistics, sources, and information is not—and should not be—tolerated by anyone.

4. The teacher gleams with energy and enthusiasm throughout the class period.

Look at the teacher's movements; he should be covering a lot of territory physically. He should be gesturing as needed, using appropriate facial muscles to show actual emotions, and varying his voice levels—volume, rate, pitch—as he speaks. Even if his students look as though they're about ready to lapse into characters from *The Night of the Living Dead*,[5] notice how this teacher never misses a beat with his energy flow. Yes, it's possible to try *too* hard and become exasperated to the point of visible frustration; but a never-say-die attitude when it comes to really getting into the role of an exciting, enthusiastic, passionate teacher takes precedence over the possibility of feeling like an idiot.

5. The teacher is definitely passionate about teaching her subject.

Does she love what she teaches? Either way—yes or no—her passion for cell mutation, semicolon use, equations, photosynthesis, etc., must radiate during her performance. Yes, I again use the word "performance" because that's what it is when you love what you teach: It's a show. You're the showman. Steve Martin said that, too; he once wanted to become a schoolteacher because . . . teaching is a show.[6]

6. The teacher generates a positive atmosphere of warmth and security throughout the classroom.

When you walk into certain classrooms, you don't have to be there for longer than thirty seconds to see that learning is taking place. The kids seem happy, the teacher is busy, and the classroom sizzles with creativity. What you find in these classrooms is an atmosphere glowing with contentment and satisfaction. These classrooms are special. The teacher you're watching is responsible for that kind of climate, that sort of atmosphere, that wholly impressive environment. The kids respond when the teacher compels them; if they don't respond to him, the teacher has not been compelling enough.

7. The teacher handles—or appears capable of handling—major discipline problems fairly, effectively, and in a timely manner.

Bedlam can happen in a blink of an eye. When a student challenges his teacher or he simply requires some instantaneous intervention, the teacher—who already has a familiar, tried-and-true discipline plan in place—knows exactly what to do. Too often in the education arena you can observe what *not* to do: yelling, screaming, threatening, swearing, crying, complaining, even wall pounding.

A teacher should avoid all of these. Since there are no longer any three-foot paddles nailed to the wall above the chalkboard—in fact, there's no chalkboard—practically nothing frightens teenagers anymore when they're at school. Guito with the tank top, tattoos, and the bulging biceps is not going to magically appear in a classroom just in time to save the teacher from a surefire thrashing. (In fact, in some schools now, there are more students who look like Guito than there are security guards who look like Guito—and I'm referring to the *girls!*)

8. The teacher appears organized.

But she may not be organized at all. As long as teachers project their lessons in a manner that demonstrates a rhyme or reason or order, they pass the muster for this category on the checklist. Clutter all over the desk, paper and pencils fallen to the floor, whiteboards crammed with writing so small even a telescope wouldn't detect what it says, and lessons that appear taken out of sequence—for instance, coloring pictures of George Washington, *followed* by a discussion of who George Washington was—are all unfortunate examples of disorganization, which do not necessarily equate with poor teaching; but they do create rumors that the teacher has lost control.

9. The teacher is likeable.

Do you like to hang with people you don't like? I don't. If you add up the hours—and it varies—students spend an average of 180 hours each school year with a single teacher (based on the U.S. Department of Education's indication that the average school year in the United States consists of 180 days).[7] This means, a child will be in the presence of—and will presumably work closely with—his teacher an average of seven to eight *full* days from September to June.

How much would you like to be cooped up in the cozy confines of a small classroom with a person you didn't like—someone who has been assigned the mission of nagging, cajoling, and irritating you? This person also has the power of life and death (maybe slightly hyperbolic) over you; she holds your future in her hands—in the form of a grade she will assign to your high school transcripts.

If they don't already own them, teachers should hone personalities conducive to being around others, especially young people. Likeability goes a long, long way toward acceptability.

10. The teacher reminds her students (without actually telling them) that they are very fortunate to have her for a teacher.

Students once told me that they had a teacher at our school who would tell them something like this out of the clear blue: "Boy! You guys ought to be grateful that I'm your teacher; in fact, I should be paid extra. If I had a teacher like me, I would pay him—I don't know—an extra five bucks per class. And per student each day, if you add it all up, it would begin to approach what I'm really worth."

This teacher escaped any official criticism for those comments, although he had, in fact, made them on more than just a few occasions. It had been his mantra: "I'm better. You're lucky; pay me more."

Why had the wrath of an administrative mallet not swung down on his head? Simple: *He was right!* Of course, high school students should never have to dole money from their own pockets to pay a daily remuneration to a great teacher; but in the minds of his students, this teacher's arrogance was justified. This teacher *was* super! He *was* special! He soared way above the mediocrity that permeated the department he worked in.

Of course, he cannot—and should not—be paid extra by his students, but he had been simply amplifying his point of contention: "Hey, kids appreciate me. Their gratitude makes them behave better, work harder, and study longer. I know I'm good; you know I'm good. Together we can foster a climate that suits all of us."

The confidence—even the arrogance and swagger—some teachers cultivate works to their benefit only if they are as deserving of praise as they seem to think they are. Unfortunately, when a poor or mediocre teacher self-toots a horn not worth, well, tooting, he strikes others as a tad buffoonish.

Study teachers who know they're excellent at what they do because they *are* excellent at what they do. They also—subtly—transmit that confidence to their students and classroom observers. When they come off with a laid back or charming self-assuredness and coolness, everybody benefits. This is an absolute *must* quality you should be searching for in your observation subjects. Obviously, excessive arrogance is obnoxious, but excellent teachers know how to straddle a fine line and help aspiring, young teachers to do the same.

Generally, there are three times we teachers observe other teachers in their classrooms: when we are studying to *become* a teacher or are being coddled by a mentor during our first or second year of teaching; when we screw up and are forced by our administrators to watch the so-called wonderful teachers in action; when we are in a program—usually mandatory—of teacher observations. (Sometimes we just volunteer to observe other teachers for the heck of it—but that's about as often as we volunteer to head a cleanup brigade in a home that has just been thoroughly throttled by seventy-five partying teenagers on a raucous Friday night.)

I am suggesting that *we observe other teachers as much as our time and energy permit us.* It can be inspiring, nonthreatening, and immensely informative to teachers who wish to better themselves or inject themselves with an intermittent shot of adrenalin. After you have seen certain other teachers in action, you may be even more excited about your own methods and your own projects. And that's part of the plan, too. Please remember to use the new checklist: highlighted qualities that really *do* matter in the classroom—not just a bunch of technical, nondescript jargon hardly anyone can figure out, making anybody who reads it hopelessly baffled, or nauseous enough to cop a lean over the nearest toilet.

NOTES

1. Student teaching never fully prepares someone to be a teacher. Getting in the classroom and having the charge of your own students, thereby, learning by

trial and error, is the only way to develop fully and move into the real world of teaching.

2. Bob Pacilio still runs workshops for teachers, presenting ideas that rely heavily on the use of music. Interestingly, even with lively, thematic music in his lessons, the students' focus is still on Mr. Pacilio; he is that charismatic.

3. Kathleen Casson, "Observing Other Teachers: Professional Development That Works," *Learn NC*, UNC School of Education, at learnnc.org/lp/pages/739.

4. Georgia Department of Education, Fulton County Schools, "School Improvement Plan," 2008–2009, 4, Item C4, Objective 4, 4.

5. *Night of the Living Dead* (George Romero's) (The Walter Reade Organization, 1968); very camp, but surprisingly scary zombies' material.

6. Steve Martin, *Born Standing Up* (New York: Scribner, 2007) 123.

7. *Ask Yahoo*, U.S. Department of Education, www.ask.yahoo.com/20050509. html.

18

Cultivate a Sense of Humor

Kids like to laugh, and they will laugh at just about anything. What astounds me is that laughter usually disintegrates within the confines of an American high school or middle school classroom. Humor seems to hide at school, as though some teachers believe they are failures if their students are laughing and having a good time. Some teachers believe they should seek a new line of work if they discover their students are actually *enjoying* themselves in their presence.

For a change.

I'm a funny guy. In the first place, I'm rather strange to look at. Not long ago I stood at about five feet eight inches tall, with square shoulders and enormous muscles. I walked like a penguin because I had a hard time straightening my arms at my sides. I had been a bodybuilder but never quite realized the hilarious persona my appearance diffused to others. When I wore a bathing suit and sported a dark suntan, I looked fairly normal—even healthy—just a regular guy with bigger than normal pectorals. But fully clothed, I stood out as this big lug, a short, thick guy with a protruding nose, loud voice, and full, rotund face.

The thing is, I knew I looked funny, and sometimes my students just laughed at me for no out-of-the-ordinary reason. I figured I could use some of this genetically gifted ugliness to my advantage: capture the attention of my students, put them at ease, and establish a mood that could—and did—lead to some frolicking good times.

Today I'm still somewhat comical to look at, *and* I'm a lot fatter than I used to be.

Which makes me even funnier, because you know how teenagers react to fat teachers; in fact, any heavier-than-normal—*way* heavier-than-normal teacher—is hilarious to children. But I'm also a droll individual, like many of my comedic favorites. Not that these guys would be shaking in their boots, but Woody Allen or Jerry Seinfeld or Steve Martin don't have to worry about a challenge from me.

Lots of times I'm funny simply because I'm desperate—*desperate*—for a laugh. And I'm probably the only one in the room at that moment who is going to provide the impetus for one.

Pretty, pathetic, huh?

My sarcasm—though it will never rival—patterns that of Don Rickles',[1] but I'm afraid if I were to ever unleash my sardonic wit in the fashion of a personally insulting, sarcastic nightclub comedian like Don Rickles, I would lose my job, or perhaps drive some poor kid to *despair*. This would be fitting (de*spair*) only if he had to change a flat tire. (Get it?)

OK, I'll leave the truly great humor to the professionals; besides, looking at the now-routine, generous sprinkling of obscenities and sexual allusions in comedy clubs and concerts, if I came even *close* to what the paid comics were able to get away with, I would eventually be fired and forced to seek a more lucrative job—maybe teaching Dick Cheney how to avoid blowing away his friends with a shotgun during quail hunting season.

Sorry. I mean it this time: I'll leave even the *moderately* decent humor to the comedy professionals.

But I know I'm at least a *little* funny. My students tell me I am. During the first week of school, I implore my students to laugh at my jokes, funny stories, and puns, even if they don't think they're funny. I (jokingly?) make their responsive laughs and smiles a part of their participation grade scores. The rate of laughs per joke I receive is normally around 20 percent, but even *this* is pretty good for a surly, old high school teacher! Sometimes I interpret a boy slapping his forehead with a resounding thud or a girl chewing her gum excessively fast while rolling her eyes as positive reactions to my jabs at clever humor.

Our schools are too serious. Worse, they take themselves too seriously! The more humor we inject into a school's atmosphere, the more students learn there. They relax and become more comfortable around their classmates and teachers. If we teachers provide funny anecdotes or jokes in our classrooms, students may look forward to coming to school. What a change of pace you would be from their sourpuss, deadbeat teachers of today!

Not everybody can make other people laugh, let alone be a natural comedian; moreover, getting down to our students' level of humor often jolts our own sense of common decency. Once, however, we realize humor can be illustrated and demonstrated in a myriad of ways, the idea of engaging our students' funny bone is less offing. But we do need to take some occasional chances, go out on a limb, *branch* out (get it?) a little bit more; but, hey, that all eventually comes with the territory!

The rest of this chapter presupposes that you are not an innately talented, naturally funny dude or dudette. If you are, then skip this part. Please continue to be funny, but focus on other suggestions in this text, those that are more challenging for you. Consider yourself lucky; bask in the luxury of knowing how jealous of you the rest of us teachers have been all the while. On the other hand, I also make the supposition that you are able-bodied, willing—even enthusiastic—to discover how to be funnier in your classroom.

You have already accepted the premise that humor is good, an enriching addition to a teacher's instructional tools reservoir. Up front, however, we need to agree that you are not a fuddy-duddy, antisocial, introverted, inhibited geek who can see absolutely no good in anything or anyone who takes school too lightly, your style of teaching too critically, or your subject matter less seriously.

This book is not a "how to be a comedian" guide; and although these suggestions are a cut above the rest, you'll probably bomb the first few times you give them a stab. (Get it?) Perhaps, some ideas here will stick; and, perhaps, tangling with these suggestions will reveal a part of you no one has discovered yet—including you. I seriously doubt, however, you will be motivated to quit the teaching profession and relegate your talents to comedy nightclubs all over America, although Steve Martin, in his earlier years as a standup comic, wanted to become a teacher; he saw teaching as a form of show business[2]:

BE UNPREDICTABLE

My students think I'm from another galaxy. This isn't a bad thing. Since they rarely know what to expect from me, they are usually leaning on the rails of anticipation. In front of a class, I like to sing. The nerve this takes exceeds the guts of the Apollo 13 astronauts—about the time they were thinking their spacecraft had become dismantled; and unless they performed some spectacular maneuvers, they were destined to float around in space for a longer period of time than it takes a professional soccer game to be completed. (Soccer is timed, I know; it just seems like a game takes an eternity.)

My musical voice sounds like a cross of an unhealthy frog and a wailing bird, after the bird had been wounded by a hunter. But I sing—and all the time; there doesn't have to be a special occasion. (Today I sang Christmas carols as I passed back homework papers—in the middle of September!)

I dance around like a goofball. I slide over the freshly waxed floors, not afraid to fall on my face (as I have already done in the past)! I use non sequitur accents, invent bad Spanish, utter silly sounds, and make idiotic faces; in other words, there is rarely a normal (or dull) moment.

Once I abandon myself like this in front of my teenagers, they expect it from me all the time; that's the downside. But I don't think it has lessened their appreciation; it's my duty to keep figuring out ways to make them shake their heads in bewilderment. Yesterday I ran out a string of puns and told my students that whoever came up with the next pun on the current subject would win a prize (which was my way of telling them I thought they had done something special; I actually had no prizes to offer them—and they knew it):

Student: Are we gonna have debates in here?

Me: You want to debate?

Student: Yeah.

Me: All right; we'll have *debate*; but first we'll have *de fish*.

A short a delayed reaction from the class. . . .
And then:

Student: Oh...

Me: Of course, most of you didn't think that comment very funny, but don't worry, you're actually better off; you can get really *hooked* on those fish puns. And that's not a *line* I'm handing you.

I waited for an uproarious reaction from my students, which hardly ever comes; in fact it never comes. My students laugh the hardest when I do something unintentionally funny to them or destructive to me, such as when I leaned back too far on my desk chair and flipped onto the floor, knocking over a small wastebasket next to my desk.

Me: OK, OK, so some of you aren't *biting*. The truth is I keep making these puns just for the *halibut*. You are just so—so *gill*able. All right, all right; I'm now *fin*ished!

You didn't think that was so funny either. However, remember, in front of forty high school seniors, in September heat, in the middle of the afternoon, right on the spur of the moment (and remember, teenagers aren't the most demanding audience in the world when it comes to enticing a laugh; for instance, they howl especially loudly when somebody passes gas), this was a pretty darn funny sequence of puns!

The best part came next with my challenge:

Me: OK, whoever comes up with the next fish pun wins a prize. . . .

After a dead pause...

A normally quiet youngster who, under the circumstances should have *stayed* quiet, raised his hand and added sheepishly, "You sure know how to *bait* us, Mr. G.!"

Most of my students didn't hear him; he was shy and his voice was soft. But some of his classmates forced a laugh (the few who didn't laugh understood not even *one* of the puns). And while I started this punning sequence having already used the word *bait*, I couldn't resist the temptation to culminate this ludicrous interchange in the English language (er, I mean, to reward him for his cleverness).

I made a sour face, as though the student had successfully provided another bad pun, and tossed him a Hostess Ding Dong. I often keep a supply of individually wrapped Ding-Dongs available for such sporadic adventures.

USE COMIC DEVICES

This is where it gets tricky, because most of us (including me) would not know a real comic device from a car's carburetor. So you have to go with the old standbys, which you may not be able to formally label; but even your fuzzy familiarity should be enough to get you through this with a bunch of video-gaming, TV-hypnotized, text-messaging, MySpacing zombies.

Here are some examples:

- hyperbole: "John came to class yesterday wearing about forty earrings—and those were on his *tongue!*" Ha! Ha!
- verbal irony: "Good to see that your pens are poised, your notebooks open, and you're ready to write down all the important, pertinent information from my lecture!" Ha! Ha!
- self-deprecation: "I have a nose for knowing who didn't do last night's homework; and one look at my nose, and you can probably see that I have a nose for a lot of extraordinary things!" Ha! Ha! (Wait a second; *that* wasn't funny!)
- acerbic observations: "Steve, if you let your hair grow any higher, I'm going to have to put you in the back of the room; people can't see over you anymore." Ha! Ha! (Be careful with that one; obviously, you may gently tease only with those who are able to roll with the punches, and even like it!)

• sardonic surprise: "It's really hot today. Maybe we should just play a game or something! How many of you would like *not* to take the test today?" After most students have raised their hands in the air: "Tough; we can't. We have too much to do. Here's the test!" Ha! Ha!

Teenagers especially love it when their teachers are capable of self-deprecation. Of those devices listed above, this one is a perennial favorite of mine. It tickles the kids who find themselves the usual butt of a joke, the object of humiliation, the focal point for caustic attention. So when they turn the tables on an *adult*—a teacher—the amount of lightheartedness that beckons from self-deprecation can't even be measured; plus, they usually show their gratitude for that teacher who exhibits his humanity, his willingness to humble himself for being far less than perfect—a recognition of the weaknesses that run through his life.

All of us have these qualities, but a humble, self-deprecating teacher may say something like this: "Yeah, the pipes under our sink at home were leaking last night, so I found a nice wrench, handed it to my wife, and told her to crawl in there and fix it. It's not that I'm a complete jerk who expects my wife to do all the work around the house or something; it's just that I'm totally *incapable* of using a wrench. I know, I know; I'm a man and all—sort of—but I can't use tools and I'm not able to fix pipes that don't work."

Crickets chirping . . .

At the very least, you'll amuse *yourself*. And during those certain forlorn moods that are bound to attack everyone at one time or another, your sense of humor may be your saving grace, that critical boost to your potential for successful teaching—ultimately saving you from a despondency that could shrink your teaching potential way down to zero.

One final comment about cultivating a sense of humor—perhaps, a point most of you thought I was going to make anyway: The kids can be funny, too; in fact, some of them can be hilarious. You should know when to recognize their sometimes offbeat, irresponsible, irrepressible brands of humor and not seem like some sort of grouchy old fuddy-duddy out to spoil their good time. My rule of thumb is as follows: If I think they're funny, I'll laugh at them, and I will do so in front of the whole class. However, I will not entertain . . .

• bigoted remarks
• hurtful or harmful comments about other students or staff
• bathroom humor
• swearing
• drug jokes
• blatant sexual innuendo

Naturally, you have to employ some old-fashioned common sense here.

The following is an actual, literal exchange in front of a class between me and one of my students who was scared to death to get up to do her oral presentation:

Sarah: I can't get up to speak in front of the class, Mr. G.

Mr. G: I know; it can be tough. But if you practice first, it'll help to relax you.

Sarah: I do practice.

Mr. G.: And?

Sarah: It's just that . . . well, I'm pretty good at doing speeches in practice; it's just that, well, I can't do them in front of *you*!

Mr. G.: Why not, Sarah?

Sarah: I'm too embarrassed to tell you.

Mr. G.: That's okay, Sarah; I know you have a great deal of respect for me and don't want to let me down. I understand that. But we're just practicing here; we're on the same side. Our intent is to get better at it.

Sarah: That's not it, Mr. G.

Mr. G.: Oh? Then what?

Sarah: You really want to know?

Mr. G.: Yes, Sarah, I do. And now, so does the whole class.

Sarah: Well, Mr. G., whenever I'm doing my speeches in front of you, you look like such a spaz, I can't even speak at all. I don't know how to explain it. It's your face—yeah, your face. It makes me wanna crack up; I can't concentrate on what I'm saying, and then I forget—so I'm, like, too nervous to do speeches in here. You should come to my house and, like, hide in the closet while I practice my speeches; just don't let me know you're watching. You'll see; I'm pretty good.

When a kid makes a comment like this, there is only one suitable reaction: I laugh.

The kids get it, too, and they usually laugh right along with me!

Although I'm not so sure being told I look like a spaz (whatever that means) right in front of my speech students generated feelings of goodwill and solidarity between Sarah and me, I tried to use the incident as a learning experience for all of us.

If nothing else, a moment of levity is usually appreciated.

Humor can be an invaluable resource for defusing a tense situation.

Jack had been noticeably irritable in class lately, and he seemingly couldn't keep his head off his desk. I have repeatedly told my students, if they wished to put their head down—if they are that sleepy—they should stay out of school. Going to bed at an ungodly hour is not an option for my students. I make random visits to my students' homes after 9:30 in the evening to see who's still awake, and who's in bed; and I play loud classical music outside their bedroom windows in order to drift them off into a deep slumber.[3]

Anyway, Jack had his head down during one of my mesmerizing lectures about the many uses for ellipses during source citations. I couldn't stand the way some of the other kids were glancing at him—and then at me—wondering what I was going to do about this disrespectful, bored-out-of-his-gourd diplodocus. If there were ever a proper time for the teacher-controlled electric seat zapper, this had been it. Practically nothing else in a classroom angers me more quickly than a kid who has his head flopped down on the desk, completely oblivious to anything or anyone else. I wanted to kick the bottom of his desk hard with my boot, but I managed to control myself; instead, I calmly walked over to him and said sweetly, "Hey—Jack! Jack! . . . *Jack!*"

Groggily, he lifted his head, "Huh? Yeah?"

Then, my demeanor completely changed, I lowered my voice, and asked him in my most conversational tone of voice, "Jack, have you ever seen *Sleeping Beauty*?"

Of course, he would answer, "No."

But then I asked him, "But you've heard of it? You know the story?" Reluctantly he said, "Yeah.

"Well, do you remember that Sleeping Beauty was, well, sleeping?" "Yeah."

"And do you remember how she woke up?

He warily proceeded, "Yeah. . . . "

"How?"

"A kiss."

"From . . . ?"

Of course, he wouldn't say any more.

So I helped him. "By the Handsome Prince! The Handsome Prince woke up Sleeping Beauty by giving her a kiss. And guess what, Jack? In this class *I* am the Handsome Prince!"

At my comment his eyes finally flashed open; I winked, exaggerated, so the whole class could see it. And see it they did, laughing loudly and enthusiastically, with a few howls and shrieks here and there.

Even Jack laughed.

With that response to Jack's obnoxious inattentiveness, I'm not sure what I had done to my own reputation; but I'm sure I had defused what may have become a volatile scene. I was proud of myself for handling the situation so well, only wishing I had been as smart and wise with him in those other confrontations I had already blown.

Finally, here are just a few solicited responses from teenagers about teachers they judge as not having a sense of humor. Please pay close attention to their comments; they imply wisdom often lost in school scuffles over hall passes and fire drills:

- "Ms. [Lim] is my favorite teacher because she's always cracking jokes. I feel sorry for the kids who have Ms. Johnson for English; she's just an old hag—no sense of humor."
- "I look forward to my classes with funny teachers [and not those with teachers who aren't funny]."
- "Mr. [Halberston] makes me want to puke; he's so grumpy all the time I don't want to be in the same room with him."

When people are funny, they make others laugh; their likeability and popularity stocks soar. When people are more likeable and popular, they communicate better. When *teachers* communicate better, they are more effective teachers. When they are more effective teachers, their students learn more from them.[4] It all goes together. A teacher does not have to be a standup comedian to cultivate and nurture a sense of humor. *Any* addition to his funny bone repertoire will enhance his students' desires to come to his class each day, and they may actually learn something about geography from him—if only by accident!

NOTES

1. From *The Hockey Puck*. at thehockeypuck.com.

2. Steve Martin, *Born Standing Up* (New York: Scribner, 2007), 123; Steve Martin's humor would have been his ace in the hole for classroom management.

3. Why not? Rap music and Barry Manilow records have been effective "weapons" for eliciting top secret information from prisoners at Guantánamo and Abu Ghraib; classical music should have some of the same effects on teenagers.

4. Antonio Luciano Tosta, "Laugh and Learn: Thinking Over the Funny Teacher Myth," *U.S. Department of State Bureau of Education and Cultural Affairs* 39, 1 (January–March 2001): 26.

19

Learn a Foreign Language

Of all the chapters in this book, this one was the most embarrassing for me to write.

No matter who we are, when we're forced to fess up that we have been eternally wrong about something, it jabs at our pride—and for men, diminishes a sense of our own masculinity.

At least, that's the way I see it.

"Bruce, you need to learn Spanish," my best friend, the Spanish teacher, had chided me for years.

"Bruce, you should learn another language," a former principal of mine had suggested half a million times—and then I lost track of the number.

"Bruce, you should listen to Eric [my best friend, the Spanish teacher] and learn Spanish," my *mother* had warned me over and over.

Naturally, I didn't heed any of their advice. I figured it this way:

1. This is America; we speak English in America.
2. If the kids don't know English, it's *their* responsibility to learn it.
3. I'm too old to learn a new language.
4. I'm already good enough with kids; learning another language wouldn't improve my teaching commensurate to the time and effort I would need to put into learning a new language.
5. When I have to communicate better with the children who don't speak English, I'll shout.

Yes, I was absolutely positive I had been right on all five counts, and, therefore, never bothered to learn another language.

And I was *wrong* on all five counts.

1. This is America. We speak English in America.

Not anymore. At least, not all of us. And what about the millions who are here, trying to learn English the best they can—or the children whose parents are too stubborn, uneducated, or mean to help them get their education? We can't give up trying to help those children.

2. If the kids don't know English, it's their responsibility to learn it.

That's right; but in the meantime, these kids need our patience, understanding, and help.

3. I'm too old to learn a new language.

That's true *now* (I'm now around 130 years old), but it wasn't true one hundred years ago when I first considered the possibility that learning another language would make me a better teacher. I should have listened to my little Spanish voice inside my brain (which, by the way, has *remained* inside my brain—and that's all).

4. I'm already good enough with kids; learning another language wouldn't improve my teaching commensurate to the time and effort it would take for me to learn a new language.

First, it *is* a lot of work; second, it's worth it. Just having the flexibility of being able to switch languages in order to communicate better with others—even those who live in the real world outside my classroom—makes it worth doing; besides, you young, single guys will seem a lot sexier to the women.[1]

5. When I need to communicate better with the children who don't speak English, I'll shout.

I still do that; I speak very loudly to these kids, the crashing volume of my voice sometimes making them cringe.

I don't think it's helped much, though.

Making the best of our talents generates confidence and enthusiasm in teachers—and in people of any profession. Generally speaking, when we do our best with the sometimes-limited talents that we have, we're proud of ourselves, basking in the knowledge we did a good job.

But when we don't do what we're capable of doing—for whatever reason—we usually run around or mope around or just sit with a nagging, irritating feeling of inadequacy. "I could have done this better," we say to ourselves. "If I had *just*. . . . And it was possible—very, very possible."

I could have learned another language. To be specific, I should have taught myself Spanish. I even bought a few compact disks for that purpose. And my Spanish teacher best friend gave me a couple of learning Spanish CDs as a gift. I never got around to it, though. All four CDs sit on a shelf—or tucked away in a drawer—somewhere in my house.

I kept making excuses to myself, most of them having to do with my age and the well-known difficulty of grasping a foreign language in the twilight years of a teaching career (although at the time it had not yet been the "twilight years"; it was something more like the late afternoon sunshine years of my career). I also moaned and groaned about having limited time to do this—and what difference would it make anyway? I mean, I'll probably be dead by the time I learn what *por favor* has to do with.

So pick any of the five excuses above. At one time or another, I've owned them all.

But I've had a rebirth; in many ways, I am more open-minded and liberal about teaching than I had been twenty or thirty years ago. Much of my pig-headedness has gotten me into trouble, embedded in a personality type I inherited from my father; I hate admitting that I'm wrong. But wrong I have been about a lot of things.

When I first sat down to write this manuscript, the most difficult chore I faced was ridding myself of the burden of clinging to my former philosophical beliefs about what teaching *should* be—and what teaching *can* be. Therein lie my former presumptions about language use, cultural acceptance, and various considerations of the old tolerance issue: I still believe that we should never tolerate behaviors in others or ourselves that are illegal, immoral, or unsafe. But at the same time, I understand the compulsion to adapt to a new look in the education landscape—especially various benign ideas and philosophies of the last decade.

Getting off *my* rear end and helping myself to better communicate with children who do not yet know English—but *will* know English well someday in the future—makes perfect sense to me today. And the fact that I had been so darn mulish about it until fairly recently, frankly, embarrasses me.

So here are five reasons for learning a second language, followed immediately by five ways to go about it. Pick only one reason out of the first five, confirm within yourself that you agree with at least that point, and then you have every reason to select from at least one category from the second list of five:

1. A BODY OF EVIDENCE SUPPORTS THAT LEARNING A SECOND LANGUAGE HELPS TO SHAPE A MORE WELL-ROUNDED, SUCCESSFUL PERSON.

By this time, duh!

Who *doesn't* know this?

If you go on a diet and lose weight—feeling and looking *good*—something can be said for the usefulness of the diet. The amount of outside research you would require to say to yourself "Hmm, this diet must be working" is rather minimal.

In July of 2007, language specialist Lisette Croese wrote extensively about the intrinsic value of learning a foreign language. She explained, "Speaking a modern foreign language today is incredibly important in both social and work life. . . . In [learning another language] you will develop a whole host of new skills. . . . [It] will also demonstrate to employers that you have the ability to learn things from outside of the norm."[2]

Croese discusses the numerous advantages to gaining knowledge of a foreign language (other than English); overall, language acquisition helps lead to greater success, increased happiness, and matured wisdom.[3]

Again, obvious is—as obvious does.

Or whatever.

2. LEARNING A SECOND LANGUAGE DEVELOPS A MORE COMMUNICATIVE TEACHER.

Of course, monolinguistic teachers can be—and some are—terrific teachers; they communicate effectively and many, many of these teachers even have won awards for their superior performances.

But the rewards for your acquiring another language flow across the board. In *Teaching English Language Learners K–12* (Corwin), Jerry Jesness contends, "[Commanding a second language] will give a teacher greater credibility in the eyes of students and their parents, as well as a certain moral authority. . . . Given that students will have more time to learn your language than you have to learn theirs, you can be forgiven if your progress is less than theirs. Nevertheless, your progress will be noted and respected."[4]

Needless to say, it also works the other way around. You begin to understand your students better, communicate more cogently with them, and relate more directly to those cultural aspects of their lives that are sometimes private and sensitive.[5]

Everybody wins; in fact, your students now may be more inclined to bring you better food and presents around Christmastime and your birthday![6]

3. SOME STATES REQUIRE SECOND LANGUAGE ACQUISITION AS A PREREQUISITE TO PROPER CREDENTIALING.

With the race—for better or worse— to multiculturalism in our schools, many states now mandate that teachers attach various appendages to their teaching credentials; one way—for example, in California—is taking classes for a minimum number of hours in teaching English learners, followed by passing a test on language and cultural diversity issues. Another method for completing this burdensome task is passing a second language test, the selected language based on the geographic location of the teacher's school; for example, in California, the most popular second languages are Spanish and Korean.[7]

4. LEARNING A SECOND LANGUAGE PROVIDES THE TEACHER MUCH GREATER JOB FLEXIBILITY.

Let's face the truth: If you know Spanish, you have a much better chance of landing a teaching position. You have a significantly greater chance of landing almost *any* position.[8] A couple of years ago a job opened up in the English department of our school, and I wanted to influence the administrator in charge of hiring to ease a good friend of mine into that position.

"Does he know Spanish?" the administrator asked me point blank.

I shook my head, "No."

The administrator bit his lip.

I quickly continued, "It's a job teaching *English*, Frank. Why should he know Spanish? I've taught English for thirty years. When we went on our honeymoon to Acapulco, my wife had to do all the talking. I never said a word; I didn't even know how to call for a taxi. But I teach kids *English*."

The administrator shrugged. "It's a new world, Bruce. We're looking for a teacher who can help English learners. We'll put them in those teachers' classes; we'll keep them out of yours."

No need to press the matter; and although I didn't think so at the time, he was right. Ironically, in those days we couldn't find a qualified English teacher who knew Spanish, so my Anglo, chest-thumping friend got hired for the job anyway, and actually stayed at our school five years, until he got in some hot water with our Indian American (as in, like, the country India) principal, who made his life so miserable, he eventually cursed the day he had accepted the job offer at our school.

But the writing has been on the wall for a long time. Ricardo Sanchez, president of the Latino Education Achievement Project, proclaimed, "Our *top priority* [italics added] this year is we want the government to invest in [training, developing, and hiring] future bilingual teachers."[9] Especially if you are a young whippersnapper, it certainly won't hurt to invest some time in learning another language—will it?

5. YOU MAY POKE FUN AT ALL THE TEACHERS WHO KNOW ONLY ENGLISH.

And that would be fun! Nobody dares—because I am big and ugly and mean—make fun of me for that reason, though they certainly have a right to. I would have loved to have said to a teacher across the hall, "Hey, Carl! Your kids are out of control because they don't understand a word you're saying to them! I told you to learn some Spanish, you moron! Let me come over there and speak with your kids in [Spanish, Korean, French, Hebrew] to your kids—and maybe I can calm them down a little."

Yeah, right. Like that's going to happen.

About ten years ago, I had decided I was, in fact, going to learn Spanish; I knew the state was about to require some kind of half-baked add-on credential, allowing teachers to work legally with English learners. Convinced I didn't need a supplement for that, I coiled up like a ball inside, refusing to expand myself, believing my record would speak for itself. "Besides," I figured cockily, "If push came to shove, they would just have to keep the kids who didn't know much English out of my classroom—and give them to teachers who did, those who *qualified* to work with English learners. *And* what would be so bad about that? Nothing! In fact, it would be good not to have kids who don't know English in my classes!"

So I procrastinated, until my wife, who at that time taught English as a second language students during night school, set me straight.

"Bruce," she said with a bit of tenseness in her voice, "just shouting loudly at the kids who don't know English doesn't reach them. I mean, you *do* know that, don't you?"

"They smile a lot," I teased, not realizing what I should have already known: My aloofness would anger her.

"I can't believe you!" she said. "You think you're so good—and you are—with a certain type of student. But more and more kids who don't understand even one word of what you're shouting at them are coming into the system. With those kids, you're not doing your job."

And then she knotted the screw. "This isn't forty years ago when you were in school!" she barked.

So I really did intend to learn Spanish.

I should have followed through. But other methods for qualifying to teach ESL students were developed by the state, and I decided to go the easiest route possible to sew up my supplementary credential. In retrospect, however, if I had been studying Spanish for the past ten years, I would have learned a great deal more than I did from those silly after-school multicultural workshops in which the teachers spent more time arguing with the pathetic presenters than they did figuring out how to teach non-English-speaking kids.

My wife had been right.

As usual.

So here are five preferable ways to learn Spanish—or Korean or Chinese or Farsi or whatever. Pick some of them. Or all of them. Or only one of them. But mastering at least *one* of them would do you a world of good in your professional life—and your personal life, as well.

1. GO BACK TO SCHOOL.

This kills a lot of stones with one bird—or whatever—because going back to school is a good idea for teachers, no matter what, especially for teachers who have been away from the other end of the classroom for a while.[10] Learning a foreign language in a university or community college setting can be intense, but then again so can learning English by a foreign national in a strange, hostile high school setting be intense. Some local school districts even offer nighttime adult school courses that cost about ten cents, not counting books and supplies.

2. BUY A VIDEO.

Do it yourself from your own television set. And then when you get bored, you can switch channels for the Car Crash Channel, with your now own special understanding of what the drivers must be feeling as they slam into the wall, explode, and burst into flames. From this experience, you may also learn some colorful swear words in languages other than English.

3. GO ONLINE.

Googling various subjects, I found no fewer than 6,128,000 sites for learning another language. Making room for *slight* exaggeration, you still get the idea. The good thing, however, is that online sites account for a myriad of different languages with varying degrees of seriousness and various lengths of time to complete the courses. Take your pick; you have so many choices now. Believe it or not, many of these courses are free, because on some sites you only work with others (no credentialed teachers) who are in the same boat—sort of the ultimate in virtual cooperative grouping.

4. VACATION—FOR A YEAR OR TWO— IN MEXICO, SOUTH KOREA, JAPAN, OR IRAQ AND LEARN THEIR LANGUAGES HANDS ON.

You may wish to consider the Iraq example as a bad joke, though Israel is a nice place to visit and learn Hebrew, which, of course, is totally useless in America, unless you are studying for Bar or Bat Mitzvah. In all seriousness, learning a foreign language in a foreign land can become a valid, meaningful experience, but it should probably be accompanied by one of the three previously mentioned methods of studying a new language. Expect it to take years before you begin to feel as though you have maximized your potential for becoming bilingual.

5. DO IT THE OLD-FASHIONED WAY: BUY SOME BOOKS AND STUDY THEM.

Take your time, too, because the only advantage to this rather lonely, archaic method of furthering your education is that you may proceed at your own pace. Be smart and don't get your books from a public library, a place in which all the books smell like cat urine. I prefer Barnes & Noble for the best-smelling books (and because they have helped me the most with setting up my book signings).

If you are an old codger, you probably should have skipped this chapter. Not much that I say here will compel you to do what you (and I) would have been much better off doing ten or twenty years ago.

The haste in which the world now progresses is sometimes frightening to those of us who have lived most of our existence without the benefits (?) of online courses, CDs, DVDs—even word processors and computers.

For better or worse, the demographics of our schools are changing rapidly, as are the demographics of the entire country. People come to this nation by the thousands every single day, with or without the intent of assimilating into American culture and one day becoming American citizens. We who are over, uh, fifty, have stories of friends and family who arrived in America from Europe, Latin America, Japan, or Pluto and did not have a clue how to utter even one word in English. Their teachers were not trained in any other language and had not the slightest knowledge about the different cultures of their foreign students—nor did the teachers care about that sort of thing. All people who lived and worked and attended schools in this country were expected to read, write, and speak English. No special dispensations were made, and no extraordinary treatment was expected. Kids who lapped up knowledge fed to them in America's schools advanced and eventually succeeded. Those children who did not, were held back; they languished in the system, until they either quit or were tossed out.

An enormous number of those who lost out were native born, Anglo—supposedly English-speaking—Americans. True, many of them looked as though they could have been sons and daughters of the folks in the movie *Deliverance*,[11] but they should have had everything going for them, since they had already won life's lottery by virtue of their American birthrights.

I am not suggesting that those were the "good old days" for the United States or American education; entrenched in your own personal tenets you may pass judgment on that particular issue. But they were certainly *different* times; and with these different times, waves of political correctness, liberal trains of thought, and a bombardment of media influence from all over the world have contributed to different standards for us, our children, and our students.

So I sigh, grimace, and then plod ahead, knowing that soon not much of this is going to matter to me personally: Eventually, I will be either retired or dead or both, and even if I had mastered Spanish and then some, it would all be irrelevant to me at that point in my existence (or lack thereof). So my strong advice is for *you*: Unless you are six thousand years old, you're going to have to compete with other teachers for quite a while; and most of them may know what you don't know and be trained in a way you're not trained.

For so many cogent reasons, learn a foreign language, and then be proud of *yourself* in this new, modern age.

NOTES

1. I have no proof for this assertion, of course; but recently a waiter in an authentic French restaurant we visited tried to woo my wife (I think for a larger tip) with his thick French accent. It almost worked; that is, until I made my usual accolade of jokes about France, getting my wife to laugh and find *me* more attractive than the handsome French waiter with the sexy accent.

2. Lisette Croese, "Reasons for Learning a Modern, Non-English Foreign Language," *Abroad Languages*, July 26, 2007, 3, at broadlanguages.com/blog/reasons -for-learning-a-modern-non-English-foreign-language_6/.

3. Ibid.

4. Jerry Jesness, *Teaching English Language Learners*, (Thousand Oaks, CA: Corwin Press, 2004) 100.

5. Ibid.

6. I have no empirical proof of this; it just seems more likely to happen in this instance. My students bring me food and presents only if they have an inkling that it may affect their grades for the better.

7. This is universally true throughout the state of California.

8. Modern Language Association and the Association of Departments of Foreign Languages (summary of article), 1999, at, ccflt.org/adfh1.htm.

9. Ken Harvey, "Cabildeo De Estudiantes Latinos Ante Legisladores," *Migrant Ed News* (Spring 2005): 2.

10. Among all the other benefits of going back to school as a student (as detailed in chapter 14), learning another language sits high on a list of those benefits.

11. *Deliverance*, (Warner Bros, 1972); Please do not die before you have watched the "Dueling Banjos" scene in this tremendous—but very hard to take—movie.

20

✦

Juice up Your Personal Life

How often have we heard comments like these about supposedly re-markable teachers?

"Mr. Thomas is an incredible teacher! He grades papers at home for hours and hours; he stays after school with kids until ten o'clock at night. He gets to school in the morning two hours early; he spends even his weekends at school-related activities!"

Mr. Thomas has absolutely no life outside his work: no family, no girl-friends, no friends, no passions, and no hobbies. Mr. Thomas has nothing but his desk in the classroom. By the way, if Mr. Thomas did have a fam-ily, he wouldn't have it for long—not with these school hours.

If I were a member of his immediate family, I would disown Mr. Thomas.

A fairly new teacher at my school—one who has become inordinately successful for so early in her career—asked me last spring if I intended to teach summer school; I told her that I didn't. She then said, "I am; I don't really need the money, but I don't know what I would do with myself, if I didn't spend the summer here [at school]!"

And she was *serious*.

While it might be nobler in the minds of men to have withstood the horrors of tedium and boredom, living a humdrum, basically lifeless existence outside the hallowed halls of academia, let it be clear to all who care: You will burn out! There are no ifs, ands, or buts about this prognostication.

Almost every teacher who gives a lick about how she does in her class-room leads a fulfilling, but stressful, life. If she's serious about returning every assignment and analyzing her students' work for exact crosses on every "t" and dots on every "i," she also spends enormous amounts of time at home reading and grading those papers.

This can't go on forever; in fact, it can't go on for very long. One of the scarier aspects about this is that it creeps up on you insidiously, like a cancer; and before long, actually doing something about it seems out of the question. Your private life is in shambles because you have ignored it. And what may be worse (at least, at the moment): your teaching will begin to stink! *Really stink!* A monotonous, menacing, marked deterioration in the quality of your instruction may—or may not— be evident to you; but what *should* be obvious to you is that you are tired, listless, bored, and indifferent. You might even think about changing careers, an idea you used to believe impossible to ponder. Very clearly, you have burned out.

Perennially good teachers have well-balanced, well-attended personal lives. They are also well-rounded folks who have more going for them than the work they do at school. They haven't put lock, stock, and barrel into teaching, because the lock, stock, and barrel soon lose their luster. It's human. You're human—at least, most of you are. Teachers who have rewarding personal lives outside school, are better—much better—teachers because, in general, they are content. They can fool some of the people some of the time, but none of the people all of the time (or something like that).

Look at it this way: Most people are happiest when they have something in their lives to look forward to in the not-too-distant future: a movie, a date, a ball game, a vacation, a baby, a new house, a pending bank robbery, etc. If there is little—or nothing—to look forward to, then the marvel of anticipation is lost. When all there is . . . is more of the same—the same school, same lesson, same students, same job, same ol' same ol'—then a genuinely deep level of fulfillment is not attainable.[1]

Most of you who slip into this profession don't do it for the money. You do it because you've yearned to do it; it's a way to make a tangible dent in society, maybe not entirely measurable, but certainly something clearly observable. And you do it because you've realized from an early time in your life that it can be *fun.* Teaching is fun. Not all the time. Not every minute. But teaching is a blast, especially—and maybe *only*—when things for you are going smoothly.

Still, there comes a time when you look around and find yourself in that swamp; and either you instantly panic (which is not good), or you frantically attempt to extricate yourself (and we already know what happens when a person is trapped in quicksand and frantically tries to extricate himself)![2]

Your profession, your job, your place of employment has begun to feel like your tomb. And even folks who have dedicated themselves completely to education, to teaching, to children need to experience the light away from the tomb every now and then.

This is where having a life—a *real* life—comes in handy. Not only does it make you happier, it helps to create a better teacher in you. Naturally, I don't know your passions, your interests, your desires; I merely assume you *have* some. And if you don't have some, you can cultivate them.

So here are some areas in your personal life you should consider. I've chosen these specifically because they have worked for me; however, the obvious caution is, you're not I (Is that really the way we have to say it?), so the outside activities and personal rewards that work for *you* may be very dissimilar to these:

PARTICIPATE IN HOBBIES.

For me, it's writing, baseball, weight training, and watching films. They are passions. Even without teaching, my life would be content, generously endowed with my interests. Since I now have two young children, I can't indulge myself too often in entertainment away from my children; I pick and choose how I spend those precious free hours—few that they are—very carefully: The movie had better be good; the book one I can't put down; the gym works only at 5:00 A.M.; the ball game on TV only from the seventh inning on—and live games at the ballpark but once a month.

Renew *your* passions, your hobbies—or find some. You think you can do it all and be it all and have it all in your classroom.

But you can't.

ATTEND SOCIAL GATHERINGS.

I hate parties because I abhor making small talk (you may like them); instead, I prefer going to the park or to a friend's home for a cookout. My girth notwithstanding, eating has become a form of recreation and distraction; besides, I just adore food. I want to eat all the time; if I could, I would eat constantly. I'm eating right now—a bologna sandwich—and there are mustard stains as testimony—on the keyboard. Friendly dinners with friends or family members quell the nerves and—when the company is right—soothe the soul.

MAKE FRIENDS.

My wife and I don't need a lot of them, but those we do have share our most important values.

I suggest to my students that they should occasionally do a house-cleaning—a cleaning out of their friends, so to speak. Sometimes friends bring us down instead of raise us up. In my ever so humble, sociological nonexpertise, our lives are richer and more profound when we eliminate friends and family who suck the marrow out of us every chance they get.

Frankly, I haven't a clue how teachers—or anyone else— thrive in an environment riddled with exhausting people to whom they feel indebted or beholden. Your personal recreation time works, only when it satisfies your need to be free from the stresses and challenges of your work environment. And you do have a need for personal time, whether you fess up to it or not.

EXERCISE REGULARLY.

I'm not body-beautiful (anymore!), but regular exercise still stimulates me in more ways than I should mention here; after I've exercised early in the morning, I always feel invigorated and ready to take on the day (or the kids). I prefer to go to the gym before work (around 5:00 A.M.); it gives me a shot of energy that lasts throughout the morning. And time by myself at the gym is spent solely on *me*. Nagging teenagers or needy children have no place in my exercise environment. The Jacuzzi and swimming pool beckon me to drift off into a sea of blissful, quiet, self-absorbed euphoria—if only for ten minutes.

ADMIRE THE CHARACTER AND ACHIEVEMENTS OF OTHERS.

A few individuals in the public sphere have become my role models, people who stir great ideas in me, rejuvenate me, and make my life even better: Dennis Prager and Dr. Laura and Bill O'Reilly are three such individuals. Barack Obama is another.[3] For you, she may be a friend or family member or someone else in the media; perhaps, you look up to a thought-provoking writer or a stirring musician. But we should all have people out there we esteem, have a high regard for; emulating them would not be a bad idea. The enrichment brought to our lives through the lives of others in the media or the print world is not just entertaining; it can also be quite profound.

EAT WELL.

Looking at many of us teachers, it's obvious that we do eat a *lot*, but whether we eat right or not is something else. Maintaining a well-balanced diet makes us feel better, live longer, and provides us energy for our teaching. (By all means, reread chapter 12; your initial shock from those suggestions may have worn off by now.)

HAVE A MINIVICE.

The controversy and possible diversion of this next point may not be worth the effort, but I find it important enough to take a chance: Teachers always—*always* have to do that acting thing—and usually, we are forced to come off like real goody-goodies or feel as though we have relinquished some of the respect we receive from students and parents. We are all, contrary to the argument of some of our students, human, and human beings require safe outlets for their vice-filled urges. Most actions we may perform to satisfy these needs are all right, if they are not done to excess.

I'm certainly not going to tell you which vices you should experience, nor am I going to reveal to you any of my own, personal minivices; however, in moderation, any of these would be okay by me, and probably by you, unless you have strong religious taboos against them: a visit to Las Vegas, a glass or two of wine (or beer), a naughty movie or magazine, an "adult entertainment" show, a raunchy comedy DVD or record, and so on.

You all have vices; just remember, not going *overboard* is the key to making your vices work for you—relaxing you and entertaining you in your personal life. Just about whatever you can think of right now should be okay, as long as it's legal. It goes without saying—so why am I saying it?— these vices should always be left outside your places of employment.

And you gotta admit: Some of this stuff sounds like a lot of fun!

Note: some vices are blatantly illegal—and I would never imply you should indulge in illegal activities (although some of *those* may look like a lot of fun, too); besides, for some of these activities, you can lose your teaching credential. Wouldn't that be ironic! Perhaps, you should wait until you retire or manifest an indifference toward going to jail before you indulge in activities that qualify for being a part of your life only after you have found out you have a terminal disease and six minutes to live. Even then, you should be wary.

GET ENOUGH REST.

For some of you "cool" people, this is an oft-overlooked virtue; in fact, rest and sleep for a swingin' teacher like you is like poison and certainly not to be mentioned in mixed company. However, it is absolutely critical—and I don't use that word often—*critical* that you get enough rest—and this also means plenty of sleep. As an experiment, spend a week sleeping each night for only four hours, and the following week sleeping each night for eight hours. If you don't immediately see the difference in how you feel and the way you treat others—particularly your students—I will come over to your house and personally eat every page of this book (if by then you haven't thrown your copy at me).

CHECK REGULARLY WITH A PROFESSIONAL ABOUT YOUR HEALTH.

You will not be viewed as a hypochondriac; you will, however, be relaxed and confident about your state of health. Few tidbits of news are as exhilarating as receiving a clean bill of health from a doctor. And if you are getting sick, isn't it better to nip it in the bud (which would be especially handy if you're growing a flower in your body). Sick teachers make lousy teachers, no matter how good their acting ability. Sick teachers also become *dead* teachers, but perhaps I've already reminded you strongly enough about your mortality and shouldn't go into any further detail; after all, you already have an idea what it may be like after you're dead: You don't teach your students that energetically, and your class is probably more boring than a Tony Bennett concert.[4]

IF YOU'RE MARRIED, MAKE YOUR WIFE (AND YOUR FAMILY) YOUR PRIORITY—NOT YOUR SCHOOL WORK.

Spend time with them. Let them know how important they are. As Emily says in *Our Town*, "We don't have time to look at one another!"[5]

Make time!

If you're single, scam members of the opposite sex; you should do some dating. And you already know how attractive and desirable teachers and would-be teachers are to members of the opposite sex (even to the *same* sex)! That snide comment aside, have fun. Go places. Take vacations. Live! And here's a little sidelight—though, perhaps, not that little and not that much of a sidelight: So you will be extra nice to your family—and *your students*—striving to have patience and thinking about what's in their best interests should be your goal, a common goal among all teachers.

However, we all have frustrations and foibles, and we need to take them out on *something*. For relief, I suggest you hang a cap from your most disappointing sports team on a dartboard and use metal darts to fire away—with total abandonment. . . . *Or* (seriously now) you involve yourself in a type of grueling competition—basketball, tennis, bowling, chess, racquetball, fantasy baseball, hopscotch—you name the activity. The pent-up frustrations, the human requirement for letting off body steam, the brain's natural tendency to immerse itself in conflict can be handled through vigorous exercise. When we have nobody to raise our voice to, take it out on, competitively bicker with, our inclination will be to do it elsewhere—in the environment we spend most of our living hours.

I certainly don't want you to smack around your own kids or yell at your wife, so I implore you to discover a safe outlet to disperse your natural quota of vim, vigor, and venom. I have found that if I don't have any of these conduits for my anger available to me, or I haven't utilized those I do have, I am much meaner to my students.[6]

Finally, on a personal note: I now possess serenity and peace in my professional life; they came to me through my personal involvement in a religious sphere. This has not been merely on a generic, spiritual plane, but in an organized faith. It became a different sort of family and friends who supported me through my most difficult times and were also with me to share my most beautiful times.

For me, it is comforting to believe there is something out there much, much bigger and more important than I am; that I am not the center of the universe. To live in an orderly time and space created by God through divine craftsmanship is a belief that has helped to mold my character and shape my views about life and death.

Only after this religious epiphany occurred, was I able to get married for the first time and have my first children (at the tender age of 48). The more I had focused solely on teaching, the less I desired to get married, and the less time I had to look for someone to marry. I needed the life structure that my religion offered me. Teaching, then, became my fourth love (behind my family, my faith, and baseball), and once I put all that in perspective, I became a much happier person. I even wound up teaching religious school every week for ten years; I count those years as among the most meaningful teaching experiences of my life.

The bottom line: Design your personal life to be the most rewarding component of your vitality; don't count on teaching to be your reason to live. You've already heard the proverbial "putting all your eggs in one basket"; and, of course, you already know that can't be a good thing. It's virtually impossible to emphasize enough how much your teaching will take on a newer, more profound purpose, as you nurture your personal contentment away from those hallowed halls.

NOTES

1. J.J. Gomez, "The Path to School-Based Management Isn't Smooth, but We're Scaling the Obstacles One by One, *The American Board Journal* (October, 1989): 20–22.

2. In an old TV show called *The Adventures of Rin-Tin-Tin,* there was an episode in which a man fell in a bed of quicksand. Luckily, just before his head went under, a sweet, caring, and very brave, uh, dog (the show's namesake) pulled him to safety.

3. It's not all politically lopsided anymore; I have a newfound faith in President Obama and Vice President Biden.

4. If this legendary crooner is dead by the time you read this, it doesn't change my analogy one bit.

5. Thornton Wilder, *Our Town* (New York: Samuel French, Inc., 1939), Act III.

6. This says a lot, and is scarier than you may think; it's frightening even for me. I need to go back and read chapter 11 (about stress) again.

21

✝

"Hey, Mr. G., When Are You Gonna Retire?"

One day, I am going to retire.

And when I do, there will be two certainties: First, I will be extremely tired—not of my work—but from the physical, emotional, and mental exhaustion that will have accumulated after nearly forty years of service as a high school teacher, baseball coach, debate coordinator, and theater director (while parenting two small children at the same time); and, second, I will be smiling—not because I had finished my life's professional work (well, maybe a little bit of that), but because of contentment in the knowledge I had always given it every ounce of energy left in me.

A wonderful highlight for teachers comes at the moment when you finally realize there is usually a proportional relationship between the efforts you have made and the results you have received.

No, not every time.

Of course, not.

But your hard day's work standing before your class or moving around from student to student, creates an attitude about success that has been woven into the fabric of your job. The feeling you acquire for having given this effort is a win-win situation; for even if the lesson went over like a bomb, and even if you saw much of the class out of control, you may still employ the One Student Philosophy: That philosophy dictates, "Even if I got through to one kid today—even if *one* student learned something from my efforts, it will have been worth it."

Yeah, I know; this is that old, stupid starfish story everyone has heard one hundred thousand times before. But consider the *reason* this hackneyed analogy keeps popping up again and again: It surfaces so often in philosophical discussions about parenting and public service and teaching because . . . *it's true.* Firemen who rush into buildings to save trapped children may be aware that some of those children have already perished—or they realize the absolute physical impossibility of saving every single child. But this never stops them from trying to rescue that one kid trapped inside the stairwell with flames blazing all around him.

And it may be just that: an *impossibility,* given the limited amount of time and resources; given the status of the victims who are trapped; given the lack of courage—or willingness—of the potential victims to cooperate. So many variables affect the success or the failure of the firemen; and sometimes they are forced to shake their heads with an absoluteness that mutters, "We didn't get 'em all; we tried the best we could, but some of 'em got away."

Still, they take pride in what they accomplished, the lives they preserved, rather than dwelling on those who, unfortunately, "got away." For most firemen, that's enough. As long as they have broken their backs (sometimes literally) to exert every ounce of available energy, knowledge, and skill into their efforts, great solace comes from saving even the few they managed to save; and an unprecedented incentive to continue, to endure, to *succeed* emerges from their memories of victories in the past.

Unwilling to admit this is a ploy to justify a lazy or bad teaching day, we recognize the truth of the starfish analogy only when we ourselves have made an effort—a heroic effort—to change, to alter, to improve what is within our grasp. We can't rationalize too well when we haven't tried our best, for having even a speck of conscience makes us unable to believe even our own excuses.

This is the gauge we utilize when we understand a glorious equation is at work:

TIME + EFFORT = SUCCESS (and the right to believe *maybe* one kid got it).

This brings us near the end of our journey. We have examined some doable—albeit weird—implementations for making a better classroom. Focused strongly on the *mind* and *mental* condition of teachers, I have argued vehemently for fixing the way we view our jobs, our lives, and our character; for I believe this is the key to improving the image we have of ourselves—and, ultimately, the comportment we have with kids.

By way of some parting thoughts, here is a very brief summary for each of the target groups of this book: what you should be considering as you turn these last few pages:

TO THOSE THINKING ABOUT BECOMING TEACHERS:

Despite what you have heard about this profession—good or bad—being a teacher is a profound, fulfilling, and incredibly important calling—that also comes with its fair share of frustrations, challenges, and setbacks. The immediate compensation is a respectable amount of money and benefits, but the life-lasting satisfaction of making a difference in the world cannot be measured in tangible form. Most teachers who have already retired are glad they chose teaching as a way of spending their lives, which is a lot more than can be said for some other professions that have led to a near-permanent status and eventually a set, sizeable retirement.

Retiring teachers are usually very glad when the time comes to retire. They're ready!

TO BEGINNIING TEACHERS:

You have a long way to go and a tough row to hoe, but, strangely, I am envious of you. You are just starting; I am preparing to stop. You have an entire career in front of you; mine is almost behind me.

Just remember that . . .

- you can't save every kid
- you can't do all that you want to do at once; it takes a lot of time
- you can't universally implement your ideas, even though you're positive everyone in education would benefit.

Pace yourself. For you, there won't be just a tomorrow; there will be more than thirty thousand tomorrows. That's a fair amount of time to change the world into the place you'd like it to be.

TO VETERAN TEACHERS:

When the going gets tough. . . . Yeah, yeah—and all that poop! But let's look at it this way: You haven't quit, yet. Retirement is far off; and you have picked up this text, presumably, with the intent of getting some ideas to make you do even a better job than you're doing now. The best part of all is that you are in the prime of your career, with the seeming strength to affect yet thousands of young people who will remember you until the day they die. Now, that is a lot of power—and a lot of influence. And it's in your hands.

My primary reminder for you is to strengthen your mind, your outlook. Yes, your body is still bitchin,' (or not), but sometimes we plum lose our heads right during the middle of our careers. We begin second-guessing, even emotionally flogging ourselves for making some of the choices we've already made and can no longer do anything about. But there's no need to do that here; just consider how the vast majority of teachers—no matter what they thought at age forty-two—by age sixty-two were at peace with their choices and would have done nothing different.[1] The only way you should be moving—mind-wise and body-wise—is forward.

TO OLD TEACHERS:

You're done. Congratulations. In just a few days or weeks or months you'll be going fishing, playing golf, watching ball games, and getting fit for dentures. I know there is probably nothing you would change at this point; you think you have nowhere to go with the ideas in this book.

My only suggestion is—since I'm probably older and crabbier than even you—you should come to terms with how you have spent your life, and consider how much better off you are now than most of the rest of America. You have a great pension and a stable medical plan, while most of the rest of the country has been wallowing in the pits of economic despair, bouncing up and down like a financial yo-yo.

Sure, I wish I could go back in time and correct a few boldface errors and incredibly stupid decisions I made, but I can't; yet, my life has been spent living my dream, and when I find others doing things to hurt education—and kids—I just can't keep it inside. Teaching is an art, and it requires a passionate force of energy and an attitude about life that never surrenders to second thoughts, regrets, or remorse.

Far from being Pollyanna, I tell others what I think.

And it ain't always pretty.

If others don't understand that, so what? Nick Nolte's character smiles at the end of the movie *Teacher*, as he proudly beckons (intended for the audience), "Of course I'm crazy! I'm a teacher!"[2]

If more of us projected that optimistic, philosophical resignation, we would be doing an even better job in our classrooms than we're doing right now.

And wouldn't *that* be nice for our kids!

NOTES

1. Nothing very substantial exists for documented proof of this thesis; however, lots of personal polling and discussion have led me to this conclusion about retired teachers and contentment.

2. *Teachers* (United Artists, 1984); Only Nick Nolte could have delivered this line with the authenticity he reflected in the movie.

Bibliography

Agne, Karen, "Acting for Teachers," Plattsburgh State College Course Catalogue 2008, at http://faculty.plattsburgh.edu/karen.agne/sy575.htm.

Allen, David, "How Eating Right Can Save Your Brain." *Buzzle*, October 17, 2005.

Allen, Woody, *Annie Hall* (United Artists, 1977).

———. *Crimes and Misdemeanors* (MGM, 1989).

Alpert, Emily, "In Tough Times a Bold Bid by a Teachers' Union." *Voice of San Diego*, August 6, 2008, at voiceofsandiego.org/articles/2008/08/06/news/+unionproposal080608.txt.

American Beauty (Dream Works, 1999).

American Institute of Stress, "Job Stress," September 10, 2001, at stress.org/hob.htm.

American Pie (Universal, 1999).

Amos, Julie Ann, "The History and Health Benefits of Hot Tubs," *Ezine Articles*, 2005, at ezinearticles.com/?The-History-And-Health-Benefits-of-Hot-Tubs&id=108347.

Asian Food Information Center, "Myths and Facts About Caffeine," January 1, 2000, at afic.org/2008/hydration.php?switchto=1&news_id=132.

Ask Yahoo, U.S. Department of Education, at ask.yahoo.com/20050509.html.

Attack of the Mole People (Universal, 1956).

Bloom, Molly. "Happy Teachers Tied to Good Students," *Statesman.com*, November 12, 2008, at statesman.com/news/content/news/stories/local/11/12/1112surveys.html.

Bosley, David E. "Better Management Policies Produce Satisfied Teachers."*USA Today*, February 13, 2008, Opinion section.

Brown, Darcia Harris. "States Target School Vending Machines," *Education Week* 23, 5 (Oct. 1, 2003).

Bryner, Jeanna "Live Science," *Fox News,* February 28, 2007, at foxnews.com.

Cabaj, Hanna and Vesna Nikolic, *Am I Teaching Well?* Toronto: Pippin Publishing, 2000.

Call Me Mr. Tibbs (United Artists, 1967).

Cassidy, Virginia R. *Academic Planning and Development,* Northern Illinois University, 2006, at ibhe.state.il.us/EffectivePractices/Featured/result.asp?Y=2006&F =001737&P=4&T=247&5=A.

Casson, Kathleen, "Observing Other Teachers: Professional Development That Works," *Learn NC,* UNC School of Education, at learnnc.org/lp/pages/ 739charlotte.creative loafingloafing.com.gyrobase/content?oid=oid%3a3284.

Clark, Ann D. "The New Frontier of Wellness," *ACI: The Specialty Benefits Corporation,* April 2, 2008, at annclarkassociates.com/news_details .php?nidi.78company-wellness-program.com.

Corporate Wellness Training, "Corporate Self-Defense Training" April 30, 2008, at company-wellness-program.com.

Croese, Lisette, "Reasons For Learning a Modern, Non-English Foreign Language," *Abroad Languages,* July 26, 2007, at broadlanguages.com/blog/reasons -for-learning-a-modern-non-English-foreign-language_6/.

Danziger, Lucy. "Pizza for Breakfast, Yes!" March 12, 2008, at health.yahoo.com/ experts/healthieryou/1/pizza-for-breakfast-yes.

Deep Throat (Aquarius Releasing, 1972).

Deliverance (Warner Bros., 1972).

Dienst, Karin. "Rewards of Teaching Inspire Students." *Princeton Weekly Bulletin,* November 13, 2000.

DiPaola, Michael F. and Wayne K. Hoy, *Improving Schools: Studies in Leadership and Culture.* Charlotte, N.C.: Information Age Publishing, 2008.

Douthat, Ross. "The Best of All Possible Games." *The Atlantic,* March 11, 2008.

"Dress for Success," July 31, 2007, at English-test.net/forever/ftopic19182.html.

Dyke, Stephanie, Ed McCormick, and Jon Weiman, *Lesson Plans That Wow! Twelve Standards Based Lessons.* Summit, NJ: Teaching Press, 2007.

Ed Data for 2008, "Teachers in California," December 2007, at ed-data.k12.ca.us/ articles/article.asp?title=teacher-%20in%20california.

Education Research, 1987.

Enchanted (Disney Pictures, 2008).

The Exorcist (Warner Bros., 1973).

The Faculty (Dimension Pictures, 1998).

Fairfield, Kathleen and Robert H. Fletcher, "Vitamins for Chronic Disease Prevention in Adults." *The Journal of the American Medical Association* 287 (June 19, 2002).

Federwisch, Roger. "Schools Enforce Dress Code For Teachers." *USA Today,* August 25, 2003.

Georgia Department of Education, Fulton County Schools, "School Improvement Plan," 2008–2009.

Gevirtzman, Bruce J. *An Intimate Understanding of America's Teenagers: Shaking Hands with Aliens.* Santa Barbara, CA: Greenwood Publishers, 2008.

Gibbs, Nancy. "Parents Behaving Badly." *Time,* February 13, 2005.

Gomez, J.J. "The Path to School-Based Management Isn't Smooth, but We're Scaling the Obstacles One by One, *The American Board Journal* (October 1989).

Griffin, Shannon. "Why New Teachers Quit." *Creative Loafing*, July 19, 2007, at charlotte.creative loafingloafing.com.gyrobase/content?oid=oid%3a3284.

Harvey, Ken. "Cabildeo De Estudiantes Latinos Ante Legisladores," *Migrant Ed News* (Spring 2005).

Hawks, John. "Health Benefits of Eating Meat," November 7, 2008. www .Johnhawks.net:84/node/689.

Hermitt, A. "Is Teacher Tenure Fair to Students?" *A-2 Education,* December 17, 2007.

Hess, Mary Albert. "Eat Right for Two," *WebMD: Live Events, Transcript*, November 28, 2008, at medicinenet.com/script/main/art.asp?articlekey=54270.

Heyman, Jon. "Why Mike Scioscia Is the Best Manager in Baseball." *Sports Illustrated*, April 30, 2008.

The Hockey Puck, at thehockeypuck.com.

Jesness, Jerry. *Teaching English Language Learners*. Thousand Oaks, CA: Corwin Press, 2004.

Juice Blog, the, at thejuice.baseballtoaster.com/archives/853276.html.

Kiui, M."Surviving the Classroom." *The Teacher* (April and August, 1998).**[AQ5]**

Kopkowski, Cynthia."The End of the Line." *NEA Today* (February 2007).

Kyriacou, C. "Teacher Stress and Burnout: An International Review." *Education Research* 29, 2 (1987).

Leave It to Beaver (CBS, 1957–1962).

Lotowycz, Lorraine. "School Enforces Dress Code for Teachers." *USA Today*, August 25, 2003.

Lucas Tanner (NBC, 1974–1975).

Lynn, Sharon. "The Benefits of Taking Multivitamins," *AC/Associated Content*, August 13, 2008, at associatedcontent.com/article/927219.

Martin, Steve. *Born Standing Up*. New York: Scribner, 2007.

Massage Magazine, "Forbes Features Massage," February 28, 2006.

McCarthy, Christopher J. "The Relationship of Elementary School Teachers' Experience, Stress, and Coping Resources to Burnout Symptoms." *The Elementary School Journal* 109 (2009).

McHugh, Beth. "Gossip Can Be Good For You!" *Families.com*, Februrary 15, 2006, at mental-health.families.com/blog/gossip-can-be-good-for-you.

Miller, Arthur. *Death of a Salesman*. New York: Samuel French, Inc.,1948.

Modern Language Association and *the Association of Departments of Foreign Languages*, 1999, at ccflt.org/adfh1.htm.

Moore, Annabelle. "Four Condom Commandments." *The Spectator*, November 14, 2008.

National Education Association, *NEA Newsletter*, November 14, 2006. www.nea .org.newsrelease/2006/NR06114.html.

NCEA Workload Health and Safety Survey, 2007, at geocites.com/conteach/OSH_ survey.htm.

Night of the Living Dead (George Romero's) (The Walter Reade Organization, 1968).

Patton, Margaret and Alan William Kristonis. "The Law of Increasing Returns: A Process for Retaining Teachers—National Recommendations." *National Journal for Publishing and Mentoring Doctorial Student Research,* 2006.

Pollar, Michael. "On the Table." *New York Times,* June 4, 2006, Opinion section.

Porky's (Astral Productions, 1982).

Rain Man (United Artists, 1988).

Ravitch, Diane. "Why Teachers Unions Are Good For Teachers and the Public." *AFT: A Union of Professionals* (Winter 2006–2007).

Reeves, Scott. "Eating Red Meat Beefs Up the Brain." *Minyanville,* September 15, 2008, at minyanville.com/articles/index.php?e=18965.

Richter, Allen. "Teacher Stress Rising, But Venting Helps." *BNET Business Network* (December 2003).

Rosekind, Mark R. "The Cost of Fatigue Is Great." *Sleep and Dreams Magazine,* October 30, 2007.

Rothman, Jennifer. "A Letter from the Editor." *Insights* 10, 4 (Summer 2004).

Serdyukov, Peter and Mark Ryan. *Writing Effective Lesson Plans: The 5-Star Approach.* Upper Saddle River, NJ: Allyn & Bacon, 2007.

Schindler's List (DreamWorks, 1993).

Searching for Bobby Fisher (Miramax Films, 1993).

Serna, Joseph. "Adams' Parents: Kids Aren't Shortchanged." *Daily Pilot,* January 23, at 2008dailypilot.com/articles/2008/01/29/education/dpt-boardmeeting23.txt.

Sheehan, George A. "And Miles to Go Before I Sleep." *Runner's World,* March 1995.

Stand and Deliver (Warner Bros.,1988).

Stossel, John. "Teachers' Unions Are Killing the Public Schools." February 15, 2006, at realclearpolitics.com/commentary/com-15-06-JS.html.

Tang, Jean. "Caffeine, More Good than Harm." *Energy Fiend,* July 14, 2006, at energyfiend.com/2006/07/caffeine-more-good-than-harm.

Teachers (United Artists, 1984).

Tosta, Antonio Luciano. "Laugh and Learn: Thinking Over the Funny Teacher Myth." Forum, vol. 39, no. 1, January–March 2001.

Trumbo, Dalton. *Johnny Got His Gun.* New York: Citadel Paperback, 2007.

Village of the Damned (MGM, 1960; Universal, 1995).

When Harry Met Sally (Castle Rock Entertainment, 1989).

White Shadow,(1978–1981, CBS).

Wikipedia: The Online Encyclopedia, at wikipedia.com.

Wilder, Thornton. *Our Town.* New York: Samuel French, Inc., 1939.

The Wonder Years, ABC-TV, "Dance with Me," Season 1, Episode 6. May 15, 1991.

Woopidoo Quotations, "Business and Finance Quotes," at woopido.com/business_quotes/authors/vince-lombardi/index.htm.

Yahoo Sports, "Seattle Mariners 2008," at sports.yahoo.com/mlb/players/6615.

Zen to Fitness, "The Simple, No-Nonsense Guide to Staying Fit While Living Life" Oct. 6, 2008, at zenoffitmess.com/a-no-nonsense-guide-to-napping.

Zhou, Kevin. "When Teachers Go back to School."*Harvard Crimson,* November 28, 2006, at the crimson.com/article.aspex?ref=516018.

Zuckerman, Mortimer B. "Attention Must Be Paid." *U.S. News and World Report,* August 18, 1997.

About the Author

In 1998 **Bruce J. Gevirtzman** received the coveted Crystal Apple Award from NBC, and in 1991 was named Teacher of the Year from over a thousand teachers in his district. Named the Southern California Debate League Coach of the Year, he also coached high school baseball for six years. An author of over twenty plays, Gevirtzman's scripts have been performed around the Western United States by Phantom Projects, a touring theater group. He is the author of the critically acclaimed book *An Intimate Understanding of America's Teenagers: Shaking Hands with Aliens*. Gevirtzman lives with his wife and school-age children in Brea, California.